STEPPE
BY
STEPPE

A SLOW JOURNEY THROUGH MONGOLIA

GILL SUTTLE

SCIMITAR PRESS

SCIMITAR PRESS
P.O. Box 41, Monmouth, Gwent, NP25 3UH.

© Gill Suttle 2000

British Library Cataloguing in Publication Data
A catalogue record for this book is
available from the British Library

ISBN 0 9534536 1 8

Printed & bound in Great Britain by
TTA Press
5, Martins Lane, Witcham,
Ely, Cambs.

For Carol

without whose help I could never have even begun this journey

CONTENTS

ACKNOWLEDGEMENTS

Firstly, I owe an enormous debt of gratitude to Rob Dean for so generously giving me full benefit of his computing skills. What little time he has had to spare after rescuing my PC from the many dire consequences of my own incompetence, he has spent designing the cover, helping with maps, wrestling with layout, and generally teaching an exceptionally dim pupil with great patience.

Thank you to my aunt, Mina Gummer, and again to Rob, for their immensely detailed and constructive proof-reading and comments.

A big thank you, too, to Jan Vegter and all at Hustain Nuruu and MACNE for their help and hospitality, and for the great privilege of seeing the first Przewalski Horses to return to Mongolia.

Most of all, my deepest gratitude to Carol, without whose tolerance, good humour - and indefatigable energy for two - this book would never have been written.

Last but not least, my thanks to the many people of Mongolia whose warmth and friendship gave us an unforgettable experience.

Thank you to those authors and publishers who have permitted quotations:

Basil Blackwell: "The Mongols" by David Morgan.
Dobson Books Ltd: "The Blue Sky" by Ivor Montague.
Clare Francis and Dr. Anne Macintyre: foreword to "ME and How to Live With It", by Dr. Anne Macintyre.
Dr. Clare Fleming: "The Glass Cage", first published in the British Medical Journal in 1994, no. 308, p. 797.

Harper Collins: "The Secret History of the Mongols" by Arthur Waley, by kind permission of the Arthur Waley Estate.

Harrap: "Land of Swift-Running Horses" by Mabel Waln Smith.

Kegan Paul International, London & New York: "The Modern History of Mongolia" by C.R. Bawden.

The Hon. Lady Maclean: "To The Back of Beyond", by Fitzroy Maclean.

"Marco Polo: The Travels", translated by R.E. Latham, reproduced by permission of Penguin Books Ltd.

University of Toronto Press: "Missions to Asia" by Christopher Dawson.

David Higham Associates: "The Mission of William of Rubruck" by Peter Jackson/David Morgan, published by the Hakluyt Society.

I

MONGOL TOUR RULES OK

As the cloud broke and dispersed, the snow-capped peaks of the Altai Mountains stood out on the horizon, a hundred miles to the south. Five miles away, measured vertically down, was Kyzyl, capital of the remote and rather mysterious Siberian Republic of Tuva. Visible at its centre were the two arms of the Yenisei River as they met and clasped hands, ready to embark on their thousand-mile journey north to the Kara Sea.

So far, Aeroflot had done its stuff. When I first conceived the idea of travelling to Outer Mongolia, it looked as if getting there would be the most hazardous part. Rather a lot of Russian Tupolevs failed to make it across Siberia; only a few weeks before one had crashed hereabouts, flown into the taiga by the pilot's teenage son. From the look of the virgin forest below, with its tens of miles between each tiny scratch made by human hand, it must have taken a month just to find the bits.

Moscow's international airport, Sheremetyevo, had lived down to most of my preconceptions. It was dark, grimy, and about as exciting as a multi-storey car-park. The menu board outside the only cafe temptingly offered "sweated bread" to the brave or just starving. The transit lounge was a tiny, smelly room draped with bodies, to which pile I added one more. When at last the flight was called, we traipsed off in a crocodile watched and counted by minders, in case the luxuries about tempted anyone to hide away and take up residence.

The plane was a creaky old bus, with X's taped on the wings; perhaps to remind the Aeroflot mechanics where the nuts and bolts went. But the flight left on time, and there was no danger of blundering into the Ural Mountains in the dark. For almost immediately the dawn broke in a cherry-pink line above the clouds, and an hour later the first rays of the sun clipped the starboard engine under my window.

The sky was unbroken blue by the time Lake Hovsgol, its waters shining with metallic brilliance in the early sun, indicated that Mongolia now lay below us. Tiny white dots, the felt tents of the herdsmen, appeared among a landscape of grass and low hills, crossed and re-crossed by a labyrinth of mud tracks. As the plane began to lose height, smaller and more numerous dots resolved themselves into grazing herds. And the first people I saw, as we circled over Ulaan Baatar Airport, were a couple of horsemen, top-heavy over their diminutive ponies.

Then the wheels touched, and a round of applause broke out from the relieved passengers.

*

I had long been obsessed with Mongolia. Its culture, still semi-nomadic, is one of the few remaining vestiges of a lifestyle going back to the dawn of true horsemanship. For most of the last three thousand years, ever since man and horse really got their act together, mounted nomads had ranged across the steppes and deserts of Central Asia, sending incursions like waves against the rocks of the settled world on their boundaries, and periodically inundating parts of that world altogether. In the process they displaced whole populations, tides of migrating peoples whose shock waves reached as far as western Europe.

I wanted to see how their descendants lived today, how many ties they preserved with that distant, romantic-sounding past. Particularly fascinating for me was the idea of a present-day lifestyle and economy which relied heavily on the horse, depending on it for transport, herding and - through its milk - even food.

But for my lifetime, indeed for centuries, Mongolia has been one of the hardest countries in the world to reach. Its very climate is viciously hostile, with winter lasting for eight or nine months, temperatures falling to -40°C with bitter winds, and even a summer's day often running through the entire meteorological gamut.

Inaccessible by distance, it used to be even more so politically. For it lies squeezed between what were for long years two of the most xenophobic states of the world, China and Russia, and was successively dominated by each. The sparse trickle of western visitors dried up almost completely after 1921, when the Communists took power. Although subsequently it was still possible in theory to travel to Mongolia, in practice the privilege was extended to just a few select visitors, paying inflated prices for a very limited and highly sanitised view.

And so the rest of the world barely knew that Mongolia existed. Even the United Nations took until 1961 to admit it as a member. Hardly, then, a great player on the international stage. Yet there was a time when its name caused the world to shudder from end to end.

From thirteenth century Mongolia came the armies of Genghis Khan, a name which has echoed jarringly down the centuries as the embodiment of brutality and horror. Welded for the first time into a single force by this charismatic and utterly ruthless leader, the Mongols carved out the largest empire history has ever known, terrorised the whole of mediaeval civilisation and, but for an accident of fate - the death of the Great Khan - would certainly have altered the entire history of western Europe. Although their westward sweep halted before Vienna, they still made their mark on the furthest corners of Britain. For it is now generally acknowledged that it was the Mongols who brought bubonic plague - the Black Death - to the West, wiping out perhaps a third of the entire population; a greater slaughter than even they could achieve by the sword.

After the fragmentation and eventual collapse of Genghis Khan's empire, the seventeenth century saw Mongolia submitting piecemeal to China. First to go were the border areas of Inner Mongolia, which remain to this day part of Chinese territory. The rest became first a client then a subject state, although retaining its territorial integrity as Outer Mongolia. Only with the Chinese revolution, and subsequently its own, did the latter manage to break free.

The Communist revolution left Outer Mongolia, now "The People's Republic of Mongolia", effectively a Soviet satellite. It has taken the fall of Communism to make Mongolia a truly independent state for the first time in three hundred years.

And, more important from the travellers' point of view, freely open at last to the West.

*

"Oh, I'm sure you haven't got ME" said the doctor, as he whipped up my sleeve and whacked in three injections. "You would hardly be thinking of travelling to Mongolia if you had!"*

This was a distinct improvement. He was the Practice member least disposed to recognise the seriousness of the illness. Not long ago, he would have been more likely to assure his patients briskly that "claiming" to have ME was no excuse for not fulfilling their ambitions to become a lumberjack, or a spaceman.

As for the ambition to travel, though, I was inclined to agree. When Mongolian Communism collapsed in 1991, I was chained by illness, and supposed, then, that such a destination had better wait for a full recovery. But, although now much improved, I was still waiting for that recovery. It had gradually become clear that, if I were not to be seeing Mongolia through bifocals from the safety of my Zimmer frame, I'd better settle for the current situation.

Hence my caution over jabs. ME and immunisations are bad friends, and many an unexpected relapse has been precipitated by, for instance, an innocent tetanus booster. If I didn't handle this carefully, I could kill the trip before I'd even packed.

But my feeble protests were swept aside. "Besides, even if you had," continued the doctor, "vaccinations won't harm you!" Bad theory; but over those three, he was absolutely right. They produced no effect whatsoever. The one that grounded me was the vaccine I wouldn't have foregone under any circumstances: rabies. Happy to chance it on lesser illnesses, even the emotive bubonic plague - still endemic in Central Asia, it is bacterial, and keels over under a few antibiotics - I almost foamed at the mouth from the very thought of hydrophobia, one of the

*for a description of ME and its effects, please turn to the Appendix

nastiest ways to die that I could think of. But the course of rabies injections, given over four weeks, kept me horizontal for six. It was lucky that, for fear of just that consequence, I'd organised it several months ahead of the journey. And during the regular visits to the surgery I learned much from the doctor, himself a keen and informed traveller, of Central Asia - and also of Tuva, a Siberian republic adjacent to Mongolia and a country which was to prove especially relevant to our trip.

The other half of the expedition was my old friend Carol Evans, a zoologist who heads the Biology department at Malvern Girls' College, where I had formerly taught alongside her. We had travelled together before my illness and, more importantly, since. Unable to walk very far, keep normal hours or even carry luggage, I was going to be a hideous millstone around the neck of a fellow traveller. It was essential that Carol knew exactly what she was taking on.

I could never have hoped for a better companion. Throughout the trip Carol took a thoroughly unfair proportion of the jobs on her shoulders; doing the errands to fetch water, fuel for the stove, bus tickets and the like, often carrying my luggage as well as her own, doing everything short of giving me a piggy-back, and never once complaining of or even commenting on my feeble ineptitude. My one contribution to the practicalities, to set against all hers, was as interpreter. During the long years of inactivity I had learned some Russian, with Mongolia in mind.

Together we planned and plotted far into the night. The respective merits of various objectives, itineraries, equipment absorbed us. An early decision was to return by the Trans-Siberian Railway. Such an opportunity couldn't be passed up, and putting it at the end would give us something to look forward to; while going out, rather than back, by Aeroflot would get the dodgy bit over quickly.

But our principal obsession, which we returned to over and over again, was food. Rumour had it that food was a luxury item in Mongolian shops. As for restaurants, recent visitors to the country couldn't dredge up a good word between them; though this was pretty irrelevant, since we planned to get off the beaten track as much as possible. We would need

15

to carry provisions, and must not rely on stocking up when we got there. The basics must come from home.

Weight was our chief consideration. We pored over dieters' handbooks; but with the opposite intention to most people, searching out the foods with the highest calorie content. Being biologically ignorant, I hadn't realised this wasn't as simple as it seemed.

Top of the list was olive oil, at a thumping 3,000 calories for each pound weight. But we could hardly go around drinking oil at every meal. Grains - oats, rice, pasta, flour - scored about half as much, but we needed carbohydrates more than fats. A pound of these would at a pinch give a day's requirements. We settled on a core stock of the first three, which we could cook easily; with biscuits, nuts and seeds, all at around 2,000cals/lb, for quick meals. Dried fruit - a mainstay of climbers and explorers - scored surprisingly low on account of its remaining water content, and we took very little. Sugar scored even worse, and was out. Instead, in went sweetening tablets, virtually weightless.

Being soft travellers used to our comforts, we allowed ourselves a few packets of sauces and dried vegetables, in case we couldn't buy any odds and ends to throw in the pot at the time. Since these are usually meant for adding to several pounds of prime steak, not to mention a pint of cream and half a bottle of sherry, we experimented to see which would add a little *je ne sais quoi* to plain rice or pasta.

To kill two birds with one stone, we did the trials in the garden, testing at the same time a variety of borrowed camping stoves for compatibility with petrol, the only fuel we could expect to find in Mongolia. More often than not the result was a cloud of oily black smoke, an inedible mess and a quick trip to the Chinese; not to mention a week of TLC with a Brillo pad before the stove was fit to go back to its trusting owner.

After several flops we stretched our budget to the MSR multifuel, a mighty midget rumoured to drink anything including jet fuel and vodka. By all accounts, the latter was probably the more available in Mongolia.

About twenty-five pounds of food each took up more than half our flight baggage allowance, but should be enough to give hard rations for the first three weeks out in the sticks. This left nineteen pounds total for personal kit, including camping gear. Actually, slightly less for me; for I used up precious ounces on a luggage trolley, being unable to carry even a fraction of this weight. Tiny and frail-looking, the trolley was the single most valuable item of my equipment. With scarcely a creak it was to bear the full weight of my possessions over some of the roughest of tracks.

Or, almost the full weight. For, despairing of getting within Aeroflot's weight allowance, I stowed as much as I could in poachers' pockets specially sewn into my coat. When the time came I rolled undetected through the baggage check looking like a Michelin woman, with a good ten pounds excess.

Through the British company which booked our tickets, we arranged a taxi from the airport and accommodation for the first few nights at an Ulaan Baatar hotel. When the details arrived, we were delighted. It seemed that the local firm called itself the "Mongol Tour OK" Company.

It was irresistible. From then on it was, inevitably, Mongol Tour Rules OK.

*

Mongol Tour Rules OK was personified in Batbayaar, a cheerful-looking youth standing by the Arrivals door with my name on a card. He was also, at this moment, looking worried; most of the passengers had already gone, as I was trailing along at the rear to avoid the crush. This was the first time I had tried out the trolley for real, and I wasn't going to win any races.

Carol, delayed by the end of the school term, was travelling later. This was very bad luck, as it meant that she would have to miss the big national knees-up, the Naadam festival, due to start the following week. It also meant that I was managing my own luggage. So I was glad to see a friendly face.

Batbayaar and I greeted each other with mutual relief. He manfully shouldered my heavy bags, and led me to a red station wagon, opulent among the few rusty heaps standing by the road. The drive into the city passed in a whirl of rap and heavy rock, which felt disappointingly un-foreign.

But only briefly. For horses, sheep and goats grazed along the airport road, while kites wheeled above. On the fringes of the city, we began to pass some of its landmarks. First was the Tuul River, a shallow, sandy stream between rather grubby banks fringed with willow. Later Batbayaar pointed out Nairamdal Park and Stadium, where Naadam is held annually.

It was snowing in Ulaan Baatar. Not real snow, although this would be no great surprise here, even in July; but white tufts of poplar seed, thickly filling the air and piling the gutters with drifts. The wide boulevards were lined with trees - very many more trees than there were cars on the road. Why, I wondered briefly, do so many countries paint their city trees white; and if there's a good reason, why don't we do it too?

Now Batbayaar turned into a pot-holed drive behind a seedy block of flats. Children watched enviously as the bright red jeep passed a row of garages and pulled up beside a big, square building: the grandly named Mongol Tour OK Guest House.

It was the usual story. The hotel was barely half finished, and building rubble cluttered the hall. I was the only guest, outnumbered at least ten to one by the staff. But I was impressed and surprised by Batbayaar's fluent English - and by that of the "Boss", a man named Sanjaa, who gave a preliminary if fleeting good impression.

Thankfully I showered and crashed out, too tired to care that "bed and board" was a tautology and the water was cold.

*

Ulaan Baatar, known to its friends as "UB", is a city of wide open spaces. The very streets are fifty yards or more wide, and the main square on which they converge is of sufficient dimension to drill a large army - a thought which perhaps wasn't far absent when it was laid out.

Named for a hero of the Revolution, Sukhbaatar Square is the centre of gravity of UB. Sukhbaatar himself is on a pedestal in the middle,

18

astride his horse - no Mongolian hero would be seen dead, alive or carved in marble without his horse - waving his hand in salute towards the *Hural*, or Parliament building opposite. To one side is the salmon-pink block of the National Theatre, its pristine white, fluted columns and picot-edged pediment looking like a very big wedding cake. It looks across to a smaller building of similar design which turns out, improbably, to be the Mongolian Stock Exchange. Along the fourth side, opposite the Hural and beyond a line of small, pleasant parks, runs Peace Avenue, UB's equivalent of Oxford Street.

This is a fairly typical third world capital. Apart from one or two showpiece buildings, it has a crumbling, slightly dingy air, even in the centre. The buildings are square, squat and rather ugly, made from cheap concrete and ill finished, while the streets below are hazardous with broken kerb-stones, or large puddles in the uneven surfaces.

This wasn't the impression received by Ivor Montague, a rare visitor in the fifties. Courteously and hospitably received by his Communist hosts, he wrote with delight and enthusiasm of all aspects of the country. Of UB he was frankly rhapsodic:

"Where Urga* was, today stands a beautiful white city. Not a great town by our standards. But 100,000 inhabitants is much for the plains of Mongolia. And beautiful... White is the town, its architecture following the imposing mood of Soviet buildings of the past decade... white are the buildings, the University, the Polyclinic, the Pedagogical Institute, the splendid headquarters of the Committee of Sciences..."

Perhaps it was newer, then.

Crumbling or not, today UB was kaleidoscopic with all sorts and conditions of men and women. Visitors were beginning to come in from the provinces for Naadam, and a cross-section of Mongolian society filled the streets. Among the city workers in their western clothes strode herdsmen straight off the steppes, in colourful costume.

The traditional garment for both men and women is the *del***, a knee-length tunic fastening high on one side of the neck and belted in by the *bus*, a coloured sash like a cummerbund. Both sexes wear long leather boots, though I could pick out the townswomen by their court shoes.

*UB's pre-Revolution name
**a glossary on page 237 lists some of the commoner Mongolian words

19

Women wear a coloured scarf, while for men, the traditional pointed hat has largely given place in recent years to a western trilby - at least for informal wear. By the time Naadam was under way, trilbies were definitely out.

It must have been pretty warm clothing for hot weather. The temperature for much of this week was in the thirties, despite a cool, gentle wind off the hills. These surround the city, and every vista down UB's main streets, straight as an arrow from a Mongol bow, is filled by green, wooded heights, sharp edged in the clear air, and set off by the famous blue of the Mongolian sky.

Set on a plateau of over four thousand feet, Mongolia has an alpine feel, with a translucent quality to the light on these warm summer days. But hints of the ferocious winter are ever present; such as the ubiquitous double glazing, panes widely spaced for packing with tufts of wool in winter, or the enormously thick, felt boot liners in the shops.

The air was as dry as a bone. Although I drank as much as I dared before going out, I was constantly gaspingly, raspingly dry-throated. The first day I was thankful to find kiosks selling drinks on the streets, and gratefully though rather shamefacedly bought two cans of Coke as well as a bottle of the local stuff. I was glad of the Coke, for the other was badly sealed, and disgraced itself all over the contents of my rucksack. When I tried to remove its leaky cap properly, it first resisted grimly and then broke at the neck, leaving a lethal edge to dispose of and a drink full of slivers of glass. I used it to water some roadside grass, and it was the only liquid I dispensed all day.

The Coke didn't go far either, as I gave up most of one can to three urchins who laid siege to me with charm and determination in Sukhbaatar Square. I drank what was left sitting under the Hero himself, until a diminutive street cleaner, barely in his teens, crossly moved me on.

So I went into the park, where a loudspeaker was incongruously playing a big band jazz-up of Claire de Lune, and prostrated myself at Lenin's feet. His statue gave excellent shade.

It was quite a surprise to find him still here. Throughout the former Communist world he has been toppled, broken up, melted down or otherwise liquidated. They say that even the original model will soon be removed from its mausoleum in Moscow's Red Square, and allowed to return to dust, like any normal corpse. But the attitude in Mongolia to Lenin and his heritage is ambivalent.

The Communist Revolution in 1921 was not only based on the Soviet model but heavily backed up by the Soviet Army, which the diminutive Communist Party invited in to give more persuasive force to its ideology. It was much the same formula as that which failed so miserably in Afghanistan sixty years later. The result here was effectively a puppet regime with Moscow pulling the strings. As in many similar cases there was even a Stalin lookalike. Mongolia's Little Brother was a man called Choibalsan, who faithfully mirrored the actions of his patron; even the infamous Russian purges of the thirties were diligently copied here.

To all intents and purposes the country was run as a province of the Soviet Union. In return for some economic assistance, such as heavily subsidised petrol, the Russians plundered the country of many of its natural resources while failing to develop others - oil, for example - that might have enabled it to become more economically independent.

In Ulaan Baatar at least, many came to regard as parasites the large numbers of Russian "advisers" who permeated every office of administration or business. For these were the élite, a cut above ordinary Mongolian society, with special status in UB. As well as controlling the best jobs, they had their own living areas of the city, their own restaurants and clubs, even their own special buses. No wonder many of the ordinary Mongolians, living under this system of virtual apartheid, often viewed the Russians with hatred.

Yet in the country, the view was often quite the opposite; for so was the viewpoint.

Few countries could have offered such fertile ground for Communist Revolution as Mongolia at the beginning of the twentieth century. For two hundred years the country had laboured under the domination of an oppressive Chinese regime, heavily taxed, economically stagnant and in increasing poverty. By contrast, in the last two generations at least, the average herdsman has seen his children educated, had access to medical treatment, and could even obtain veterinary care for his livestock. Now, in the period of change and economic uncertainty which has similarly rocked most countries of the former USSR, the system which provided these securities is breaking down, and has not yet been adequately replaced. And so the people of the provinces mostly regret the departure of the Russians.

Among rural people of any land, memories are long-lasting. Life under the Chinese was so difficult, and for so long, that change could hardly fail to be for the better. The horrors attending the first couple of decades after the Revolution were comparatively brief, and followed by relative prosperity; in many ways the Mongolians had never had it so good as in recent years. No wonder that, alongside the loathing of the Chinese which runs deep in the Mongolian psyche, there is sometimes a respect for the Russians verging on reverence.

It is a confusing polarisation of views, and one which I spent much of the following weeks trying to unravel.

*

It was time to leave the bosom of Mongol Tour Rules OK. At fifteen pounds a night it was over my budget, and I could stay for a few dollars at the Altai Hotel on the other side of town. And it would be a relief to escape from being woken by the builders at six every morning.

But there was a problem: Sanjaa, the boss, had my passport. He had taken it away to register me with the police and, the destined reception desk being still only a pile of bricks, he had kept it on him.

"Sanjaa is at the restaurant" said one of the staff. It was, she implied, just round the corner. I set off with Otongbayaar as guide.

"Bayaar", a common constituent of Mongolian names, means "happy". Otongbayaar, a cheerful, obliging youth with a perpetual sunny smile, was well named. Unfortunately he spoke only Mongolian, and I couldn't explain why I wasn't keeping up with him.

At my own pace - Dead Slow - I can walk a good half-mile, and further with rests. But Oto, anxious only to solve my problem, set off like a marathon runner; and became increasingly mystified as I lagged further and further behind, desperately trying to slow him down.

When I slumped on the pavement for the fourth time, his creased brow suddenly cleared. He shot off at a tangent and reappeared a moment later with Batbayaar, whose office was just round the corner. In his good English, Batbayaar soon put me in the picture.

He was the good news; the bad was two-pronged. Sanjaa's restaurant, it turned out, was miles away; while Sanjaa, rot him, had forgotten all about my passport until tipped off by the lady at the hotel that I was chasing it. At once he had sent a minion to the police station with it, leaving poor Batbayaar to cover for him. Had I reached him he wouldn't have had it anyway.

The two lads were keen to make amends. This, I began to learn, was Sanjaa's modus operandi. Full of get-rich-quick schemes - the restaurant, the guest house, an embryonic tour company - he wasn't running anything properly. But somehow, he had contrived to surround himself with a devoted, loyal and diligent band of people, who spent most of their working lives protecting him from the consequences of his frequent cock-ups.

Somehow, Oto and Batbayaar borrowed a car and got me back to the guest house. At least now I needn't feel embarrassed at decamping elsewhere. It was the poor staff who were embarrassed - my good luck, for Oto was sent with me, managing taxi and luggage, explaining at the registration desk why I had no passport, and promising to deliver it himself that evening - which he faithfully did.

The Altai was familiar territory, a typical backpackers' hotel. Slightly down-at-heel, it nevertheless had clean sheets and very comfortable beds. The light switch was ingeniously hidden behind the mirror, and the radio didn't work - the dust that pinged into the air when I flicked the switch showed how long it was since anyone had been naïve enough to try. But what price the ostentatious colour telly chez Sanjaa, when it was in Mongolian anyway?

23

And at seven dollars a day it was undeserved luxury to have my own bathroom. True, the loo seat was detachable, which made using it quite a balancing act, and flushing it was an intelligence test - you had to dismantle and rebuild the mechanism anew every time. But I would have jumped through a lot more hoops than that for the reward of the ultimate discovery: that the water coming out of the tap was hot.

*

The Altai had one more advantage over the MTROK Guest House. It was right by a bus stop. On a route, what's more, which took a rare bee-line into town, and dropped you by the Ulaan Baatar Hotel, with its essential restaurants and exchange desk.

Normally, the buses weren't so obliging. Although, like most third world cities with little private transport, UB had plenty of them, they were hardly user-friendly. The stops were often more than half-a-mile apart, little use to feeble knees. Worse, I never found a map or timetable; more often than not, the moment I jumped on a bus going my way, it turned straight round and carted me off in the wrong direction.

At first when this happened I would sit and grind my teeth until the bus stopped and I could escape, find the "opposite" stop (usually miles down the road) and catch the same number back to where I'd started. Soon I learned to take it philosophically, and even explore some parts of the city that I might never have found otherwise.

To the west, at the end of Peace Avenue and along by the railway, industrial suburbs and modern apartment blocks stretched to and beyond where the power station belched out its thick smoke into the prevailing wind and thus all over UB. Here, too, was the hot water plant, which supplied the whole city via enormous green pipes - four feet in diameter, of which three was for insulation - bending in a series of awkward right-angles to cross over road, river and other obstacles. Can there be any country other than Mongolia, which suffers winter temperature of -40°C, yet supplies all its hot water communally and through external pipes?

North and north-west lay the older, less developed parts. A typical Mongolian suburb consists of a grid of streets with individual plots of regular size laid out behind wooden fences. Inside these each family erects its own choice of dwelling. This might be a wooden shack; but far more often it is a *ger*, the domed felt tent known as *yurt* to the Turkic peoples west of the Altai range. With little change, this has sheltered the steppe nomad since well before the time of Genghis Khan.

Streets and streets of these "ger cities" surround the capital. As he migrated off the steppe in his search for a living, the herdsman-turned-townsman simply brought his home with him. After all, if you already possess a dwelling which is big enough for the family, designed for the life-style you know, warm and windproof against the savage Central Asian winter and, above all, portable, what more do you need?

One unscheduled detour took me up the hill behind the old monastery of Gandaan Hiid, and I wandered through the back streets of one of the ger settlements for a closer look.

The poverty here was indescribable. The nomad may have few possessions, but his wealth lies in his animals. These people had neither animals nor possessions, and in the yards surrounding the gers was little save bare mud and rubbish; here and there a motorbike, and very occasionally an old truck which provided somebody's living. The children playing in the streets were grubby and tattered, the smallest usually wearing miniature dels, the older ones much-worn western style clothing - cheap T-shirts and tracksuits imported from China.

And all of them happy, laughing kids. Few could have been more deprived, but they made their own fun with football or sticks and, in one street, the simple game of throwing stones from a distance into an old suitcase. They invited me to join in, and within moments were laughingly bringing me monster rocks. Hitting the case was a doddle for anyone over three feet tall, but that wouldn't have been playing the game. I kept missing narrowly, and applauded when anyone else got a bull's-eye.

By the time I left them the sun had set dramatically over Gandaan's temples, and the eastern mountains were pinkly incandescent in the pure mountain air. There were compensations for living in this grim, comfortless suburb. To the north, though, black lowering clouds threatened one of Mongolia's abrupt changes in the weather, and within minutes lightning split the sky.

I was going to get wet, I thought resignedly, in between the next six or so changes of bus. But for once one was enough, and I was safe in the Altai before the rain bucketed down.

*

The food situation, in UB at least, wasn't as bad as Carol and I had feared. In the State Department Store on Peace Avenue, the only sizeable shop in all Mongolia, the shelves were well stocked with basics. We could have bought our rice and biscuits here, and even noodles. There was plenty of flour, if we only had the means to cook it, and before leaving town we could stock up on sugar.

While casing the joint I was approached by an elderly Mongol, hostility written all over his grizzled face.

"Russkii?" he growled.

"Niet - Angliiskii," I replied quaking, making two mistakes in the one word to prove my credentials.

His face creased into a broad grin. "Then... Good... LUCK!" he roared, and thumped me on the shoulder. It was the nearest I got to trying out my Russian for several days. Afraid of being wrongly identified as a Russian before I had had the chance to demonstrate, through my linguistic incompetence, that I was just a foreign capitalist swine, I clamped my mouth shut on anything but English.

Perhaps that was why I didn't manage to get tea in the cafe along the street. First of all the waitress brought me a large bowl of thick soup. I shook my head, risked the Russian "chai" and sent it back. She returned with a small bowl of thin soup, at which I gave up and drank it. Straight from the bowl; there was no spoon. The two ladies at the next table had spoons, and must have thought me hopelessly uncouth - probably a Russian. Much later it dawned on me that this was probably the milky, salty Mongol tea which I'd been dreading. If so, here was the key to surviving it: just think of it as thin soup.

As for restaurants, there were plenty of them, serving perfectly adequate meals - if you weren't too choosy. For the food was unvarying.

The menus tried very hard. In the Altai it was "bifsteks" one day, "kotlet" the next. But the meal, when it came, was always the same: boiled mutton. About the only variation lay in whether the mince was served up loose or glued together into a rissole. Always mince, or at best small bits; you only fed large bits of Mongolian meat to a cement mixer. It was usually accompanied by plain rice, occasionally by potato. If you were lucky there might be boiled red cabbage, or raw red cabbage - or both together if no other vegetables were available - and, on a red-letter day, a teaspoonful of chopped carrot. Guest houses the world over are supposed to smell of boiled cabbage; those in Mongolia, from the early hours of the morning to late at night, reek of boiled mutton.

There was better food about - if you knew where to go. By the time Carol and I left UB, we had just about worked out how to eat properly. But I couldn't shop around, as I needed all my legpower for higher things.

The Ulaan Baatar Hotel was my lifeline. As UB's biggest and most expensive hotel, it represented the fleshpots. There were three restaurants: a posh one at the top where I never ventured, a middle one where a decent meal cost only a few dollars, and my usual bolt-hole on the ground floor, a cheap and popular eating place for travellers, serving mostly the usual mutton but more imaginatively disguised than elsewhere.

And the Altai bus stopped immediately outside. This was a mixed blessing, for it was the busiest bus route in UB.

To watch a Mongolian crowd entering a packed bus gives some insight into the successes of Genghis Khan's army. For one thing, there's no nonsense about allowing disembarking passengers to get off first. This would make the game too soft. So the process is a fight to the death between the opposing teams, with the leaders furiously using feet, elbows and teeth, and the rearguard leaning all their weight into the scrum.

Sometimes a spoilsport driver took matters into his own hands, driving a hundred yards beyond the bus-stop before opening his doors so as to separate the combatants. The ensuing hundred-yard dash gave the leavers time to escape, while nicely spreading the entrants and giving a breathless wilt to their aggression.

The first time I tried this national sport I got caught in the middle. After a few moments using my elbows to defend myself and the frail, elderly lady beside me, I'd had enough, and the bus sped off without me while I sat gasping in the gutter. After that I learned the lesson, avoiding the hotel bus-stop at peak hours or eating elsewhere altogether.

If all else failed, there were always the kiosks. Mongolia's earliest private businesses, they lined the streets in busy areas or near bus stops. Most were plain, wooden cubes; a few mimicked Chinese pagodas. One imaginative lad had painted his box as a bright blue ghetto blaster, with black daubs for the knobs.

One or two sold bread and even, occasionally, a few wizened potatoes. Most were good for a bar of chocolate, or some locally bottled drink, and all sold cigarettes. The main stock, though, was cheap, imported stuff mostly from China - soap, washing powder and other basics. Plus the most widespread and depressing sign of the impact of western culture on Mongolia so far: Coke, Snickers and chewing gum.

One thing I was desperate for: tea. All I ever managed to get was the Mongolian version, which was indeed the thin soup I'd been given in the cafe.

Looking one day through the open door of the *djournaya*, or caretaker, on my floor of the Altai, I spotted a row of thermos flasks. My blood pressure surged: could they be for the guests? Certainly they suggested facilities for boiling water. And I had my own teabags in the food bag.

Rather grudgingly, the djournaya agreed to put the kettle on for me, and I went back to my room in high excitement to wait. After half an hour, there was still no sign of her, so I went looking. But her door was locked against importunate foreigners, and no-one answered my knock.

A long time after I'd given her up, she unexpectedly arrived at my door with a pot. I was almost pathetically grateful; but then I took the lid off.

The inside was greasy with mutton fat, and a thick scum floated on top, along with two dead flies. Desperate for tea, I actually went through the motions of making a brew. The result looked almost drinkable, and I almost drank it. Then I remembered the flies, and they tipped the balance.

It worked. I didn't bother her again.

*

On one of my mystery bus tours, I accidentally washed up on the road to Zaisan, where the Tuul River, running wide and slow right under the sacred mountain of Bogd Uul, is a popular swimming spot for small boys.

Here, where the road forks off to the village-suburb of Yarmag, and beyond it the airport, is a grandiose tank monument. It commemorates the last battle fought on Mongolian soil, against invading Japanese troops in 1939. Never inclined to brevity, the Communist authorities labelled it "World War Two Revolutionary Mongolian Tank Brigade Monument". Behind it lies a rather more absorbing piece of history: the Winter Palace of the Bogd Khan.

The last Bogd Khan, the Holy Ruler, was the eighth Jetsundamba Khutuktu, or re-incarnation of the Living Buddha, and in the Buddhist hierarchy third only to the Dalai Lama. Like the latter, each successive Khutuktu was "discovered" re-incarnated in the person of a very young child, a few years after the death of his predecessor. The Khutuktu was the spiritual head of the Mongolian people; and when independence from China was unilaterally declared in 1911, the Eighth Incarnation was the natural choice as Head of State.

It was the presence of the successive Jetsundamba Khutuktus in Urga (Ulaan Baatar) which made it the leading city in Outer Mongolia. At first a shifting tent city, grouped around the Khutuktu's camp, it became a fixed settlement only in the latter half of the eighteenth century. At the same time other Mongolian towns were beginning to grow up around lamaseries, military camps and Chinese trading posts.

The Winter Palace is comparatively recent, dating from 1903 when the Manchus still ruled here; hence its Chinese style. Demons guard its gateways, and the rippling green tiles and swept-up frills of the roof are replicated in pagoda-like structures about the grounds, their ridges crowned by the silhouettes of lions and deer.

Inside, it is preserved as a museum, with contemporary furniture and artefacts. There are also, they say, pornographic pictures painted behind the mirrors.

This hint of hidden scandal is the tip of an all-too-visible iceberg; for the Holy Ruler wasn't in fact as holy as his title pretended.

Most of the few travellers to Mongolia in the late nineteenth or early twentieth centuries were far from impressed by the morals of the lamas they met. Experiences - and, in their absence, tales - were rife of theft, promiscuity, perversions. They spoke of visiting lamas demanding *droit du seigneur* over the lady of the house; of the clergy being largely instrumental in the spread of venereal diseases, estimated by medical sources to affect nine-tenths of the adult population.

Head of the lamas in all spiritual matters, the last Khutuktu apparently wasn't far behind in such temporal things. Certainly he openly defied his duty of celibacy to maintain a wife. Her photographs show a fierce-looking lady not unlike the "Granny" in Giles' cartoons, so perhaps it isn't surprising that her holy consort preferred the company of little boys. Not that her looks had much to do with it, for advanced syphilis had left him blind for many years.

Pathetic figure as he was, the Khutuktu was allowed to retain a symbolic position as Head of State after the Revolution. He was needed to give credibility to the new regime among his simple and pious subjects. But he obliged his new masters by dying decently soon, and even without being helped on his way. His debauchery had brought ultimate disgrace on his position. Perhaps for once it wasn't entirely due to religious intolerance that the Communist government decreed there would be no successor.

For whatever reason, his people seemed to accept the declaration that he was the last of his line, and there would be no Ninth Incarnation. From now on the country would be a Republic.

30

Now, with the resurgence of Buddhism in Mongolia, will some young child emerge from an obscure position to be proclaimed a ninth Jetsundamba Khutuktu? Or even a tenth, since it is a generous threescore years and ten since the death of the last one recognised? It is a fascinating possibility.

II

FUN AND GAMES

At ten o' clock sharp the brass band, smart in red and blue braid, struck up a fanfare.

It was a pity they'd forgotten to collect all their members. The result was chaotic, with musicians running from the stands and elbowing through the ranks, bashing a path with trumpet or tuba, to take their places halfway through. Meanwhile, the loudspeaker prattled patriotic waffle, effectively drowning the music. It wasn't a promising start.

But the opening ceremony, which began an hour later, was magnificent.

The band - complete now - launched into martial music. It probably came straight from Hollywood but here, in the wide arena thronged with people and framed by sharp-edged mountains, it was spine-tingling.

The gates at the far end were thrown open. In came nine warriors, clad in worn, boiled leather plate-mail and helmets, mounted on identical palomino horses and each carrying the yak's-tail banner symbolic of the armies of Genghis Khan. Twice they circled the arena then, attended by cavalry units, processed up the centre. Dismounting, they planted their banners ceremoniously in a circular stand. The Naadam games were officially open.

Now the members of the cast came on stage. From the gates at the near end strode the archers, some hundred men and women, carrying long recurve bows and dressed in colourful dels, leather boots and round, pointed hats. The racehorses followed, a token number only of the hundreds waiting to come under orders. Their child riders wore the bright tunics and strange, peaked caps that are the traditional jockeys' dress. All made a circuit of the arena before taking their positions around the edge.

An aerial display brought the ceremony abruptly into the twentieth century. Suddenly appearing from low over the hills, a helicopter flew the length of the arena, with a man dangling precariously from a line underneath and holding high the Mongolian flag. It flew a number of passes overhead, each time releasing three or four parachutists who spiralled skilfully down, trailing a coloured smoke canister or a flag, to make a succession of perfect landings on one of two small crosses of white fabric laid out at each end of the stadium.

At last the show was over. To prolonged applause the riders remounted, and led the crowd of performers from the arena. As the tailenders left, more than five hundred wrestlers flooded on to the field. The serious stuff was about to begin.

*

"The history of Naadam," says the English translation of the local tourist booklet *This is Mongolia*, "is rooted in hoary antiquity." For centuries the Mongolian people have come together on high days and holidays, celebrating their festivals by competition in the *Eriyn Gurvan Naadam* (Three Manly Sports) of wrestling, archery and horse-racing. After 1921, July 11th - Revolution Day - became the occasion for the National Naadam held in Ulaan Baatar, now extending over two days.

For more than a week the *arats* - Mongolian herdsmen - had been streaming on to the steppe between Yarmag, on the airport road, and the Holy Mountain of Bogd Uul. Here a ger city suddenly sprang up, like a crop of mushrooms after autumn rains, as they made their temporary camp for the duration of the festival.

It was a timeless scene. For hundreds of years the nomads of Central Asia have gathered just so for their markets and festivals; or to go to war.

Many, uprooting en masse with the whole family, brought their herds with them. For a few days the mountains echoed to the bleating of thousands of sheep and goats. The Yarmag bus was held up by mobs of twenty or thirty horses at a time, on their way to water at the banks of the Tuul. Groups of children on half-wild ponies raced each other around the suburbs, and riders in their best clothes trotted down Peace Avenue, or crossed Sukhbaatar Square.

Best clothes were the order of the day all round. Ladies went shopping in beautiful silk dresses of a pattern adapted from the del, while sober townsmen replaced their trilbies with the traditional pointed hats. Incongruous in the department store was one formidable old countryman, sweating under a thick del and *gutuls*, the ceremonial leather boots with upturned, pointed toes and inch-thick felt lining. If his party outfit was designed for winter wear, that was no excuse to leave it at home.

The pre-Naadam parade through the city was a technicolour pageant. Groups from every section of society and representatives of every contemporary organisation wore costumes from every period of Mongolian history. There was even a troop of drum majorettes, with white teeny-bopper knee-boots under their short, black, gold-braided skirts.

At irregular intervals a deep clang sounded from one end of Sukhbaatar Square. It came from the "World Peace Bell", a heavy brass thing some two feet high, hung in a Chinese-style pagoda in the small park between the Square and Peace Avenue. A horizontal wooden beam was slung alongside, and passers-by stopped to dong the bell, swinging the beam as a clapper.

Standing hard by the main bus-stops and on a pathway through to Sukhbaatar, it was much used. As the city crowds thickened, queues began to form at the pagoda, and a gentle benevolent ringing sounded an ongoing bass line to the music of the Square.

*

To the south of the city, between the line of the Trans-Mongolian Railway and the Choijin Lama monastery, is Nairamdal (Friendship) Park, where Naadam is held.

The park runs some miles along the line of river and railway, and at its near end a few hand-cranked roundabouts cater for minuscule riders. All, of course, gallopers; what else would the junior Mongol expect in a fairground? Even in children's playgrounds the amusements are all shaped as horses or camels.

For once I managed to catch the right bus and, with a short detour to dong the Peace Bell, arrived at the Park gates with an hour to spare. It was only a short walk from here, over the footbridge which crosses the hot-water pipes - when the system was renewed a few years ago, the old pipe was left to disintegrate alongside the new, producing a double barrier. Across the park, holiday-makers were settling themselves for the day, bagging the shadiest spots to spread their picnics under the trees.

People streamed in from all directions to the stadium, like ants to spilled sugar. Places filled fast for the opening ceremony, and by the time the wrestling began the stands were heaving with people.

Wrestling is to Mongolia as football is to Britain or baseball to the States. If a couple of English kids meet and play together, the chances are that they will soon be kicking a ball about. In Mongolia, they have each other in a half-nelson before introductions are completed.

Certainly the men now congregating in one of the doorways looked frighteningly professional. And terrifyingly large. There are no weight divisions here, and although the Mongolian wrestler may be a few hamburgers short of the Sumo expert, it was obvious that no-one under six feet tall or less than fifteen stone stood a chance. Their size was all the more striking for the fact that their countrymen are, generally, a small race.

All were dressed alike: short tunics of pink or blue silks, with trunks of the same colour, and heavy gutuls. Their pointed hats were held during the bout by each man's *zasuul*, or second. The stewards wore carmine-pink dels, with a golden sash; one particularly hulking brute, someone said in a hushed whisper, was a "Titan", a former multiple champion.

As soon as the helicopter had quit the arena for the last time, they poured on to the field, a solid phalanx of bone and muscle that would have gladdened the heart of Genghis Khan. Spreading out, they performed the mystical "eagle dance", a slow-stepping, arm-waving ritual. Supposed to imitate the flight of Garuda, the legendary bird of the east, this is really to impress the spectators - and psych out the opposition.

Within a few moments they had paired off, handed their hats to the zasuul, and closed in a murderous clinch.

These were the cream of Mongolia's wrestlers, men who had already come through qualifying rounds at local meets. Yet some of the bouts ended surprisingly fast, the victor taking just a few seconds to make the winning throw, or force some part of his opponent's body other than hands or feet to touch the ground and end the contest. The winner headed for the yak's-tail stand to perform another eagle dance, this time one of victory.

Meanwhile, track races were in progress. Although very much a fringe event of the festival, this was nevertheless high-class stuff. I timed the women's 100m at under thirteen seconds, pretty sharp on an undulating concrete track criss-crossed with grassy cracks; and this from a nation with no running tradition. Except that, when it comes to anything physical, the Mongolians are up there with the best of them.

The thrills were over for today in the main arena. With several hundred wrestlers fighting on a straight knock-out basis, it would be well into the next day before the real excitement began to run high. Meanwhile, competition was getting under way at the archery stands behind the stadium.

Here, at the head of a range stretching about eighty yards, competitors were busy stringing their bows and flexing their shoulders. Almost as many women as men took part, and classes were held for children. But the archers who really stole the show were the veterans, a venerable troop of wizened old men whose seamed faces and bright, deep-set eyes might have seen as many as eight decades.

One ramrod-straight old man, resplendent in black del and gold-tasselled sash, was the image of Sir John Gielgud. He was a past champion, and the crowd held its collective breath with every arrow he shot. For the rival to his immediate left, the spectators simply didn't exist; concentration in every sinew, he struck an attitude after each arrow, feet apart and eyes staring straight ahead while he centred his thoughts afresh. He might have been alone on the steppe with never a soul for miles.

They shot at a strange target: a pyramid of small felt cylinders, to be toppled like skittles. Hard by each pile stood a team of four judges.

36

Regardless of life and limb, they followed each shot closely, occasionally lifting a casual foot to let a stray arrow pass underneath. They then faced the archer, arms outstretched in a gesture meant to show his degree of accuracy. Every such gesture looked, to my ignorance, identical.

Blunt plastic cylinders tipped the arrows, but no further regard was given to safety. The stands were at the competitors' end, but spectators could sit along the full length of the range, or wander where they chose. Imbibing the general laissez-faire, I walked carelessly across behind the butts, and a skidding arrow nearly took my foot off.

*

The horse and the bow were the mainstay of the Mongol hordes. They could hardly fail to be experts at mounted archery, for their Central Asian forebears had spent more than two millennia getting it right.

In the mid-twelfth century, though, they were mostly practising on each other. Asia east of the Altai Mountains was inward-looking, the home of many small, endlessly warring tribes. The land was nominally under the control of the Chinese, who exercised a divide-and-rule policy. Only if one tribe looked like getting too big for its boots did they intervene, to prop up a rival and restore the balance. Thus they got what they wanted - safety from the threat of nomadic incursions - for minimal trouble. That was, until one of the least of these tribes, the Mongols, came to dominate and unite the rest, and bequeath its name to history.

Tradition wasn't short of myths to attach to the child born in 1167, the Year of the Pig, to the petty chieftain Yesugei, and named Temujin. Old wives remembered how he emerged from the womb with a clot of blood the size of a knuckle-bone in each tiny fist; contemporaries related without censure how the eleven-year-old boy had killed his half-brother over a minor disagreement.

Temujin's early life was the stuff of legend. Exile with his family from his tribe, and precarious living off the land; capture and enslavement for several months by a hostile tribe; the gradual forming of a fragile camp of friends and allies, only to be raided and dispersed into hiding on the slopes of the holy mountain Burkhan Khaldun. Eventually,

37

ASIA in the EARLY THIRTEENTH CENTURY

KIEV

RUS

Caspian Sea

Aral Sea

L. Balkhash

KHORESMIA

KARA

BUKHARA

SAMARKAND

MERV

SYRIA

BAGHDAD

PERSIA

HERAT

CAIRO

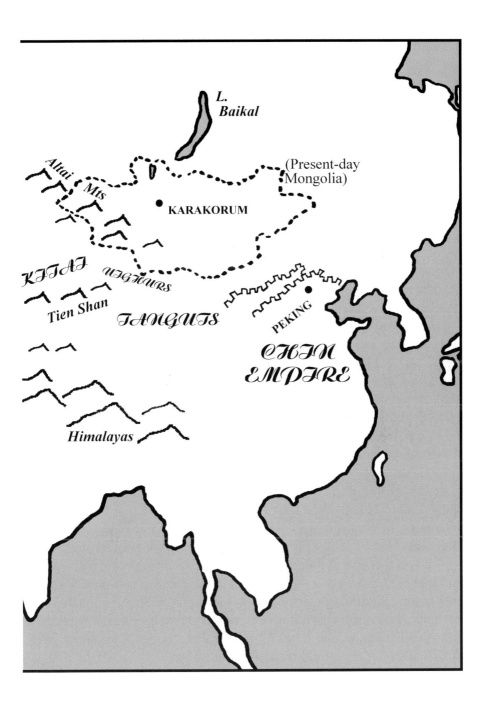

L.
Baikal

Altai
Mts

(Present-day
Mongolia)

KARAKORUM

KITAI

UEGHURS

Tien Shan

TANGUTS

PEKING

CHIN
EMPIRE

Himalayas

with the patronage of his father's *anda* - blood-brother - Toghrul, Khan of a powerful clan, and the help of his own anda Jamukha, he became the head of a strong force, more an alliance than a tribe. They elected him their Khan, whereupon he took the name Genghis. Its meaning is disputed; one interpretation is "Oceanic"; that is, Universal. It was a pretentious title for the head of a few miscellaneous nomads. He now proceeded to justify it.

From precarious infancy to local warlord had taken him twenty years. He spent the next twenty consolidating his power, mopping up rival tribes one by one and eliminating both Toghrul and Jamukha in the process. The path to leadership was arduous, with many reverses, and more than once he nearly lost everything. By the time he was proclaimed Khan of all the people of the felt tents, Emperor of the Steppes, he had learned to trust rarely and forgive almost never; and had acquired the few shreds of ruthlessness that he had not already been born with.

He had also become an outstanding general. From his early days as a warlord, he had drilled his gradually increasing army with a discipline never seen before on the steppes. And as he absorbed new tribes, he was careful to break up their warriors, distributing them among the *tumans* - units of ten thousand - under his own commanders. By 1206 he led over a hundred thousand men, and nobody gave much thought to the Chinese any more. Except, that is, the Chinese themselves. They were now getting understandably twitchy.

Throughout Genghis Khan's rise to power, the driving aim was not so much power itself as raw survival. Having unified the tribes and gained control of all of the steppe east of the Altai, what next? What leap of imagination transformed the aspiration to live and rule, into that of becoming lord of a world greater than he then knew even existed?

It was the natural progression of military unity, says David Morgan in his book *The Mongols*. "Unless something decisive was done with the newly-formed military machine, it would soon dissolve into quarrelling factions again... If it was not used against external enemies, it would not remain in being for long. The only matter that required a decision was in which direction the armies were to advance."

Lev Gumilev, Soviet historian and gloriously described in *This is Mongolia* as "author of global humanitarian biospheric ideas", is rather more indulgent. "I've come to a fantastic conclusion: the Mongols' wars were defensive. All the time they were pestered and forced to defend themselves. They retaliated so strongly that it brought them victory."

Aggressive expansionists or innocent victims? Or was there ever a Great Plan at all, offensive or defensive?

Genghis was a child of the steppe, not a graduate of a military academy. His combination of genius and charisma had brought him via survival to greatness by a progression composed of risk, of impulse, of a series of lucky throws of the dice. And the next step was written almost indelibly into his fate. The proper course for a nomad warrior was decreed by more than two thousand years of history. It was to plunder the lands of his settled neighbours for the rich pickings of civilisation. With a certain inevitability, he began to raid China.

Against the Tanguts of Central China, the Mongols had their first experience of attacking walled cities. As ever, they learned rapidly. Captured engineers taught them siege tactics. By the time three campaigns over six years had prostrated the Tanguts, Genghis was ready to take on the Chin Empire. In 1215 the Mongols crossed the Great Wall and sacked Peking. Three years later they conquered the Kara Kitai, a powerful people of eastern Turkestan. The Mongol Empire was up and running. Yet it was even now only in its infancy.

With it came a new lesson to be learned: Administration. This was provided by the Uighurs, neighbours of the Kara Kitai, who had early seen the writing on the wall and submitted voluntarily to Genghis. To add to the biggest and best army in the world, he now had an embryonic civil service. He had become a statesman. To prove it, he left the continuing war against the Chin to one of his generals, and opened communications with the other great Asiatic empire.

Ala-ad-Din Mohammed II, the Khoresmshah - that is, Shah of the Khoresmian Empire of the Oxus delta thousands of miles away in western Turkestan - was considered by most people, not least himself, to be the greatest ruler in the world. He had recently added the ancient, fabled cities of Samarkand and Bukhara, wrested from the Kara Kitai, to the empire he had inherited from his father Tekesh, and now ruled from the Euphrates to the borders of China. His self-esteem was badly dented, therefore, when an emissary arrived in Samarkand from somewhere Mohammed had never heard of, bearing a lump of gold the size of a camel's hump and a promise from an obscure nomad chief to love Khoresmia "as he loved his most cherished sons".

Genghis may not have been a diplomat; but nor, it now emerged, was Mohammed. When a Mongol caravan arrived on his border at Otrar to implement, as they expected, a trade agreement, the governor there - doubtless acting on orders - butchered the lot. Genghis' response was, by the standards to come, mild: he sent three envoys to Mohammed to demand reparation - and the governor's head on a plate. Mohammed replied unequivocally. He executed one of the envoys and sent the other two back with their beards singed, the crowning Asiatic thumbed nose. By this act of careless derision he condemned millions to death... including himself.

It took two years of careful preparation before Nemesis caught up with Mohammed. When it did, he realised too late that he was confronting not a bunch of mounted thugs but an army, maybe as much as two hundred thousand strong, of unprecedented discipline and sophistication. With the help of their tame Chinese siege engineers, the Mongols employed ballista and trebuchet, Greek fire - even explosives. But their greatest weapon of all was terror.

"I am the punishment of God," thundered Genghis from the pulpit of Bukhara's central mosque, while his men picketed their horses in the courtyard beneath and prepared to sack the city. In his vengeful pursuit of Mohammed, Genghis visited that punishment on the great cities of Central Asia in turn. At Samarkand, which he approached behind a human shield of Bukhariot prisoners, the entire garrison of thirty thousand was massacred, the population enslaved. At Merv, the Mongols slaughtered every living thing then retired into the desert to lie in ambush for the few survivors who crept back prematurely into the smoking ruins. Worst carnage of all was at Herat, which committed the unforgivable sin of submitting then turning again in rebellion; estimates of its dead ranged at around two million.

Rumour preceded the Mongol juggernaut, turning knees to water and paralysing resistance. Rumour expanded their awfulness with mystique, with the fear of the unknown. The civilised peoples of ancient Silk Road cities saw the Mongols through the eyes and ears of Rumour much as students of Middle Earth see trolls and orcs through the imagination of Tolkien - except that the Mongols existed for real. "They have the heads of horses," people whispered. "They give birth to children like snakes, and eat like wolves." "They live for three hundred years..." And they stank. You could smell them coming before you saw them.

The first scent to be carried downwind must have belonged to the Tatars, as they were usually in the vanguard. Former tribal enemies of the original, nuclear Mongol clan, they were perhaps put there by Genghis to share the fate of Uriah the Hittite. The cry: "The Tatars are coming!" that went up at their approach led to the name often being associated with the entire Mongol army, rather than just one division. Genghis Khan's men came, quipped King Louis IX of France, "ex Tartaro", which finds an echo in the idiom of our time: the Soldiers From Hell. The label stuck, with or without the extra "r". To this day the name "Tartary" is loosely applied to Turkestan, the lands wrested from Mohammed and others by the Mongols; and the descendants of Mongol invaders in southern Russia are known as Tatars.

As for Mohammed himself, he eluded capture throughout a long hunt across Afghanistan and Persia. A fishing boat took him, dressed as a beggar, to the island of Abeskum in the Caspian Sea, where he made his only sensible move of the whole fiasco by succumbing to fatal pleurisy before the Mongols reached him.

Genghis survived him by a mere six years. Now the master of the largest empire in the world, he was still looking for fresh challenges. Campaigning once more against the Tanguts in China, he took a fatal fall from his horse - surely a rare exit for a Mongol, even one of sixty. His body was brought back to Mongolia and buried with great secrecy. "He who witnesses the death of a Khan," ran the saying, "becomes a pillow under his head." Genghis' head rested on forty jewelled slave girls and forty horses. After the burial a thousand horsemen rode back and forth over the grave to obliterate it. They succeeded entirely, for the site remains undiscovered to this day.

*

Five miles up the road at Yarmag I found the other half of the Mongol military equation, the horse. Here was the real hub of things, the pulsating ancient core of the Naadam festival.

By now the arats' camp stretched away up the hill for half a mile. Across the road, a double row of trucks formed an impromptu market selling everything imaginable. In between was a constant flow of traffic. Mounted traffic; spectators on foot were in the minority, and a lesser breed altogether.

The chief excitement lay over towards the airport. The finishing post for the races was marked partly by the rickety green wooden stand, but mostly by the thronging pedestrians - and the horse lines pressing up close behind them and outnumbering them greatly. Word had come back from the steppe that the race had begun, and all were staking out their positions early; even though it would be the best part of an hour before the finish.

"Hoary antiquity" plays its part here, too. The Naadam races evolved from the *Yam*, the communications system set up by Genghis Khan nearly eight hundred years ago. Even the distance - one *urton*, or nineteen miles - commemorates the stages between successive posts of what was a kind of Pony Express. Although it wasn't a new idea for Asia - Genghis borrowed it from the Kara Kitai, but the Persians had been doing it rather well nearly two thousand years earlier - the Yam's efficiency was astonishing. At the peak of the Mongol Empire dispatches could be sent from eastern Europe to the Chinese coast in a matter of days. Marco Polo estimated a travel rate of two to three hundred miles a day. What, I wondered, would he have made of the tiny riders performing today?

Mongol ponies are small, between thirteen and fourteen hands by western measurement; that is, standing just over four feet high at the

44

shoulder. Incredibly strong, they may carry a tall man, plus saddlebags, all day over rough terrain. The Mongols reckon them the toughest horses in the world, and no-one would disagree. But the lighter their load, the faster they can run.

So the jockeys are boys and girls mostly aged from six to eight; never more than ten, and sometimes as young as four. The herdsmen's children grow up in the saddle, quite literally riding before they can walk. To gallop nineteen miles isn't unusual for them; to prove it, many race bareback to minimise weight.

Assembling by the camp, they ride together with the marshals and officials to the start, miles away on the steppe. On the way they pass the "Wailing Stone" - actually an *obo*, or sacred cairn. Tradition demands that all circle it three times, singing the "Wailing Song", a cautionary tale about Gin and Gu, a boy and horse who won when illegally entered.

And then the flag goes up and the cavalry charge is off; and the crowd back home wait in tense anticipation.

I found a spot on the rails, with horses breathing down my neck. Just behind was a friendly chestnut pony, tolerant of human contact - a rare thing, here. I was very glad that I'd made a pal of him, for after some time standing I began to feel very ill, and had to lean against him. Five minutes later my legs gave way altogether, and I ended up slumped on the ground, squeezed between spectators on one side... and the pony's hock on the other, an unthinkable liberty with a Mongolian horse. It said much, too, for the human watchers, that nobody pinched my place while I was down.

For despite the rising excitement, the crowd was impeccably quiet. Yet suddenly a line of riot police arrived, complete with perspex shields and vicious-looking batons. I wondered what they knew that I didn't.

Ten minutes later, I made it to my feet again. And none too soon; for, with a rising buzz at the sighting of the still distant leaders, drama broke prematurely.

As heads began to turn and the spectators to lean out for a better view, one end of the tottering grandstand gave way, spilling people and heavy boards together down on to those below. A few remained, clinging to the remaining rail, or swung down harmlessly in a controlled fall. Helpers converged quickly to scrabble among the wreckage towards those groaning underneath, or to catch children passed down to safety from above.

One more moment, and the disaster was forgotten by all except those caught up in it directly; for the first horses were thundering up the finishing straight. Cheers went up for the gallant winner who had galloped nineteen miles. A moment later, all hell broke loose.

Through the increasing dust cloud galloped horse after horse, still tightly packed and racing hard after all those miles. There must have been well over a hundred finishers. And on both sides of the course a stampede began, as those supporters who had followed the last few miles on horseback scooped up the mounted spectators at the finish, and all raced pell-mell together beside the finishing funnel to greet their own competitors.

Despite the heavy rain of the last few days, the air was thick with dust. The later homecomers were barely visible, and my sympathy went out to the horses who had galloped their hearts out all that way in the thick of the pack, with never a breath of clean air. As the backmarkers trailed in, they were overtaken by the first of the ambulances, threading a path from the broken grandstand through the dust and horses to escape at the funnel exit. It was utter bedlam. To be a spectator on foot felt like walking through a herd of charging buffalo, and about half as safe. The riot police wisely took cover.

As for the tiny jockeys, there were no tears of exhaustion, not even a few buckling knees. They dismounted from their gruelling ride as nonchalant and impassive as if they had just been for a quick canter. One little boy sat a few yards from the finish, burying his face in an enormous slice of watermelon, while drips of juice made puddles in the dust on his racing silks.

I needed some fuel myself, if my legs were going to get me home. From one of the trucks I bought a handful of bars of some sort of Chinese nougat. Solid enough to finish building the Mongol Tour Rules OK Guest House, they were the more packed with calories for it, and saw me back to the Altai.

I was sated with Naadam; but there was no escaping it. In the entrance hall, a huge old colour telly had appeared for the occasion. On its screen wrestlers heaved and grunted far into the night.

*

They were still heaving and grunting the next day. But now the numbers were much reduced, giving plenty of space for the lengthy rituals of the later stages.

The third round begins with a song from the zasuuls. "Hear us, people on the other wing..." followed by endless praise of their own particular protégés. From now on, the competitors of the right or senior "wing" (roughly, the top seeds) may choose their own opponents from the lower wing. The zasuul gives the challenge:

"Zasuuls of the left wing, hearken! I challenge your wrestlers!"

"So be it," they reply.

"At this joyous and great Naadam, my chief of wrestlers, captain of the mighty, most eminent of the host of sinew, foremost of ten thousand battles, strongest of the strong, bursting with bravery, gloriously invincible before the people, challenges wrestler... (name), of... (province and district), in the family of the mighty, joyfully to match strength, in the flower of his manliness and might!"

"Thankyou for the honour," answers the zasuul. This posturing continues with the eagle dance and a lot of fierce glowering; and battle commences.

Those men who make it through to the sixth round are given the title *Nachin* (Falcon), while the semi-finalists are *Zaan* (Elephant). The champion, with echos of Narnia, is called *Arslan*, or Lion. The ultimate accolade of *Avraga* - Titan - is reserved for those who win two titles.

So what does that leave for the champion who wins again and again? The answer is simple. With each victory his title is celebrated by a further tribute. The greatest Mongolian wrestler of all time, Khorloogiyn

Bayanmunkh, was thus described: Eye-pleasing Nationally Famous Mighty Invincible Titan. Truly, madly, deeply a champion.

Only one stand had any tickets left. To my great good luck, this was at the very end of the arena, where the prizewinners in the racing were assembling.

Just across the barrier from me thirty or forty horses grazed loose; a few wandered far up the arena to stare in amazement at the wrestlers between mouthfuls of grass. Soon preparations for the prizegiving ceremony began. Horses who had probably never before seen a brush in their lives were lovingly polished, ornamental saddles were girthed up, riders patted down their silk pyjamas and gave a final tweak to their peaked caps, which looked like Christmas paper hats. Manes were braided with coloured tapes, forelocks twisted up into a top-knot, bridles draped with the ceremonial blue silk scarf known as a *khadag*.

At last their moment of glory arrived. In seven groups of five - one for each race - they paraded right round the ring, escorted by mounted stewards, then halted in front of the yak's-tail stand for a lengthy panegyric.

"Racer, flying like the wind at the head of ten thousand,
Racer, straining on your iron bit,
Racer, straining tirelessly against your silken bridle,
Racer, whose teeth gleam like ivory,
Stretching your supple neck in the gallop,
Pricking your wondrous ears,
Your black eyes shining..."

Then the children dismounted and were led up to the VIPs, to return each bearing a large parcel wrapped in spotted paper; while the unfortunate horses received a libation of mare's milk poured over their heads.

The shadow of the low stands was now halfway across the field, but the wrestlers were still only on the semi-finals; each of these had already lasted over an hour. Even this crowd was finally losing patience, hissing when either pair stood back for a breather. At last, a bout came to an appropriately dramatic end when one contestant, seemingly the loser in a final convulsive clash, turned the tables and cleanly upended his opponent in a flying shoulder-wheel. The crowd went wild, and applauded with a slow handclap as the winner performed his victory-dance around the yak's-tails.

Four Elephants, and one of them a Lion. I didn't find out which. It was time for home.

*

The Naadam winners may be almost deified, but the losers aren't entirely forgotten.

The two-year-old racehorse which finishes last is honoured by its own special song. Called Bayan Khodood, or Full Stomach, it is given a bagful of excuses. The trainer was incompetent, the rider too young, while the racecourse was strewn with potholes and sharp stones. At next year's Naadam the horse will win, and its fame will rise like the sun and glitter like gold.

III

LONG WALK TO FREEDOM

The day's work turned into a zoological treasure hunt, beginning on the dusty streets of Ulaan Baatar and leading to the glorious mountains and steppes of Hustain Nuruu. The clues were a series of increasingly accurate directions, the stepping stones a string of offices, the progress a pattern of ever decreasing circles narrowing to the penultimate goal; and the treasure, one more step away, the exotic, prehistoric Przewalski horse.

Extinct for twenty-five years in its last natural homeland of Mongolia, the Przewalski or Mongolian Wild Horse continued to exist only in zoos and private collections. In recent years a number of schemes have been considered for re-introducing it to the wild. And now a group of visionary Dutch enthusiasts had succeeded in doing so, with the help of the Mongolian Association for the Conservation of Nature and the Environment.

John Knowles, Director of Marwell Zoo and a leading world expert on these horses, had kindly given me the address of this Association, but my preliminary letter asking to visit the release site had produced no response. I had to find its office; and, Mongolian addresses being cryptically framed with little reference to sequence or location, the many people I asked were as baffled as I was.

In desperation, I asked at the British Embassy. Try the Academy of Sciences, they said. Someone there is bound to know. And the hunt was on.

The Academy, behind the UB Hotel, was the tallest building in town. A concrete monolith flanked by two single storey blocks of one room each, it was a phallic symbol drawn in right-angles. No-one inside had the slightest idea of the Association's existence. On a whim, I went into one of the side annexes. It had nothing to do with science, being a privately run art shop. But the charming lady owner was my best lead yet.

"You want the Ministry of the Environment," she told me, briskly giving concise directions.

The trail was getting hot. Here I found the offices of the Mongolian Biodiversity Project, and a delightful lady called Suufd, with excellent English - and a knowledge of the Przewalski horses.

No, I still hadn't reached the Association, said Suufd; it was an NGO - non-governmental organisation - based elsewhere. But she took me to meet a couple of Canadians, both called Chris, who were working in various fields to assist the government's embryonic interest in conservation. Yes, they both knew about the re-introduction scheme. In fact, Chris no. 2 had been present when the horses were released. Frantically busy, he nevertheless found time to tell me about them. But for most of my questions, he referred me to Dr. Tserendeleg at MACNE. The acronym for the Association sounded vaguely familiar, although it was the next day before I remembered why.

Following Suufd's sketch map, I set out on the last lap. MACNE remained elusive to the last. In a little square with some promising offices such as UNICEF, it hid on the third floor of a building whose brass nameplates admitted only to banking and finance corporations. By now exhausted and demoralised, I nearly gave up and turned away; then gave myself a dressing down and went back for a closer look. I was exploring its different levels rather pessimistically when I met someone who recognised the name Tserendeleg; and nearly hugged the poor man.

And now I struck gold. By a rare coincidence, there in the office was Jan Vegter, Project Manager for the Dutch Foundation. He was travelling out to Hustain Nuruu Reserve the next day... and had a spare place in his jeep.

*

The Mongolian Wild Horse is named for the Russian explorer Nikolai Przewalski, who "discovered" it on his expedition in 1878; that's to say,

51

a hunter gave him a skull and hide which he brought back for examination by Moscow zoologists.

It is the world's only true wild horse, as opposed to "feral", or escaped domestic, horses like the Australian brumby or American mustang. Genetically different from the domestic horse, it bears the same sort of relationship to it as do the zebra and donkey. Closer, though; it is the only equid which can hybridise with the domestic horse to produce fertile offspring.

It is also probably the oldest of the species. The distinctive red-gold coat with lighter belly, black upstanding mane and chunky head and neck are depicted in cave paintings such as those at Lascaux and Vallon-Pont-d'Arc in France, dating from before 20,000 BC. In prehistoric times it roamed the grasslands which extended almost unbroken from central Europe to eastern Asia, reaching as far west as the Atlantic seabord.

Opinion is divided as to whether it is the still-living ancestor of the domestic horse, or a sub-species which evolved in parallel from a common parent. Most experts incline to the latter view, although many believe that Przewalski blood found its way into the domestic horse. Given its prevalence in ancient times, particularly in the Central Asian and Russian steppes where horses were first domesticated and selectively bred, it would be difficult to argue with this.

That it survived at all as a separate entity is remarkable. This was probably due to its intractability; like the zebra, it doesn't relate well to man. If such a horse approached domestic herds, it was more likely to be driven off - or killed and eaten - than captured and added to domestic stock, in case its genes produced wild and unmanageable offspring.

The spread of human population and livestock, with increasing settlement and agriculture, caused a degree of competition for grazing lands and water which drove the human-shy Przewalski into smaller and more barren areas. The invention of firearms probably accelerated its demise. The last survivors fetched up in the Jungarian Gobi, an arid land of mountain and semi-desert where the Altai range runs into the Gobi Desert. There were infrequent sightings of the horses in the fifties and sixties; then nothing.

But it escaped total extinction; for despite its shyness it was able, handled tactfully as a wild animal, to thrive and breed in captivity. From an original handful of captured specimens, there are now around a thousand scattered about the world.

From the time when it became a certainty that the Przewalski horse had died out in the wild, enthusiasts have dreamed of re-introducing it. The Foundation for the Preservation and Protection of the Przewalski Horse, brainchild of Jan and Inge Bouman, was founded in Holland in 1977. Since then, its handful of dedicated members have established a database of genetic and other details of the world's population of Przewalskis to aid breeding programmes worldwide. But their primary aim was more ambitious: restoration of the horse to its natural homeland.

Patiently, they set about collecting horses, establishing a number of "semi-reserves" where they could become accustomed to living in open spaces and fending for themselves with minimal human contact. Meanwhile, a team from the Foundation began to investigate possible release sites in the Ukraine, Kazakhstan and Mongolia. The choice fell on the former hunting reserve of Hustain Nuruu, a beautiful region of mixed mountain and steppe possessing a rich diversity of flora and fauna.

With the Dutch and Mongolian governments now involved, work began to set up an official nature reserve at Hustain Nuruu. And in June 1992, sixteen Przewalski horses were brought back to their native land.

They weren't set free at once. Instead, accommodation in three large pens gave them time to acclimatise to the fierce Mongolian winters, under the careful eye of Reserve staff. Some years on, they had passed all their tests with flying colours.

And just two weeks ago eleven Przewalski horses had been released into the wild.

*

The day started in such a way that it could only get better.

Jan was leaving from the Baigal Hotel, bought by MACNE from the Russians in 1982 and run to raise money in support of the Hustain Nuruu project. It was at the end of town diametrically opposite to the Altai. I left in plenty of time, but halfway down Peace Avenue my trolleybus broke down. When the passengers started crawling on to the roof to disconnect the antenna my nerve broke. I abandoned my sinking ship and jumped on the next passing bus; which promptly made two ninety-degree turns and galloped off back towards the Altai.

Eventually I walked much of the remaining distance, arriving hot, bothered, exhausted... and late.

No Jan. No sign of his jeep outside. Inside the Baigal, I asked at the desk. The receptionist, who had only a word or two of Russian, managed to indicate that Mr. Vegter had gone out.

"How far 'out'? Out of town, or nearby?" Incomprehension.

What followed was my second stroke of luck in two days. I had decided to give it half an hour before going miserably home, just in case Jan had only gone out on an errand. With five minutes to go, along came Baigal.

I thought I had misunderstood her, with my feeble Russian; had she said something about the hotel? No, that was her name. She was called, she said, like the hotel, after Lake Baikal in Siberia. The two different spellings were just a matter of local transcription. The word meant "nature". Perhaps it wasn't such a strange coincidence.

Baigal was a medical student whose brother worked at Hustain Nuruu as a ranger, and she was taking the chance to get a lift out there and visit him. She was able to tell me that Jan hadn't left after all. He had been held up, though she didn't know why.

It was another hour before Jan arrived, and he was as hot and bothered as I'd been earlier. He had been thrashing out a visa problem at the Foreign Office in UB. The Belgian government, he explained, had given generous grants for the establishmnent of Hustain Nuruu. Now they would like to send a delegation to have a look at the work. The trouble was, the xenophobic Mongolian Embassy in Brussels had blocked their visa application. It was left to Jan to try and convince the Powers That Be that, if you want people to give you money, it helps to be nice to them.

It was mid-day before we all packed into the jeep and set off. "All" included Jan and his driver, with a mysterious brown paper parcel wedged on the seat between them; Baigal and me; and a journalist accompanied by a photographer. Suzanne was Russian correspondent for the New York Times. Permanently based in St. Petersburg, she had been rushed out here to research an article on the newly released Przewalski horses. Igor was her photographer. They made an odd contrast; she small, neat and all-American, he tall and leggy, looking more Gallic than Slav. They huddled close in their corner of the jeep's back seat, talking privately in intimate whispers. It was apparent that their relationship was more than just a professional one.

We turned on to Peace Avenue and were led west out of the city, beside the railway, past the belching power station, and under the crazy multiple arches of the hot-water pipes. The concrete and smoke thinned and fell behind. At the city limits we forked left, away from the road to Siberia, to follow a line of green hills. But for the environs of Yarmag, this was my first real taste of the Mongolian countryside, and my face stayed greedily glued to the window.

All around, wide grassy plains curved up to meet low hills, sometimes close by, sometimes miles distant. Everywhere I looked there were grazing herds; huge ones of sheep and goats, smaller ones of horses and cattle. Four of the five mainstays of the Mongol economy; only the camels were missing. Here and there groups of two or three gers huddled together; once only did we see houses. A hamlet of beautifully painted bungalows, the village had been built for railway workers, said Baigal. They were out of place, interlopers on the timeless landscape.

But then so were the trucks, loaded with revellers on their way home from Naadam. As if to emphasise their inadequacy compared to the horse, several of these had given up the ghost and stood forlornly on the roadside, while baffled drivers peered helplessly into ailing engines. The passengers meanwhile waited philosophically, regretting their horses left behind at home. The scene was to become depressingly familiar over the coming weeks.

But most of the people streaming out of Ulaan Baatar on their way home were travelling the old-fashioned way. The steppe beside the road teemed with herdsmen and their families, still resplendent in best dels and Genghis Khan hats. Many drove herds before them, while a few towed strings of hard, fit-looking horses on leading reins: the local Great White Hopes coming home from the racing. Had any, I wondered, paraded in the ring with braided manes, to suffer the sticky anointing with mare's milk that was the sole reward for all their sweat?

An hour out from UB was a rare area of cultivation. Strips of wheat, alternating with fallow, ran alongside the road. The plot looked, in this immense landscape, comparable to an English field. It turned out, though, to be over a mile long.

But for this, the land was pasture, short, scrubby grass interspersed with flowers. And what flowers! In Mongolia's short summer, there is no space for succession, for spring flowers followed by summer flowers followed by autumn flowers. Everything blooms at once in brief exuberant profusion, racing the calendar to set seed before the bitter winter turns all to brown nonentity. Their carpet ran thickest in the disturbed ground beside the road, where I could see surprisingly many familiar friends: wild larkspur, willowherb, cranesbills and, twisting around the feet of its taller companions, the feathery yellow haze of lady's bedstraw.

At last we turned off the road, on to a rough track distinguishable from many others only by the row of telegraph poles running beside it. A golden plover flew from under our wheels, pipits piped overhead, and the occasional wheatear flashed its white rump. But for a single hoopoe, we might have been in the north of Scotland. That was, until we came to the dunes which loomed up suddenly out of the green steppe. Possibly the result of disturbing soil too sandy to cultivate, they housed, said Jan, a wolf's lair.

After some miles we breasted a rise and stopped at an obo. This is the traditional Buddhist monument, a mound of stones with a tall stick rising from the centre and heaped with offerings of every description: money, of course, scraps of cloth, pieces of bone, a horse's skull, even an old pot. Obos mark anywhere of moment in Mongolia. Boundaries, as here; mountain tops, passes, crossroads; or other places where it is felt that a spirit may dwell. Scratch a Buddhist Mongol and you find traces of a Siberian shamanist. The Old Religion runs deep in the national psyche.

Even we who, with the exception of the driver, were neither Buddhist nor shamanist, wouldn't have dreamed of passing the obo without stopping to pay our respects, by making the obligatory clockwise circuit and placing a stone. For it signified the entry to Hustain Nuruu Reserve; and as such stood for the Przewalski horses, whose roots go back deeper even than human spirituality.

"Place of the Takhi!" warned the sign nearby. *Takh*, Mongolian for the Przewalski horse, was a far more elegant name than the spluttering Russian one. From then on, none of us used any other.

Ten minutes later the jeep pulled up at the stone bungalow and cluster of gers that is the nerve centre of the Reserve. Waiting for us was a group of new names and faces. Lee Boyd, an American Przewalski expert, here for two months to make the first ever study of takhi in the wild; Dr. Perenlein Galragchaa - otherwise known as Dr. Gala - from MACNE, Director of Hustain Nuruu; Sukh, a tall, young Mongolian with fluent English who was here as interpreter; and Hans Hovens, a Dutch biologist, whose personality matched both his six foot three frame and the constant grin on his sunburned face.

And now the mystery of Jan's large parcel was solved. Almost before hallos were exchanged, Hans pounced on it and ripped it apart. Inside were several boxes of Cuban cigars. His supply had run out the week before, and he lit up with the desperation born of five days' cold turkey. Within moments he was groaning in ecstasy, while the rest of us choked in clouds of thick, black smoke.

In the cosmopolitan society of Hustain Nuruu, the everyday language was English. It was a great relief, as I had expected to have to blunder through somehow in Russian. But, as Hans later pointed out, most Dutch are fluent in English. Besides, he had his own reasons for avoiding Russian. The language has no "h", and replaces it in foreign words with a "g". (I had already been thoroughly confused by references to the "Gollandski".) This meant that his own name became "Gans" - rather bad luck, as in Dutch it means a goose.

After lunch (wonderful - I hadn't expected to be fed, and the enormous meal of soup, stew and rice, with real vegetables, was way above the dry loaves in my pack) we set out, anticipation and excitement mounting, to find the takhi.

Two "harem" groups, each of a stallion with four or five mares, had been released. The nearer, that of the stallion Khaan, was usually to be found in the next valley to where we were now, or on the hill in between. Lee took the lead. She had been shadowing this herd, and knew its movements better than most.

Hustain Nuruu Reserve straddles a wide valley running south between two mountain ridges to join the Tuul River at its lower end. On the west side the ridge is dominated by the horseshoe peak of Hustain Nuruu mountain, which lends its name to the Reserve.

The pink stone ridges, spotted with granite outcrops like Devonshire tors, are harshly beautiful. In contrast, the valleys that seam their hillsides are gentle, intimate places. Their lower slopes are alpine meadows covered with edelweiss and gentian, while the stream banks bloom in riotous colour with every flower imaginable.

We followed the beck which rises in the combe of Hustain Nuruu mountain, and waters the two nearer takhi enclosures before joining the main valley just below the Reserve centre. The scent of sage and chamomile, crushed under the feet of the leaders, drifted back to those of us behind. Each stride produced an explosion of grasshoppers; smaller ones leaping a few inches to safety, and monsters with red undersides flapping away in a series of clattering swoops, like flying football rattles.

Making a handsome living from them were the numerous black kites, hovering menacingly overhead. A family of choughs lived just upstream from the office; while here and there pairs of honey-coloured Isabelline wheatears tutted crossly at us from above their holes at the upper edges of the river banks. Outside the larger holes lower down stood tall, narrow pyramids of brown fur. Animals about the size of a large fox, they gawped at us briefly, before diving underground with a shrill whistle that warned every relative within earshot. Steppe marmots, *tarbagan* to the Mongolian, are as common to Central Asia as rabbits to Britain.

The gers were now falling behind and, but for the unfamiliar creatures, I had to pinch myself to remember that this Nature Reserve wasn't the Island of Rhum, or the edge of the Cairngorms. Such places had featured large in my former healthy incarnation. Despite the frustration of lagging behind and my difficulties when the party turned uphill, I felt back in my element, and almost light of foot. And when we came over the brow of the hill and saw the takhi, it was the gold-plating on an already silver day.

About a hundred yards away on the upland meadow stood a small group of stocky, thick-necked horses, their colour, but for the black manes and tails, matching the pink-red granite tor nearby. Behind them the land fell away, and continued to fall in a series of hills and valleys all the way to the Tuul River; then rose again to a further ridge in the blue distance. Yet the horses were completely at ease on this tremendous stage, not remotely awed by their surroundings, as if they had spent all their lives here, instead of in dull European fields. As if this were the most natural place in the world for them to be; which, of course, it was.

And we were among the first of our generation, among only a few non-Mongolians for centuries - maybe millennia - to see takhi in the wild. No-one said a word. We were all conscious of immense privilege.

Too bad they didn't feel the same about us. After sizing us up with a brief withering look, the "boss" mare Svetlaya led them off at a sharp trot down the hill. We stalked them at a respectful distance, coming closer only when they reached the bottom of the hill and relaxed at what was obviously a favourite watering spot.

Here a curve in the stream had scooped out a bank which must have held a rich mineral vein. They used it as a salt lick, taking turns to nibble at the raw, red earth and bickering gently for precedence.

Now at last we could watch them properly. There were nine of them: a stallion, four mares, three foals and a yearling. The last had been the first takh foal born on Mongolian soil for a quarter-century. He was named Macne, said Lee, in honour of the Association. Now I knew where it was that I had previously heard the acronym: in the Dutch Federation's newsletters.

59

Their reddish colouring blended perfectly with the landscape; natural selection might have designed them for this very place. The foals were lighter, more chestnut. They would darken after their first winter or two; Macne was still more baby than adult colour. All the foals had been born within the enclosure. Just as well, Lee commented, as one had had a serious case of fly-strike, and needed to be caught and treated. Svetlaya's foal this year had been born dead. But the hundred per cent fertility was a good sign: it proved both the potency of the stallion, Khaan, and the comfortable adaptation of the takhi to their new surroundings.

Khaan stood aloof from the squabbling of his wives and children. Long after our presence had become intolerable and Svetlaya had led the herd officiously up the bank and away, he took his own leisurely nibble at the natural salt lick. When we came to within forty yards he climbed the bank and followed the others without haste. "Thoroughly laid back," said Lee, with deep affection.

We now stayed behind to allow Igor, armed with camera and a bagful of lenses, to do his stuff. He crept furtively closer, bending low in the deep grasses for cover. Unfortunately he straightened his long legs at every step, making for a bouncing progress about as stealthy as a dwarf on a pogo stick. Nevertheless Svetlaya suffered him to approach, perhaps through curiosity at this strange creature, and he got some excellent shots.

But soon they were on the move again, with the innate restlessness of all wild things. This time it was downhill and away from home, and I threw in the towel. The haste of the early morning had caught up.

There was compensation in going back early, for I came over a low ridge to find myself staring into the eyes of a steppe eagle. Visible only from the neck up, he stared back at me for a frozen moment; then rose laboriously, his great wings seeming to take for ever to lift him into the air.

As I fell into bed, the last thing I heard was the chattering of nesting sparrows in the eaves of Lee's ger, and the sound of a cuckoo away down the valley.

*

Now that the Przewalski horse thrives all over the world, it is almost too easy to forget how close it came to total extinction.

When Nikolai Przewalski brought his prize back to Moscow in 1878, interest was keen but purely academic. Mongolia was far away, and about as accessible as the moon. Twenty years later, though, things had changed. By the end of the century, the Trans-Siberian Railway had reached Lake Baikal and skirted the edge of Mongolia on its way to the Pacific. Mongolia was now on the map. A scramble began to capture living specimens of its strange and primitive wild horse for the collectors of Europe.

A trader by the name of Assanov quickly cornered the market. He began to buy takhi captured by local herdsmen and transport them west by the new railway. To present-day sensibilities, his methods were barbaric. He encouraged his hunters to shoot mares in order to capture their foals. These were loaded into cattle trucks for the long journey, many days and thousands of miles, to Moscow and beyond.

It is hardly surprising that every foal in his first two consignments died. Nevertheless he persisted, and in 1900 succeeded in bringing back four fillies alive. They were sold to F.E. Falzfein, the owner of the Ukrainian estate of Askania Nova. Of the four, just one grew to maturity.

By the end of the following year, Assanov had brought 28 foals to Europe. He now embarked on a profitable alliance with the international animal trader Carl Hagenbeck, who supplied American and European zoos with rare animals. Through Hagenbeck, Przewalskis found their way all over Europe and even to the USA. One of his clients was the Duke of Bedford, who bought some of the horses to grace his Woburn estate.

But the high death rate continued, as the animals were too highly strung to adapt well to a new existence. Of all those captured, just thirteen survived to pass on their genes to a new generation. Ironically, though, it is to the Przewalski diaspora ruthlessly engineered by Assanov that the takhi owe their continuing existence.

Four breeding centres emerged: Askania Nova, Woburn, Prague and Berlin. After World War II these were joined by Catskill in the USA. The

Askania Nova stud was destroyed in the War, but re-established and re-stocked with horses from Europe - and one more Mongolian import. This last was the only Przewalski horse to be brought from the wild after successful breeding in captivity had been established. Perhaps methods had improved greatly by her time; in any case, she lived to a ripe old age.

The survival of the Przewalski still hung by a thread; but with each new generation that thread became stronger. In recent years, better communications have allowed exchange of stock between breeding centres, vital if the already frighteningly narrow gene pool wasn't to be further weakened by inbreeding.

Meanwhile, the number of takhi left in Mongolia dwindled rapidly, until only a few remained in the inhospitable reaches of the Jungarian Gobi. Herdsmen still came across them occasionally in the valleys between Baitag Bogd Uul (Baitag Holy Mountain) and Takhiin Shaar Nuruu, or Yellow Wild Horse Ridge.

Eventually, after a series of exceptionally hard winters, even these occasional sightings ceased. By the mid-fifties, expeditions were being sent in search of them; and returning without a glimpse.

In 1966, however, Dr. Z. Kaszab of Budapest Zoo came back from a trip to Jungaria with photographs of a herd of eight takhi. The next year an expedition sent by the Mongolian Academy of Sciences, under zoologists Prof. Dashdorj and Dr. Dondogin, sighted a mare and yearling on Takhiin Shaar Nuruu, and in 1968 the same group saw a single horse and a pair. This was the last validated proof of the Przewalski horse in Mongolia. It is generally accepted that by 1970 it was extinct in the wild.

Yet reports of sightings continued to trickle in. The takhi are similar in size and colour to the kulan, a wild ass found in Jungaria, and at a distance the two could easily be confused. But it is more likely that the horse became a sort of folk myth, conferring a spurious fame on any who claimed to have seen it: a Mongolian Loch Ness Monster. Local herdsmen queued up to win a slot in the record books as the last man to have seen the takhi.

Such claims continue to this day. On Operation Raleigh's expedition to Mongolia in 1991, the Veterinary Adviser met a herdsman who boasted that he had seen a takh not long before. Pressed for details, he told the group not to bother going in search; for he had shot the beast.

*

Lee's ger, where Suzanne and I were staying, was strikingly furnished as a guest-room. The door, bed frames, chest, low table and even the two wooden stools were all beautifully hand-carved and painted orange. The bed-bases, though, were of humbler stuff: they were made from the crates in which the takhi had travelled from Europe.

From inside, you could fully appreciate the ger's simplicity and utility. Its two basic building blocks are a wooden lattice which compresses very small for moving and extends to join up in a circle forming the wall; and the *toono*, a wheel mounted horizontally on two *bagana* or vertical posts. The toono is both smoke hole and roof tree, for it supports around sixty roof poles extending downwards to rest on the tops of the lattice. Felt wraps the structure snugly, covered by a waterproof layer of canvas. Ventilation is controlled by a square of felt sitting over the toono, manipulated by hair ropes whose hanging ends are tucked under the tie-ropes of the canvas and twisted for luck into patterns of squares. The door, of carved wood or just hanging felt, must always face south.

The result is comfortable, efficient - and supremely mobile. Warm enough to keep out the vicious winter winds, it is easily cooled in hot weather by raising the felts around the base to let the air flow through. Two or three people may dismantle or erect it in an hour, and the pieces fold, pack or collapse small enough to fit into a truck - or, in times not so long ago, a wagon.

That evening, the chance came to see for real how the ger functioned as a family home for the Mongolian arat. We all - Jan, Hans, Sukh, Lee, Baatar the driver, and I - piled into the jeep and followed the road down the valley to the southern edge of the Reserve. Here, where the mountains levelled out abruptly to meet the flat plain of the Tuul valley, lived Davadorj, one of the wardens.

We drove into a mêlée of sheep and goats. Bleating loudly, they were being crammed into a wire corral, their night refuge from the wolves. The milch mares were already gathered; for they do not stray far from their foals, tethered to a long rope pegged to the ground at either end. It seemed a tough system. The youngsters stumbled over the line and wrapped themselves up in it as they struggled to reach their mothers, and kicked each other in the confusion. The mares, too, squabbled irritably.

Davadorj was still away in UB for Naadam, and his wife welcomed us into their ger.

"*Sain bainu*," she said, taking my hand with a gentle smile.

The correct answer was, "*Sain. Sain bainu?*" (Well. Are you well?). Uncomfortably aware of my ignorance I rather feebly answered "Hallo", carefully keeping an eye on the others so that I might do better next time.

She led us inside, and when we were seated (men at the top, women visitors down the left side, women of the house down the right) brought us each a bowl of *airag* - fermented mares' milk, that staple drink of Central Asia known as kumiss on the other side of the Altai Mountains. Slightly sharp, it wasn't as unpleasant as I'd feared, and to my disappointment didn't taste remotely alcoholic.

Taking Davadorj's place, Sukh did the honours with the hard stuff. This should by rights have been Mongolian *arkhi*, distilled from the airag; but, as usual nowadays, it was Russian-made vodka arkhi. Pouring it into tin cups, Sukh gave one to each of us with the prescribed courtesy: right arm extended with the cup, left palm supporting the right elbow. We each received it with a similar gesture.

The ger bulged with all the necessities of daily life. Beds ran down both sides and across the far end. Garish cartoon characters frolicked across the brightly coloured spreads and hangings. On the right near the door was the kitchen, an area of shelving piled high with neatly stacked utensils. Pots and other implements hung from the roof poles. Near the centre stood a low table, behind an iron stove whose chimney pipe led out through the toono. An antique sewing machine was squeezed into a corner. It was a real family home. A big family at that, and swelled at present by visiting sisters and daughters from UB, fleeing the locker-room atmosphere and drinking sessions of Naadam for the chance of a female get-together, as women do the world over.

The floor was of beaten earth, and a rank smell of sheep filled the air. Its origin became apparent after a few moments when a nearly grown lamb scrambled from under a bed, forcing its way rudely between the elegantly stockinged and suited legs of a city relative then, alarmed at the influx of strangers, baaed loudly and galloped out of the door. A few minutes later a goat kid wandered in.

The arkhi flowed, and conversation inevitably centred on Davadorj's Naadam racehorses - he had entered five runners, ridden by his daughters, aged eight and six. Hans and Sukh began to challenge each other with drinking boasts, Sukh claiming that he could down ten litres of airag at one sitting. Jan, visibly mellowing, shed the last of the tensions raised by dealing with obstreperous diplomats, tensions which had begun peeling off him that morning in perceptible layers as the miles diminished between himself and Hustain Nuruu.

Someone had the impudence to joke that we would drink the place dry. No way, said Mrs. Davadorj, gesturing to the generous supplies of airag. As well as the traditional goat-skin at the door, topped up at every milking, there were hefty reserves in the huge, open trough from which we had been served, and in which a large bluebottle was dog-paddling vigorously.

As she spoke, the children brought in more frothing buckets. They tipped the contents into the goatskin, and began to thump the bag rhythmically with wooden paddles, to mix old and new and hasten fermentation. Outside, the last of the mares was being milked. The rest of the horses and cattle were coming in, but just as the stock total was nearly complete the sheep found a hole in their fence and began to restore the status quo. No-one took a blind bit of notice; the trickle became a torrent of sheep, climbing on each others' backs and spilling out two deep. Soon the corral was completely empty, and the sheep had spread out over a large area a quarter-mile away.

With milking over, Hans beckoned me to join him in the neighbouring ger. This belonged to Davadorj's sister-in-law, who proudly introduced us to her twin daughters, eighteen months old and dressed in matching outfits of purple miniature del and orange bus.

As soon as I sat down, I realised my mistake. I couldn't now leave without drinking the obligatory bowl of airag; to refuse would have been a frightful social gaffe. As I swallowed in desperate gulps, Hans whetted my appetite by describing the traditional Mongolian method of slaughtering an animal.

"They make a small incision in the chest and reach in to squeeze a main artery, which makes the heart stop." He had hoped to see this done tonight, but was disappointed. More humane, he thought, than western methods. He was, I agreed, entitled to his opinion.

The Mongolians, said Hans, wasted nothing when they killed a sheep. All the internal organs were consumed. The favourite bit was the intestines, which were filled with blood and grain and boiled as a sausage. It sounded a bit like the habits of some of our own northern tribes. My airag was tasting better and better.

"When I first met Davadorj," continued Hans, "he offered me a pair of sheep's balls to eat. I didn't want to make a bad impression, so I managed to eat one. The worst part was that I thought - actually, I was wrong - that it was raw."

After this tale of heroism I could hardly refuse something from the plate of goodies passed round. I took the smallest thing I could see. My cowardice was duly rewarded, as it was a piece of goats' cheese guaranteed to clear a bad head cold. I furtively slid the lump into my pocket; when I re-discovered it the next day, it hadn't improved with keeping.

Back in the jeep, we bounced over the puddles and potholes at a swinging pace, sure to jolly up stomachs awash with airag. Hans and Sukh continued their sparring, while Jan was singing quietly to himself.

The party continued back up at the top end of the valley, in the ger of the other warden. It turned out a riotous evening, culminating in the ceremonial fitting of Jan's del, made for him by the warden's wife. He was toasted in arkhi and entertained by communal singing, for which Mongolians are renowned.

A pity I heard it only by report; for, by now completely rubber-legged from the long day, I'd shown the white feather, jumped out as the jeep passed base, and crashed out heavily.

*

The next morning we awoke to heavy rain. Lee went out early to take a look at Khaan's group; no-one else stirred.

At ten I found Hans lying outside his ger. He was apparently pinned to the ground by what looked like the corpse of an uprooted lamp-post lying across his chest, its concrete roots still attached to both ends. *Both ends?* With a grunt he began to heave it upwards, and the mystery was explained. Weight training. Soon Sukh emerged, looking mildly rumpled from the night before, and joined him in the routine.

Jan didn't appear until early afternoon, except for frequent trips down the field to the loo. This was a wooden hut over a cavernous trench, fortunately a good hundred yards downwind of the office.

Poor Jan. He was beginning a bout of Mongolian tummy, regularly suffered by foreigners after a couple of months of the unremittingly greasy mutton diet. But everyone attributed his distress to too much good cheer, and it was two days before he got the sympathy he deserved.

A delegation from Thailand was expected to visit today, and a carload of Mongolian officials arrived early to greet them. Friction surfaced at lunch when one of these suggested rounding up Khaan's herd and driving them up to the office to put on a floor show for the Thais. Hans was outraged, and went off to mobilise Jan. Lee was distantly philosophical; such things had clearly happened before. But the dispute resolved itself. The Thais never materialised, and word later went round that they had feared bogging their bus down on the muddy tracks, and had turned round to go home.

At three we gave them up, and went up the path leading to the horseshoe ridge of Hustain Nuruu mountain. North of this was the area chosen by the other herd of takhi released, the harem group of the stallion Patron. They, however, usually stayed in the forested area behind the mountain, so it was unlikely that we would see them.

Both herds had been freed from their enclosures two weeks before. The timing corresponded to the optimum moment prescribed by Buddhist lamas: at the Hour of the Horse, on the Day of the Horse, and in the Month of the Horse. It would have been most satisfactory if the Year of the Horse could also have been observed... but this wasn't due to come round for several years.

The takhi were blessed in a special ceremony held at the obo on top of Hustain Nuruu itself. Here, to the accompaniment of Buddhist monks blowing conch shells, Mongolia's Chief Lama, Derembel Choijamts, said prayers for the horses, and sprinkled a libation of airag on the obo. As the procession descended the hill, the gates were opened at last.

The two herds responded in very different ways. While Khaan took a full three days just to lead his group outside their pen, Patron was both intoxicated and terrified at the idea of freedom. Taking off at high speed into the forest, he left his mares completely for several days. When he rejoined them, it was to lead his mob twelve miles away, outside Reserve territory. Reluctantly, the wardens suspended their policy of non-interference, and drove them back. Now they had settled to range an area on the north-east slopes of the mountain.

Khaan's former enclosure was the "first fence", half a mile from the office. It was around seventy acres, incorporating both open hillside and sheltered valley, with the little stream off the mountain running through its centre. Six feet of wire surrounded it; this had been electrified, to keep the horses in - and the wolves out. Lee pointed out the "stud pile"; a stallion always produces his droppings in one place, so as to mark his territory. The conical pile was as neat as if dropped straight from a dumper truck.

And now Lee's binoculars picked out the dumper himself, way up on the hillside with his harem. A million miles from me; at my feeble speed it would have taken me all day to get up there. Sadly I gave my camera to Lee and watched the party scramble up the bank; then turned back down the valley.

But I couldn't be gloomy for long in such a magical place. I followed the tiny river, its crystal clear water running over coarse granite sand, its

68

sheltered pockets of riverbank thick with flowers, so dense as to crowd out almost the last blade of grass.

Alone, I saw far more of the animal and bird life. The tarbagan were braver than yesterday, watching me until I was quite close before diving below with a shriek. Their furry pyramids resolved themselves into identifiable shapes; bottoms squatly supportive, back and shoulders stretched more thinly, noses pointing skyward for maximum viewing height and optimum scent. Ludicrous creatures; Walt Disney could have had marvellous fun with a marmot.

Back at the centre, there were still no Thais. When Lee, Suzanne and Igor returned we said our goodbyes and crammed into two jeeps bound for UB. Two, because there was a party in UB, and a large Hustain Nuruu contingent was invited. Sukh wore his best del for the occasion, green velvet with an orange bus. Where the neck flap lay open for coolness - the del fastens with toggles high on the right shoulder - I could see his blue T-shirt underneath. "Be Ambitious!" was written across his chest.

Just as the first engine fired, the clouds rolled back at last and the sun streamed down. Ironic timing; but it was good to see Hustain Nuruu by sunlight, and it was unimaginably lovely.

In fact, we had plenty of time to appreciate the view. For, with the Reserve not quite out of sight, our jeep picked up a piece of wire somewhere in its tender parts. Lee saved the day by producing, magician-like, a pair of wire cutters from somewhere in the depths of her handbag. Poor Baatar, in his best party clothes, grovelled in the mud putting them into action.

The rest of us lay on our backs in the grass, watching the skylarks. One minute the sky would be thick with them, spreading a curtain of song from one horizon to the other. Then a black kite would pass over and they would vanish into the grass, to reappear in their hundreds once the menacing dark shadow had disappeared.

The minutes passed, and Hans produced his mouth-organ, entertaining us with a brilliant performance of his "Ulaan Baatar Blues". Back home, he told me, he led a blues band. The desultory conversation passed to music, and he asked if I had heard of a famous British blues player. I hadn't, and he was scandalised. Desperately scrabbling for Brownie points, I asked if he had seen the film of "Cannery Row", with its soundtrack of blues music. He hadn't. With the score at fifteen all, I was saved. The jeep was suddenly cured, and we could continue.

Much to Jan's relief; for the World Cup was in full swing, and Holland was due to play Brazil that very evening.

IV

THE BOUNCING BOMB

Carol's plane was due in at eleven. This time it wasn't Batbayaar but Sanjaa who turned up to meet the plane, in a flash new "Mongol Tour OK Travel Company" bus - his third money-raking venture after the restaurant and the Guest House. Too posh to drive himself, he sat with a lordly air alongside a chauffeur. Presently he took out a Japanese electronic pocket game to ping and zap away mindlessly, pouring adverse gut reaction on top of my already plunging opinion of him.

We watched a small propellor plane take off; then nothing. Then: "delayed until 4 pm." Poor Carol. We went back to UB.

Next time round, the timing was perfect. The big Tupolev touched down as we arrived, and a few moments later I could pick Carol out among the crowd crawling distantly over the tarmac. Mongol Tour Rules OK bore her off - I hoped her shower would have hot water by now - while I went back to the Altai and booked her in for the next day.

For the rest of the week, while she found her bearings in UB, I went to bed. We had some serious travelling planned, and I needed to go into training.

They were days of self-indulgence in more ways than one. For Carol, a veteran of Chinese travel, had cracked the tea problem. You simply asked for "Lipton chai", and along came a cup of hot water with a Lipton teabag steaming fragrantly. No more pale soup.

It was the last taste of easy living for some time.

*

The Mongolian airline's internal flights were still disrupted after Naadam (no reason; just a good excuse for MIAT to save aviation fuel, said a

71

cynical fellow-traveller). There would be nothing airborne before next week.

We were anxious to hit the road. On a recce at the bus station we learned that there was a bus going our way - to Hovsgol *aimag* (province) in the far north - the next morning. And MIAT, we reminded ourselves, had a reputation for keeping its planes in the air with Sellotape and rubber bands. Staying earth-bound wasn't all bad news.

Our other errand was to change some travellers' cheques. Outside the capital, nothing but cash would be of any use. This meant walking around with frighteningly large wads of dollars and *tugrigs*, and in constant fear of being mugged. I had sewn pockets into the inside of my loose-fitting jeans for security, so that for the first time in my life I had million-dollar (well, hundred-dollar) legs.

At eight the next morning Carol was sitting on our pile of luggage outside the bus station, while I went to find the bus.

There was no bus.

In vain, I insisted that the man behind the desk yesterday had promised a bus to Hovsgol, but the snooty lady who had taken his place today was adamant. There simply weren't any buses to the further provinces. Ever.

Somewhere in her repeated denials, the word "official" crept in. No official bus. It should have tripped a switch in my brain, but didn't. Light only dawned when Carol, after much asking around, discovered that the ranks of trucks behind the station were taking passengers. Yes, of course there was one going to Hovsgol. The fare was 4,200 tugrigs, about ten dollars.

In no time we were on board, sharing nibbles with the other passengers, and feeling very pleased with ourselves. It was as well that we only found out by stages that of the five hundred miles to go, most was on unmade roads, that the journey was to take two days and most of the night... and that the truck had no springs.

What was immediately obvious, though, was that this was no Pullman coach. Its wooden sides, perhaps three feet high, were surmounted by an iron frame of mismatched pieces wired together. The roof was a thin piece of rotten larch tied on with baling twine, to which two heavy planks were loosely wired, lengthwise. This contraption supported a moth-eaten tarpaulin which, more patches than original material and more holes than patches, must have seen at least fifty Mongolian winters.

At the front stood a forty-gallon petrol drum. Later, when it had been filled, petrol slopped all over the sides of the truck. I was relieved to see a fire extinguisher fixed beside the drum, but less relieved at the labyrinth of wire binding it in place; the truck might burn to a cinder before it could be released. I needn't have worried, for after all the extinguisher was a fake. We later found that it carried spare petrol.

Yet another hazard appeared when an army ammunition crate was thrown up beside us. After the first few potholes had rattled our bones, we were to name our coach the Bouncing Bomb, with scant apologies to Barnes Wallis, Guy Gibson et al.

Our fellow travellers were a mixed bunch. A young couple were accompanied by a lady in a mauve shirt, blue leggings and orange stockings, and a shell-suited teenage girl whose lame leg gave her great difficulty in climbing in and out of the truck; for its tailgate was seven feet off the ground, with only a couple of footholds. When he was comfortably seated the young man took off his boots, carefully unwinding and rewinding around his feet the strips of cloth that served him as socks.

Two middle-aged ladies completed the payload. Above their traditional dress of del and leather boots, their headscarves, knotted gipsy fashion at the back of the head, framed lined, weathered faces of a beautiful serenity. They endured the rigours of the journey with uncomplaining patience, emerging at the end still straight-backed and poised, an object lesson to their knock-kneed, gibbering companions - one of them, at any rate - and reinforcing the picture that was already well-formed in my mind: that of the inner strength and stoicism of these extremely tough people.

We sat for three hours, waiting to be off. One by one, the other trucks started their engines and rumbled on to the road, and still we waited. And waited.

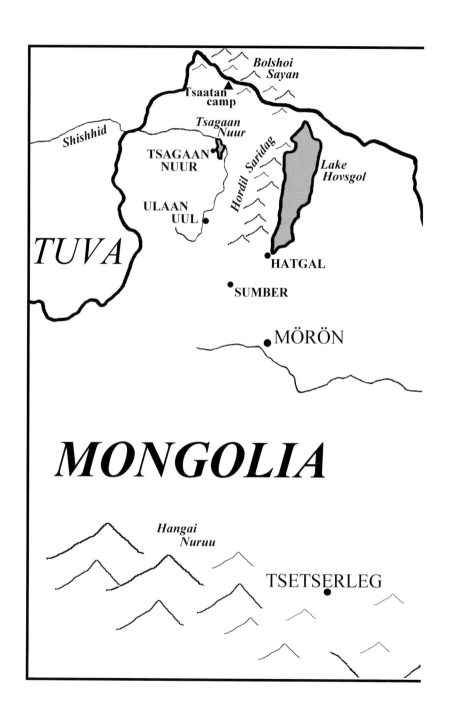

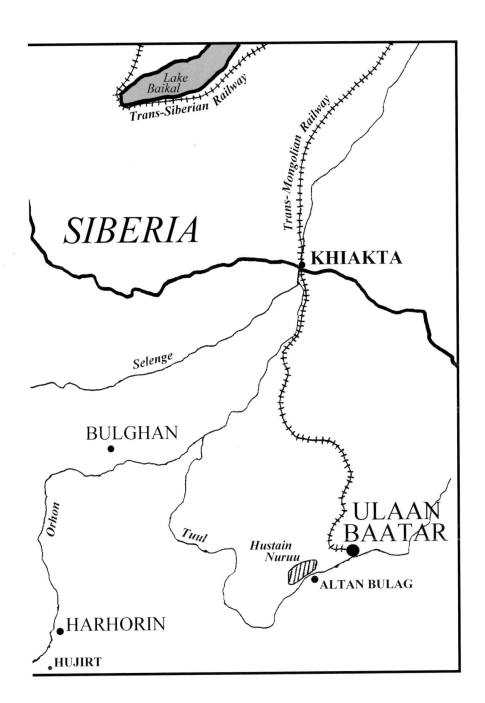

At eleven, more passengers arrived, a family with a young baby. The slender wife was dwarfed by her colossal husband, a man-mountain of enormous breadth and even greater musculature. He must surely have spent the previous week wrestling in the Naadam arena. When the child began to cry, he took it from the mother and nursed it with incongruous gentleness, its tiny form almost hidden under his vast biceps.

Now at last we could go, although there was nothing to hurry for. We pottered around UB picking up odds and ends; petrol here, there a huge iron bracket, filling the width of the floor by the tailgate. How we would come to loathe that innocent-looking lump of metal!

It was past mid-day when we finally hit the road west. The truck bucked and jerked over every pothole. And that was the easy bit. After sixty miles the tarmac gave out, and the real fun began.

From now on our road was a rough track straight across the steppe. Here and there, where the mud was particularly bad, the odd stone had been thrown into the ruts, but for the most part beaten earth formed the surface. Where a track became more eroded than usual, you just left it to strike a new path alongside, the subsequent traffic following this route while the old path recovered to the point of re-use or simply faded back into the steppe. Sometimes three or four of these roads marched in parallel over the grassland.

Never out of second gear, we lurched over such tracks for an eternity. The constant jolting of the unsprung lorry was indescribable; it rattled our bones and made our teeth chatter and turned every moment into pure hell. In vain we tried to cushion it with rolled-up sleeping bags. But there was no escape anywhere. It was a hell that continued throughout most of the night until the end of the following day. They were two of the longest days of my life.

The iron frame was a hostile travelling companion. Displaced by the jolting, it crept backwards towards us to squash or batter or both. Over and over we heaved it back to the tailboard, only to be painfully overwhelmed again after another five minutes. Later - much later - my deadened brain flickered briefly and produced a solution. With a couple of twists of the orange baling twine I had thrown into my rucksack as an afterthought, I tied it firmly to the tailgate. The strong twine frayed a little but held, and that particular purgatory ceased.

Our road led westward across the rolling steppes and into the depression east of Tov, the aimag that encloses Ulaan Baatar. In the mid-afternoon we stopped for food at a roadside ger, "a sort of Mongolian Greasy Joe's", commented Carol.

Immediately on climbing from the truck we were pounced on by hordes of the vicious mosquitoes which bred in the marshes nearby. We at least could stave them off with bug-cream, but the wretched animals around were plastered. The constant blood-sucking had left them poor and thin, their coats thick with scurf.

Also plastered, in more ways than one, was mine host. He seemed unconscious of the flies on his face and neck as he invited us all into his ger and sat Carol and me at the head, or honoured, position. He spoke some Russian, and we managed a conversation of sorts. But he had been, and still was, on the arkhi, and his speech became more and more unintelligible.

He possessed, he said proudly, three hundred horses, four hundred cattle and five hundred sheep. Yet his ger looked very poor. The furniture was basic and the usually intricate winding of the roof-rope was skimped. Various dripping, fly-ridden bits of a newly-slaughtered sheep festooned the roof, and hideous unidentifiable innards made a pile beside my stool. Instead of the usual goat-skin, the airag was in a plastic tub. It was so sharp as to be almost undrinkable.

It was Carol's first taste, and she bravely emptied the bowl. Within a short time, we had made a pact: she would deal with my airag, and I would take on her cheese.

A few tugrigs changed hands, and the wife and daughter of the house began to prepare fresh noodles for a mutton stew. Outside, the hide which had formerly belonged to the stew lay steaming over a hurdle, while cheese and curd were spread over the roof to dry. I admired the horses, with more courtesy than honesty; and then walked over a small rise for a loo-trip.

Out of sight of the ger, I could have been the only creature on the planet. Nothing was visible this side of the hills which reared a mile or two away, except, of course, for the black kites and the crickets. But the steppe was full of flowers, crowding the meagre spiky grass. Among the chamomile were yellow daisies, a carmine-pink dianthus and a dozen unfamiliar faces.

As I looked about, a cloud of dust appeared on the horizon. After a few moments a lorry materialised out of the cloud, taking shape and becoming clearer every minute, as if it had put on a spurt and was slowly but surely leaving its dust-trail behind like a comet's tail. It recalled the famous mirage scene in "Lawrence of Arabia"; with the flowered steppe taking the place of the desert, a jolting truck that of the shimmering camels.

I had missed my moment of privacy, and had to wait long minutes until the newcomers had passed out of sight behind me. What an innocent! By the following day I had learned to be less frowstily spinsterish.

Too much time had elapsed, and our host came to look for me. Now far gone, and with a lecherous gleam in his rheumy eye, he tried to pinch my bottom on the way back. By the door he stopped me, and leaned close, with a conspiratorial whisper: had we any arkhi with us? No? Disbelief. But surely, we must have just one bottle...?

Inside, lunch was almost over; a blessing, as I got away with only a few mouthfuls of the greasy mutton stew before the truck engine revved warningly. My stomach, shaken beyond endurance by the constant rattle, was in open revolt, and food was abomination.

Now we sank into a kind of stupor, brains firmly in neutral, from time to time rousing ourselves to stagger to our feet and look at the slowly-changing scenery. In late afternoon we swung north-west into mountainous country; away to the left, beyond a single line of hills, was a sort of void, the sense of another great depression tracing a parallel path. Towards dusk the clouds began to gather, framing a shattering pink sunset over the mountains ahead. An eagle owl sat on the hillside, not ten feet from the truck, watching us pass.

A line of telegraph poles converged with the road, suggesting that we were drawing close to civilisation. By ten we were in Bulghan, capital of the aimag of the same name and halfway point. Surely we would stop here, and stagger into some truckers' hostel for a few hours' merciful rest? But Boria, our driver, seemed to be indestructible. After a brief fuel stop (the fuel cap, refusing to turn by hand, was hit with a hammer until sparks flew), he swung back into his cab and continued until one in the morning before allowing himself a few hours' sleep.

His wife and child emerged with him from the cab, and the three climbed into the back with us. And here, among all that incendiary stuff, Boria lit a cigarette. Unable to close my eyes until it was safely extinguished, I watched mesmerised as the glowing tip, the only thing visible in the utter blackness, described a wide arc from his lips and back to the full extent of his outflung arm, casually resting on the ammunition box. It wasn't until the following day that I saw him open the box, and realised that it, too, was a fake; it contained his lunch, and little else.

Now, with the extra people, plus the iron frame and the luggage, it was impossible to lie down. At last I found a space for my legs, only to have someone pick them up, dump them in someone else's lap and promptly lie down in the space they left; while I struggled to apologise, disentangle myself, and squash my body even smaller. And now it began to rain. Water streamed through the tarpaulin to soak our luggage, our sleeping bags and, of course, ourselves. It was a welcome relief when at first light, about half-past five, Boria yawned, stretched and prepared to resume his personal marathon.

The growing light showed us a beautiful land, despite the lowering grey clouds. We were now passing the tail end of the Burengiin mountains. Their tops were invisible, but their valleys, crossed by clear, fast streams, were alpine meadows waist-deep in lush pasture and thick with flowers. The shorter grasses alongside the road were full of edelweiss.

After a day of bare steppe, we had reached the fringes of the northern woods, where the pine and larch forests of the Siberian taiga stretch their fingertips down into Mongolia. Here the trees favoured the northern sides of the hills; the side away from the potentially fierce sun, perhaps, or that towards the rain-bearing winds? From the south, or barren, side, just the edge of the forest was visible, a line of trees marching in single file across the precise top of each hill like a row of dinosaur spines.

With such raw materials to hand, the impact of man on the landscape, elswhere minimal, increased. Small railed paddocks gave the gers a more permanent air; some had little wooden store huts, their cracks sealed with dried dung. A hitching rail shaped like a goal-post replaced the usual tether rope pegged along the ground.

Wooden privies made our loo-stops more private, if less wholesome. "Where do they get their fibre?" wondered Carol; the Mongolian diet of meat, milk and flour was hardly conducive to healthy peristalsis. Yet, if the privy trenches were a reliable indicator, the Mongolian arat has a uniquely vigorous digestive tract. Paper from all possible sources was pressed into service: food packings, rare bits of newspaper, even old letters. *Dear Sir, As I write I have your letter before me. Soon it will be behind me...*

The cloud rose and whitened, and a cheerful sun broke through. Butterflies drifted into the truck. From time to time the flying grasshoppers passed through, too quick to be seen, discernible only as a sort of flying raspberry that came in at the open front and promptly disappeared over the tail. For a long way, the old track running alongside had been colonised by blue flowers, its blue parallel lines stretching out before and behind us as if to mock our dull brown ones.

There were a couple more ger stops, with much goodwill and hospitality. At the second, three or four gers were spread out at a distance of half a mile apart around a spacious green bowl, watered by the stream we had just forded. At intervals single riders or pairs galloped flat out from one ger to the next, in what was obviously an ongoing social round. Summer to the Mongolians is a holiday, a few short months when the animals are in milk and the fodder is plentiful and the hard work of making a living under the grudging climate is temporarily eased.

At last we crossed the final mountain ridge into Hovsgol aimag and began the long descent to its capital town, the attractively-named Mörön. Various detours delayed us when the track grew boggy, and Boria was forced to drive a new path through virgin steppe. Filling the very last valley was a wide lake, its shores densely crowded with the lama ducks which Mongolians never kill for fear of bad luck. Their brown and white bodies were almost the size of geese. And could those possibly have been herring gulls wheeling above?

On the final hilltop the statue of a red deer marked the local boundary. Piles of stones and money offerings gave it the status of an obo. Grazing around it were yaks, our first sight of them; they were hump-less and smaller than Himalayan yaks, their short legs scarcely longer than the fringe of stomach hair which swung below them at each lumbering step.

And there below was Mörön, the shining goal which we had thought of ceaselessly for two days.

It looked strangely squat, like a settlement seen in two dimensions from an aircraft. As we neared it, this resolved itself into an absence of high buildings, with only a handful reaching a second storey. It was as if some frightful apocalypse had flattened everything in sight.

The houses of the suburbs, which made up most of the town, were mainly cubes of rough-hewn wood surrounded by coarse palings. They might have belonged to a Wild West frontier town, the comparison reinforced by knots of ponies tied at the gates. Boria navigated their identical streets unerringly, dropping off his passengers at their own homes. Last to leave were the two middle-aged ladies, who climbed down with the easy nonchalance of the Naadam riders dismounting from their epic races, and fell into the embrace of their waiting families.

That left just us, and the iron frame. The town centre - when we finally tracked it down, even Boria seeming not to know the way - was more solid than the rest. Its concrete buildings included a cinema, a theatre, a grandiose sports stadium with Chinese-style entrance gate, and the usual enormous empty square with the usual enormous posturing statue of a local hero.

The one hotel was a mouldering building with two horses and a motorbike parked outside. Yet after the last two days it seemed to Carol and me a veritable Ritz. Briefly.

Boria dropped us outside, helped us out with our baggage, and set off at last for his own home. He had driven for twenty-seven of the last thirty-two hours, over frightful tracks allowing not a moment's lapse of concentration. Now he had just two days to rest before setting off once more, his family living with him in the cab, on the weary road to Ulaan Baatar. Yet another very tough Mongolian.

We waved him off, then, feeling "like tenderised beef" as Carol put it, thankfully staggered into the hotel. Paying an inflated price for the privilege of staying there, we were impressed to find we had our own bathroom attached. And met the final straw: no water.

The dust in our clothes and bodies was an inch thick, our ears and noses silted up and our throats crackling. Between us we had perhaps half a pint left of our carefully hoarded water. Desperately we begged for something to wash with, but the little, wizened woman sitting at the reception desk smiled with contempt and shook her head. The water, she told us, would come on at six in the morning. For half an hour.

A kindly resident found us a spare pint, with which we were able at least to wipe our faces. The "bathroom", a purely theoretical luxury, was the only treat we were to get. The main room was tiny and thick with grime, the paint was peeling from the walls and bits constantly fell off the ceiling.

I hardly left it for a week.

*

To lose so much time, still relatively early in the trip, was bad news.

Normally, I expect to waste a large part of every day in bed, trickle-charging for the rest of it. Obviously I couldn't stick to that pattern rigidly while travelling; instead I just kept putting one foot in front of the other for as long as possible, and accepted the loss of a couple of days when I hit the buffers. It was partly to allow for such time-wasting that I'd come out ahead of Carol.

The present meltdown was way over the top, given that just two days' rough handling had caused it. But there was no arguing.

As well as the suspension of all physical and mental functioning, I'd had on arriving here one of the protracted, frightening heart spasms which had characterised my illness from the start. Although I knew by now that these were more threat than substance, it was a warning that I was out of the game for a bit. Some serious repairs were in order.

I hardly left my bed for the best part of a week, while the old, irreconcilable enmities of ME rolled and clashed jarringly, like Naadam wrestlers, within my skull: my brain and will raging for activity, for stimulus, for release from their imprisoning carcass, for the chance to explore this strange place that we had striven so hard to reach; my body screaming for rest, for respite from being endlessly driven beyond its limits, for the desperately needed sleep denied to it by my fractious, boiling mind.

By the time I left I knew every feature of the filthy, dilapidated room, every crack in the glass, every patch of flaking paint on the ceiling. The last, at least, was an ever-changing landscape.

*

Carol, meanwhile, was busy.

After all too brief a rest, she set out for the airport to scout for foreign travellers going, like us, further north, who might be prepared to share the cost of a jeep. MIAT, to spite us, had resumed operations almost as soon as we had left UB. What an irony, to see the passengers disembarking fresh after an hour's flight from the capital, and to think that, but for some patience - and a crystal ball - we might have been among them, and with no time lost.

In one short afternoon, she made a number of interesting contacts.

First was the man from the Hovsgol Tour Company. He was bolshy and off-putting, refusing to tell Carol where his group was going, or at what price, and parting only grudgingly with his phone number. Later, when he succeeded in leaving before we did, he crossly wanted to know why we hadn't gone with him. Some local rivalry, perhaps? A few days after, we learned that he had run out of petrol at Ulaan Uul, and hoped that he'd had to walk the rest of the way to his jealously guarded destination.

83

Then there was Thibault, whose name seemed better suited to a twelfth century Crusader from Outremer than to a twentieth century French journalist. He was a horse enthusiast, but had never heard of the takhi. He was on his way back to UB, and was most interested to learn of Hustain Nuruu.

It was his companion and interpreter, Alta, who was the real find. A native of Mörön who was studying French at UB University, she had been working for Thibault for a spell of several weeks. From now on she gave us endlessly of her time, using her local influence and contacts to mobilise us rather more cheaply than most foreigners here.

But Carol's most interesting new acquaintance was David Edwards, an American photo-journalist and professional wilderness guide. Here to lead a private party into the mountains about Lake Hovsgol, he was a third generation Welshman, and struck up an immediate rapport with Carol. The previous year he had visited the Tsaatan, nomadic reindeer herders from the northern frontiers of Hovsgol. It was in the hope of finding the Tsaatan that we had come here, so his experience was pure gold to us.

David came to see us at the hotel. Over a cup of tea which Carol had brewed on the tiny stove ("How very British!" he said), he told us about his trip, on which he had worked with a journalist writing for a Canadian magazine. He brought with him four packets of photographs of the Tsaatan and a copy of the magazine article, which he entrusted to us to deliver. It was to our mutual benefit; he had found some postmen, while we had the perfect means of introduction to these remote and shy people, whose potential reaction to a couple of strangers was an unknown quantity. "I knew you'd make it," he said to us much later. "Anyone who could conjure up a pot of tea in that pit was bound to get where they wanted to go."

David's enthusiasm for, and knowledge of, the Tsaatan were boundless, and he gave us every encouragement and much practical information as to how to reach them. A hugely interesting man, he held a fund of stories of his expeditions to all parts of the globe.

I could have listened to him until the sun rose, but was still half-dead from the truck journey. Some days later I discovered that I'd taken a whole page of close-written notes from his information, without the least recollection of having done so.

*

When I finally set foot outside the hotel, I found that I hadn't missed much. Mongolian towns tend to be as dismal as the countryside is exhilarating. Mörön, a miserable dump surrounded by spectacular mountains, was no exception. Perhaps it derived little inspiration from its name; but then we were, we reminded ourselves, in a country whose first democratic president was called Batman.

The Wild West feel persisted. Horses were almost the only traffic on the street, or parked by the the roadside. There wasn't a single car, only the odd truck or jeep. For how would you bring a car here across hundreds of miles of steppe, other than by flying it in?

Mechanical transport consisted almost entirely of motorbikes. There was even a whiff of bikers' culture: young men sitting all day on their bikes in yards, revving up on street corners, or riding slowly around in pairs, sometimes with a girl. There wasn't a sign of the petrol shortage later to be invoked in delaying our own transport.

The roads themselves were pretty hazardous, pitted with potholes and criss-crossed by excavated trenches, slowly filling up with water as if they had been dug weeks ago and then forgotten. A few small parks, in which Chinese-style pavilions stood waist-deep in weeds, separated the roads, as did large patches of indeterminate wasteland.

On one of these was the market, a sort of car-boot sale with prams instead of car-boots, at which you turned up with whatever you had to sell. Here Carol found some riding boots; not leather ones such as the arats wore, which are Russian-made and expensive, but cheaper and very serviceable rubber ones. Watching my dollars, I decided to do without, and later cursed my tight-fistedness.

All other shopping was done at one of the "department stores", two or three single-roomed general stores selling anything from food to plastic dolls and Chinese-imported sweets. Their "trapper store" feel was perfectly set off by the ponies tethered outside. We could have bought our rice here, but not much else. There was a temporary supply of sugar, and we stocked up; but all other food they sold was in tins, too heavy to carry.

Alta's help here was invaluable. As a local resident she was able to buy bread, which was in very short supply and sold literally from under the counter. Coaxing three loaves out of a friendly baker, she kept one herself and bundled two more into our rucksacks. These fed us for days, their last solid crusts softened in soup.

We also found a number of suitable gifts to take to the Tsaatan. Bus material, enough for two or three, of a bright orange colour particularly liked, said Alta, by the men; blue khadags - the ceremonial scarves I'd seen at Naadam - for the women; practical things like needles, thread, matches, candles; and also, on a last-minute inspiration of Carol's, two or three coloured rubber balls for the children.

On our last evening we walked along the river which borders Mörön to the south. There was a lot going on here - washing, watering horses, or just idling - but little actual life. "Eutrophic" was how Carol described it: but for a few stunted weeds and some tiny fish it was dead; not even algae dared to grow. The only birds to be seen were a couple of sandpipers.

You didn't have to look far to see why it was so lifeless. Several times in a couple of hundred yards we stepped over raw sewage outlets spewing greasy filth straight into the river. Some of the waste came from what appeared, from the piles of coal outside and hefty transformer within, to be the power station. Its blackened walls and heaps of rubble looked more like the remains of some terrible nuclear catastrophe; or as if the Bouncing Bomb had been driven within its walls and then dynamited.

The one restaurant was dead, too, closed for lack of support, and the hotel cafe evidently hadn't functioned for years. We got stuck into our own supplies, using our tiny, fierce petrol stove to cook precariously on the windowsill, and hiding the evidence furtively if anyone came near. The only creature to cotton on was a thin, half-grown puppy, which arrived punctually at every mealtime and importuned us with irresistible charm.

The high spot of Mörönic culture was the museum, a typical result of Soviet influence. The Soviet attitude to culture and heritage was always ambivalent. While attempting to reduce to grey uniformity the peoples they governed, the Russian overlords were keen to show the world their recognition of and respect for local culture. That their notion of doing so was to remove it far from its context and pickle it in aspic was rather a pity; but pickling beats total annihilation. It is one of the reasons why some of the best museums in the world are to be found in Russia and its former satellites.

So it shouldn't have come as any surprise to find an excellent local museum in this remote backwater. Its treasures began with a wealth of information on local history and geology, little help to me without an interpreter; but much also on flora and fauna, which were labelled with Latin names and often Russian as well. The wildlife here, I discovered, would have crammed a zoological textbook. As well as wild boar, lynx, elk, wolf and Altaic ferret there was the exotic snow leopard, alongside familiar, homely creatures like badgers and hedgehogs. And here, sure enough, was the herring gull, though minus the distinctive red spot on its beak.

The most interesting rooms were those filled with treasure looted from the local monasteries. By his treatment of the Buddhist monasteries in the thirties, Choibalsan, Stalin's Mongolian clone, would have made Henry VIII look like a kindly old bishop out of a Trollope novel. Applying his final solution to the lamaseries, Choibalsan had the monks turned out to beg, or simply massacred. It was said that, by the end, his commissioners were being given execution quotas to fulfill.

Priceless collections of religious artefacts were shipped back to the Soviet Union to fill its museums, or to be sold or melted down. Some, though, didn't travel so far. The treasures of Mörön museum were a foretaste of what was to become familiar when we later visited re-established monasteries: gold, silver, bronze, coral and wood-carved figures of dragons, elephants, lions, demons. And, of course, Buddhas, in all sizes from thumbnail to twice life-size. There were paintings and hangings, often inscribed with prayers and sacred writings; prayer wheels; and laboriously hand-scripted copies of the *Kangur* and *Tangur*, a collection of Indo-Tibetan treatises on arts and sciences.

There was a section, too, on shamanism, the ancient, animist religion marginalised by Buddhism but still practised among some of Mongolia's remoter peoples, especially the Tsaatan. And here were the Tsaatan themselves, relegated to folk-history and personified by their reindeer-skin coats and their skis. Life-sized photographs all along one wall showed how the collective system had gathered them to its bosom, bestowing order and plenty, and pinning down their free-ranging reindeer herds into nice tethered, orderly rows, ready to be milked all together for maximum efficiency.

The Mongolian ger and its various trappings were on display too, dismantled and labelled; in preparation for the time, perhaps, when they, also, became folk history, and the Mongolian people could all live in tidy, sanitised apartment blocks.

Among the cooking pots and goatskins was an exquisite little *morin huur*, the trapezoid two-stringed cello decorated with a horse's head. Rarely played now, this was once the mainstay of traditional music, and historical records show it to be very old. Records such as the Mongolian epic "Janjar", which, according to the accompanying note, says of Janjar's wife Aoot, "In her hands the long stringed instrument sang as the swan that had hatched an egg in the reeds, as the duck in the rushes..."

*

Alta was trying to find us a "taxi" for the journey north to Tsagaan Nuur. In reality this meant a jeep, as the road, leading into one of the most remote parts of Mongolia, would be much rougher than the one from UB to Mörön, and the heavy rains would mean that the rivers in its path could be expected to be high.

Mongolian aimags are divided into *sumoins*, roughly equivalent to English counties, each with a central town called a *sum*. The sumoins in turn are sub-divided into parishes, or *bags*. Tsagaan Nuur, or the White Lake, is the second largest lake in Hovsgol, and gives its name to the sum lying on its southern shore. Over a hundred miles north of Mörön, it

88

would be the starting-point for our journey to the Reindeer People. It would also be the end of the road as far as mechanised transport was concerned; from here on we must travel with horses.

First of all, we had to get there. There was no regular transport, and we must hire our own jeep and driver. After a few days the friend of a friend obliged, and Alta told us to be ready to leave at mid-day.

This meant mid-day, Mongolian Time. At four an embarrassed Alta arrived with our prospective driver. His vehicle, he explained via Alta, needed a spare part. Tomorrow morning...

Tomorrow morning arrived, and now we couldn't leave because there was no petrol in Mörön. Priority was given to medical services, police, fire vehicles. Could we produce proof of urgent need? Maybe one of us was a journalist with a commission? We told Alta of my previous work, and the book I was writing on Mongolia, and she went off to try and work miracles. Meanwhile, in case our credentials were inspected, we went to work and concocted a file. Starting with a voucher from our travel company, smartly headed and replete with official stamps and compliments to the Mongolian Embassy in London, we pinned David Edwards' card to it, zipped it into a plastic folder with the photographs and magazine article, and designated Carol an official company "courier".

Alta waved this under a few noses with some success. On her next visit we learned that she had now arranged the petrol, but "the elecricity had failed and the pump wasn't working".

By now it was patently obvious that we were being strung along for the driver's convenience. He didn't want to go until the end of the week, and knew very well that there wasn't a lot we could do about it except walk.

But from a selfish point of view, the delay was to my advantage. While Carol justifiably fretted at all the gerrymandering, I was still reeling from the rigours of the truck ride; and the prolonged negotiations, in a mixture of Russian and our joint excruciating efforts in French, were draining in themselves.

I would willingly have put my best foot forward at the first opportunity, but we had no other option than to sit tight. And when the "off" was at last truly imminent, my fogged brain had cleared for the first time in a week, my legs were beginning to work again, and I could look forward with genuine pleasure to the coming adventure.

V

RIDING THE TAIGA

We left at eight, Mongolian Time. That's to say, we sat on our bags outside the hotel until mid-morning, when the driver finally rolled up. After the manipulations of the previous week, it was the last straw. I wasn't polite, and he grinned feebly.

As well as a driver's mate there was another passenger - the reason, of course, for the week's delay - and Alta's husband, Tulgha, who came with us in case we needed a helper or interpreter at the other end. So four of us shared the back seat. It was quite a squash.

Alta came to see us off, bringing her three-year-old daughter. Tonga was a laughing child, impossibly sweet in tiny pigtails and lime-green best dress. How Alta juggled a university course in Ulaan Baatar with the demands of a family in a town hundreds of miles away was a mystery. When, on our return, we discovered that she had flown to Beijing "on government business", we decided that there was rather more to Alta than met the eye.

The countryside was glorious, and we couldn't stay angry for long. We left Mörön by the airport road, then climbed out of the valley bowl by a pass across the shoulder of its surrounding mountains. On the far side the road entered a narrow gully between two cliffs. The sward here was thicker with flowers than we had ever seen, even in Mongolia. We stopped and climbed out for a couple of minutes to enjoy it. An eagle flew up from under our feet, to alight in a sparse covering of trees on almost sheer granite walls; trees that cackled with eagles and screeched with kites.

Beyond the first line of mountains the terrain levelled out into lush grasslands dotted with lakes. This was the richest country we had yet seen; supporting a ger every mile or so, it was positively crowded. Everywhere herds grazed, mostly of yaks.

Their calves gambolled like lambs in front of the jeep, woolly tails held high over their backs. Even the adults joined in, with a skittishness that sat oddly on their ponderous bulk. Often the herds strayed on the road, and would explode in all directions as we drove towards them, bucking and snorting just for the hell of it.

No marmots lived here; instead the common form of wildlife was the *souslik*, or ground squirrel. They fled from the track before us, their outraged tails sticking up vertically like the yaks' then spiralling stiffly down behind them as they dived into tiny holes. Great flocks of waterfowl gathered on the lakes, and we saw many more lama ducks. Later there were demoiselle cranes, in flocks or pairs, and once with grey, woolly chicks.

Around mid-afternoon we made a ger stop. And here for the first time we tasted a Mongolian cream tea.

Steaming bowls of milky, Mongolian tea were passed round, and then out came a great tin bowl. Carol and I could hardly believe our eyes, for it was full to the brim with clotted cream. There was at least a gallon of it, so thick that it was cut into solid slices and piled in a heap, and another vat was already bubbling on the stove. We ate it on delicious sour-dough bread with a sprinkling of sugar, and I'd never tasted anything so close to ambrosia.

On a rack outside six or seven different sorts of cheese and curd were drying in the sun, more evidence of the brief but generous plenty of the Mongolian summer. Erdenebilet, our hostess, was a lady of many talents. Her ger was sparklingly clean and comfortable, with beautifully painted furniture. Proudly she introduced us to her twelve children, the youngest a tiny baby tightly swaddled like a papoose.

Soon we were chatting like old friends, with only minimal help needed from Tulgha. As we rose to leave, Erdenebilet presented us with a khadag as a token of friendship, draping it formally across both forearms. Carol received it in the same way. Then, "*Bayar-teh*," we said; "Goodbye." And it was time for the road again.

Now the terrain grew harsher, with rocks in the path; like driving over a Scots grouse-moor. We began to ford streams. Progress became very slow. After climbing to a pass with an obo and panoramic views, we came on a broken-down truck. No help for its driver for some time, we thought.

About one-third of the way came the *sum* of Sumber. Its now familiar wooden shacks and storehouses were relieved by a dazzlingly smart village street, whose brightly painted palings and multi-coloured gates surrounded compounds with equally cheerful houses. For the first time we saw gardens planted with trees.

At Sumber the route turned north-west between two low ridges. We crossed our first sizeable river, driving along its bed in a wide S-turn to find the best ground; afterwards following its course for some miles. It was very rough going. All too often the tyre marks led up and away from the valley floor, winding high up the sides to find a passable route. Years ago someone had built rough log bridges across the many gullies which scored the hillside, but most of these had been carried away or undermined by flood water. No-one had bothered to repair them, even when only one log was missing; easier by far to lurch off the track and cross the stream by the line of least resistance. Yet even in this austerely barren land the mountain was thick with flowers, purple willowherb and the sinister dark blue of the deadly poisonous monkshood.

Throughout the valley we saw perhaps one ger. But people had been here long before the Mongolians.

At intervals along the valley floor we came upon mounds of stones, perhaps twenty yards long and six or eight feet high. There could be little doubt that we were looking at Scythian kurgans.

The Scythians were a loose confederation of nomad mounted tribes who, two and a half thousand years ago, rode the steppes of eastern Europe and Central Asia from the Black Sea to the fringes of Siberia. They did not use writing, so that our only recorded history of them results from their collisions with the settled world on their southern borders, notably Assyria. In their more respectable latter days they settled parts of the Black Sea coast, where they became well known to Greek traders. It is the Greek historian Herodotus who leaves the most complete account of them.

Although some of Herodotus' tales about the more distant tribes of Asia smack of taverna gossip after one amphora too many, archaeology has proved him remarkably correct in much of his account of the Scythians, particularly their burial rites. The vertical shaft to an underground tomb, the precise methods of embalming, the golden vessels, the strangled attendants buried alongside, the inhalation of hemp fumes during burial rites... All these details and more have been verified by excavation in just the last few decades.

Perhaps the most exciting tombs are those at Pazyryk in Siberia, near the point where Mongolia, Russia and China converge. Here excavation of kurgans just like those we were now passing yielded astonishing treasures, deep-frozen due to water seepage through the permafrost. Instead of imperishable items and a few bones, archaeologists unearthed artefacts of leather, fur, fibre and wood, including the first known pile carpets; and among them complete mummies, many heavily tattooed. Horses buried around the chamber wore saddlery and felt masks decorated in the Animal Style of Scythian art. One tomb held plates of horsemeat and mutton, the deceased's last meal.

The latitude of permafrost was very close to the kurgans in our Mongolian valley. Under the ground just a few yards from where we were passing might be more tattooed mummies, more sacrificed horses, unimaginable carpets, tapestries, saddlecloths. It was enough to make the skin prickle.

At last we left the valley to its ghosts, and took a long pull upward. Here was the watershed between two great river systems, that of the Shishhid which runs north and west to join the mighty Yenisei, and the Delger Mörön which becomes the Selenge and ultimately feeds Lake Baikal in Siberia. A towering obo marked the top of the pass, piled high with sticks until it resembled a dense wigwam, or a huge Guy Fawkes bonfire. It was draped with scraps of material, and its hollow interior held a Buddha figure surrounded with offerings. We all left the jeep and circled it three times, before making our own contributions to the shrine.

The backdrop was breathtaking. The high, jagged peaks of the Hordil Saridag range, covered with snow, stood to the north. Perhaps I

94

had seen these very peaks from the plane. For the first time I began to get an idea of the type of country we were bound for, and my pulse quickened.

By the obo was a gate arch in a line of lesser obos, the entrance to Ulaan Uul sumoin. A sign gave the good news: "Ulaan Uul 12 km"; and the bad - 102 remaining to Tsagaan Nuur. It was already late afternoon. We would be lucky to make it tonight.

Ulaan Uul was laid out along the banks of the Shishhid River, in a beautiful, peaceful valley whose wide pastures stretched away east towards the magnificent line of the Hordil Saridag. The town itself was extensive, a good mile in length. As well as the rarity of a petrol station, it had its own policeman, and a school. Yaks kept the grass short on the playing fields.

There was once also a sizeable monastery here. It suffered worse than most during the purges; it is said that the foothills nearby are littered with the skulls of the slaughtered lamas.

Here we picked up a decent road, and some speed; and also another passenger. She was a rather bossy young woman who seemed to have some odd ideas about route-finding. Carol became increasingly caustic as we left the road at the insistence of the newcomer, fording the river several unnecessary times. At the last of these apparently random crossings the jeep became hopelessly bogged in mud and smooth-polished stones. Tulgha and the driver's mate threw rocks under the rear wheels and eventually managed to fish out the sinking vehicle.

The inhabitants of the nearby gers lined up along the river to watch the shenanigans, open-mouthed. Afterwards, heartily sick of the road, we accepted their invitation to supper.

By now Carol and I were well educated in ger etiquette. We knew that we mustn't step on the threshhold as we entered (a prohibition mentioned by Marco Polo in the thirteenth century); nor lean against the *bagana*, or two central poles, for as symbols of the stability of the ger and its link with heaven they must be treated with respect. We wouldn't have dreamed of whistling inside, even if we'd been so inclined. And we would avoid the, to us, natural gesture of throwing rubbish into the stove.

There are various taboos concerning fire in Mongolian social customs; as, for instance, that no knife should be allowed to come near it.

The significance of the hearth may have its roots in ancient fire-worship, and the annual ceremony of relighting and blessing the fire goes back centuries. So does the ritual of purification by passing between two fires, described by the monk John of Plano Carpini, who visited the Great Khan Güyük's court in 1246.

Tea must always be brewed in the presence of the guest. We watched politely as our hostess took out the pressed brick of imported Chinese tea and cut off a few thin shavings with a knife, then sprinkled them on a pan of water and added at least as much milk again. We were getting to like the strange Mongol tea. And this time, two bowlfuls of mutton noodle stew on an empty stomach tasted pretty good.

It was nearing dusk, and I asked Tulgha what was the plan.

"It depends on you," he answered with punctilious but totally vacuous courtesy. In fact it did nothing of the sort, as we didn't know the way, the distance or the difficulties of the road ahead. Nor, it was rapidly becoming clear, did the driver.

So circumstances made the decision for us. We fetched our sleeping bags and bedded down on the long carpet runner which covered the beaten earth floor. The ger was sparsely furnished, but the usual painted cupboards gave up a heap of blankets which were piled on top of us. Carol and I, next to the stove, were warm as toast.

"And," I said as the candle was blown out, "we'll have the mountains to wake up to in the morning."

*

But the Hordil Saridag was disappointingly hiding in cloud when I went out next morning to make suitable use of the privacy behind a pile of yak-dung. In a corral beside, a dozen yak calves stumbled sleepily to their feet to watch me.

We had assumed that the driver would take advantage of the delay to check his route. But immediately after leaving the ger we turned two complete circles, then set off hopefully up a blind-looking valley, still under orders from our new passenger.

She was something of an enigma. "A poseur" was Carol's opinion; she was as irritated by the girl's expensive sunglasses, unnecessarily worn well into the dusk of the evening before, as by her interference in our journey. Yet this was no ordinary townie. Under her unsuitable city clothes were the spare, hard limbs of an athlete, and her taut face with its high cheekbones was alert as that of a wild animal... even while she was directing us astray.

According to the map, we were on the opposite side of the Shishhid from the road, in an area of marsh and streams. Tulgha admitted that this was the first time the driver had been to Tsagaan Nuur. It was no longer news to us.

We asked at a ger, where an ancient lady gave us croaky but authoritative instructions. Off again confidently into a forest; but a mile later we stopped for more directions. The Shishhid had completely disappeared.

The track now entered a valley where two-humped camels grazed among more burial mounds and fast, deep rivers flowed over mercifully hard, stony beds. At a couple of crossings the water flowed right over the floor. There was more than one way to flood a carburettor, we thought nervously; and how the hell would we rescue our baggage if we conked out in the middle? But the tough little vehicle was built for the task, and took us to dry land with no more than a short halt afterwards to allow the water to drain from every orifice.

At last we found a firm track and made haste, and my hopes rose; to be rapidly dashed when the tyre marks vanished into a bog which even our driver baulked at. In search of an alternative he made a detour through woods on higher ground.

Three sets of wheel marks ran abreast on ground sloping at a good 30°. When, having started on the highest, the jeep slid slowly and elegantly to the lowest, with the bog below, the passengers made for the doors. Nothing daunted, the driver carried on until the jeep tilted perilously and rocked on two wheels; at the last moment it sideslipped, righted itself and struggled bravely on. We watched with our hearts in our mouths; firstly for our luggage, and secondly for our prospects of ever getting to Tsagaan Nuur. If the driver featured at all in our prayers he was a long way third.

This was the final trauma, and we now made good speed, skirting the edge of the marshes on a stony track which led round a sharp limestone outcrop to a sudden view of endless lakes ahead. Our last ger stop was at a permanent settlement, the main "ger" being of wood. Rough-cut logs made an octagonal base, with one massive purlin supporting the roof, and a carved hatch formed the chimney hole. The usual beds and chests were arranged around the walls, and on the floor was a single goatskin surrounded by a worn tarpaulin. A lean-to alongside housed a motorbike.

The settlement bore the marks of extreme poverty, borne out when the children appeared, dirty and dressed literally in rags. The family were long-faced rather than Mongoloid in their features; Kazakhs, perhaps, here a long way east of the main Kazakh population in Mongolia's westernmost province.

Somewhere we regained the main track, having cut out Dzöölön, through which we should have passed, and taken - on paper, if not in fact - a short cut through the marshes. And very soon we came over a rise between two welcoming signs, and saw Tsagaan Nuur, town and lake, laid out below us.

*

We might never have got any further without David Edwards' help.

From now on, things would become more difficult. For a start, we could travel no further by motor transport. The Reindeer People were away to the north, and to reach them we would have to enter the southern fringes of the taiga, the great Siberian pine forest. This could only be crossed with horses. Moreover, we needed a guide with good local knowledge, if we were to find the Tsaatan at all.

But the governor, who we hoped would help us find a guide and horses, was away on business.

Against this apparently impenetrable wall of difficulties, David's photographs were an Open Sesame. Among their subjects was Erdenejav, who with his partner Tokhtbat had acted as guide for David's party the year before. Tulgha took on the hunt - the driver, and most of the locals, spoke no Russian, so Carol and I were helpless - and waved the pictures under the noses of the next few people we met. Within half an hour we were sitting with Erdenejav in a side room of the administrative building, which, together with a school and a communications HQ with huge satellite dish and red-striped aerial, formed the centre of Tsagaan Nuur.

Erdenejav was a rather solemn young man, with a disconcerting habit of drawing back his upper lip when speaking to show long, bared teeth. It probably only meant he was concentrating hard, but it gave him a wolfish air.

The first question was the most crucial. Did he speak Russian? For setting off into the wilderness for some time with no common language between us and our guide was a non-starter.

"Of course," he answered, and I could have hugged him. Did I but know it, this was the first and last time I was to feel so inclined.

*

We spent the remainder of that day camped in Erdenejav's garden, brewing tea; or, rather, Carol brewed tea, and later supper, while I slumped guiltily.

The house, like the town, was to the standard pattern: a wooden building set in the corner of a fenced compound. The building was unfinished, and its bare walls, which would later be covered by plaster, showed a lattice infill similar to the lattice wall of a ger. The rest of the compound was occupied by a wooden privy, a large woodpile, and a dog tethered by a rope near the gate.

"Don't touch the dog," warned Erdenejav. "It's a bad dog!"

Nervously we gave it a wide berth. Yet it showed no hostility; far from it, it wrinkled its upper lip in a grin, and wriggled its backside ingratiatingly at us. Soon we were stopping to give it a cuddle every time we passed. "When we get back," I said to Carol, "I'm going to ask if I can take it out for a run." In the event, I didn't.

*

That evening two small, grubby faces appeared over the boundary fence. Only their eyes and noses showing, they regarded with that motionless, unblinking inscrutability of toddlers the two alien creatures wriggling in and out of their strange green cover, like Martians who had suddenly invaded their familiar world.

Soon they were joined by a third face, larger, immeasurably cleaner and far from inscrutable. To our astonishment this face spoke to us in English.

Eighteen-year-old Soyolmaa was a language student, and couldn't believe her luck to find two Brits shacked up next door. Her English was staggeringly good for a beginner, and all three of us were thirsty for information. We put the billy back on the stove for the nth time, and settled down to compare notes.

Universal access to education, even in the remotest of places, was one of the triumphs of the old order. Soyolmaa had been educated here from the age of seven - Tsagaan Nuur even had its own secondary school - and then won a place at university (further education is competitively, not automatically, allocated) in Erdenet where her eldest sister lived. Now she was home for her long summer break.

We shuddered at the thought of her horrendous journey by truck every term, nearly as far as UB. But her thirst for learning, her obvious desire to be in at the sharp end of Mongolia's renaissance, and the importance she attached to English as the key to entering the wider world, pervaded all she said.

"Now our country has diplomatic, economic, trade and cultural relations with many countries: America, Japan, England, Russia, China... for example, there are nine foreign teachers in our institute."

Her favourite was Carleen, her American teacher of English. "We visit Carleen's house, cook American food, and hear about life in the West. And we listen to English songs - I particularly like the Beatles!" *She's got a ticket to ride, and she's OK* - was there a hint of escapism here, where getting about was such a nightmare?

Carleen had started up an English newsletter, "Future". Soyolmaa showed us the first issue. It covered travel, western and Mongolian films, life and aspirations at Erdenet, all treated in refreshingly buoyant mode. There was even an agony column.

"Dear Gonchig, My husband is terrible. He eats too much like a pig, is too lazy and doesn't wash his face. He smells so bad and all of my money is used for his food. What should I do? Love, the Housewife." *"You can separate from him. There are many good-looking men in our institute and you can make a good choice. They aren't terrible, don't eat too much, they aren't lazy and always wash their faces!"*

Soyolmaa - and, through her, her friends - were a window through which we glimpsed the intellectual life of Mongolia: young, vibrant, full of optimism, meeting with resilience and good humour the restrictions imposed by old inflexible systems, out-of-date Marxist textbooks, lack of resources. "Dear Gonchig, I want to use the computers three times a week. How can I do this?" *"Calm down, please! One wonderful and sunny day the institute directors will solve this problem and we can use them as many times as we want."*

They will, too, if mountains have to move. Meanwhile, in case we should become complacent at the superiority of our own affluent society, one contributor to "Future" - a young Mongolian who had travelled in England - made a disturbing comment. Most things there had delighted her, but she had one reservation. "The English do not care after old people, it is the main thing that I do not like."

*

The bush telegraph had been at work. The following morning Tokhtbat, the arat who had been David's other guide last year, arrived at Erdenejav's house, having somehow divined that he was needed.

Tokhtbat, himself half Tsaatan and familiar with the remote area of the Tsaatan's summer camp, was to be our other companion for the trip. He lived on the way, some fifteen miles from Tsagaan Nuur on the very northern edge of the steppeland, and we would camp at his ger for the first overnight stop. I had explained to Erdenejav that I was unwell and that Carol hadn't ridden much. So we had arranged to spread the ride over three days instead of the usual two. David, said Erdenejav, had done the same, finding a beautiful camping place. We all agreed that that would do very well.

Of my ill health, I said merely that I had "a problem with my heart". I could no more render a complex neurological illness into Russian than I could imitate the mating call of a haddock. But the phrase was more than just a cop-out hiding a cause behind a single effect. Rather, it was easily understood and carried all the right implications. So it wasn't necessary to explain that I was unable to walk fast or far, and would become unnaturally exhausted by the journey.

Tokhtbat was much more laid back than the rather stiff Erdenejav, with a merry face under his battered trilby, and a lop-sided, gap-toothed grin that he used readily.

He brought two horses to add to Erdenejav's three, which left one spare as a packhorse. Heads were scratched over our luggage, which we had already pared to the bone. Reluctantly we gave up most of our food, having previously been determined not to scrounge off local hospitality, but instead to give more food than we took. We weren't prepared, though, to leave any of the gifts - at least those would only have to be carried one way. At a brusque "*ne nado*" - "unnecessary" - from Erdenejav we unwillingly ditched our cooking gear, for which we were later to curse him. That left us with next to nothing besides sleeping bags and tent, which made the bulk of our goods, and some basic medical kit.

Before departure Naran, Erdenejav's sweet and beautiful wife, fed us wonderful home-made bread with clotted cream. As we ate, we learned a little of Erdenejav's background. Via the military service compulsory for all young men, he had spent a fair bit of time in Russia, and showed us photographs of himself soldiering in Irkutsk and working in the fish factories of Murmansk. He was much travelled, and we were impressed.

Now Naran crammed a last-minute loaf of bread into Erdenejav's saddlebag; and we were ready for the road.

My pony was a skinny little black beast, the smallest of the five. From on top, his short neck and drooping head gave the impression of nothing in front of me, a feeling accentuated by the unnatural height above his back of the Russian saddle on its thick layers of felt. I might have been sitting on a little black beetle. Carol's was a fatter, stolid-looking animal whose mouse-grey colouring, dorsal stripe and zebra leg-markings were distantly familiar. Perhaps the steppe tarpan - ancient cousin of the takhi - wasn't, after all, entirely extinct.

We set off at a brisk trot, all the more knackering for the Beetle's stride being so short: he took three steps to the others' two. How on earth, I wondered, would I survive several days of this, even with a break in the middle?

Several days, too of more than just physical strain. For it soon became apparent that the real problem was going to be Erdenejav himself.

Carol, as an inexperienced rider, was safely attached to Tokhtbat by a leading rein, and thus under satisfactory control. "I feel like another bit of baggage!" she laughed, as we rode along the lakeside. But I was loose, and therefore by definition a liability.

If the Beetle jogged to keep up on his short legs, Erdenejav crossly told me to stop. If I moved any part of my body a fraction, adjusted my stirrup, patted the pony or pointed at a landmark, he shouted at me angrily. "This isn't a European horse," he said. "Mongolian horses are different!"

We had already seen that for ourselves. If you went near his horses, they cowered in fright. And it was obvious why. The more hectoring he became with me, the more he jerked his own horse in the mouth, or hit it with the end of the rope.

"Hoosh!" he roared at it. This is the Mongolian equivalent of hush, or whoa; a gentle noise to soothe a fidgety horse. Erdenejav used it like a curse.

Eventually the Beetle, who was more lively than he looked, had a bucking fit, and this gave Erdenejav his excuse. He firmly put me on a leading rein, dragging me along beside him on a twelve inch length of rope that spoke volumes about his approach to other people. We were on a steep, rough hillside at the time. While he firmly held his horse to the narrow track, mine had to stagger along on the slope beside him. For now I held my peace; confrontations could wait till later. There were plenty to come.

As we rode, Erdenejav told me something of the way ahead. It was rough, steep and bad riding. (He had already said this several times while we planned the trip.) "Have you done it often?" I asked him. He hadn't; only once, when he and Tokhtbat accompanied David last year.

"I don't like taking tourists," he said disparagingly. Besides, he went on, it was dangerous, because of the wolves, bears and other wild animals; and of course bandits on the Russian border.

I let it wash over me. He was obviously out to make us wish we hadn't come. But his dislike of "tourists", as well as, we became convinced, his dislike of women who didn't know their place, was a clue to his behaviour towards us throughout. Whyever, we wondered, had he come with us?

Despite all, it was a glorious day's ride. We followed the lake north-west, until it narrowed once more into the Shishhid River flowing towards the border with the Russian republic of Tuva. This was the end of the road for anything on wheels, as the river was far too deep to ford.

For us there was a ferry, a simple raft riding on oil drums and pulled across manually via a wire hawser. Passengers walked on almost dry-shod by a plank, while the horses were led into the river and persuaded to jump aboard. They did so with aplomb, being obviously hardened sailors.

The furthermost drum leaked. As successive horses came aboard, it took in water with audible slurps, and the raft sank a little lower. By the time the last horse was loaded, the first was standing with his hind feet in the water. Yet we made it safely, and at the other side the process was reversed, the drum spitting water at each unloaded horse until the whole contraption was horizontal again.

From now on we followed the Hogrog River, tributary to the Shishhid, up a wide basin; now high above it on the hillside, now low down among the rocks in the valley. Repeatedly we forded it, the horses splashing us with water for some way after as they swished their long, wet tails.

I sweet-talked Erdenejav into letting me off my tether, which he did with many a grim warning about my bad horse, the bad road, the danger of falling and hitting my head on the stony path, the danger of being kicked, the danger of going too fast. The rest of us rode in high good humour, with Tokhtbat singing raucously. The Mongolians often sing as they ride, rousing songs with a good rhythm that encourage the horses to step out.

Now, Tokhtbat indicated, it was our turn. We conferred and treated them to Jerusalem; then some lively Welsh hymn tunes, Carol's Welsh choral background standing her in good stead.

Even Erdenejav relaxed a bit, although his dignity baulked at singing. He brought up various European pop songs which he had heard in Russia, and asked me if I knew them. I didn't, which got me more black marks. Fortunately Carol was able to step in and uphold British prestige.

Black clouds were building, I was dizzy with fatigue and Carol was getting saddle sore, so it was a relief when at last Tokhtbat's gers appeared in the distance. For the last mile the storm broke behind us, and we outran it at a gallop across a marshy stretch strewn with stones. As we tied up the thunder was crashing all round us; we raced the rain to the ger entrance, just in time to avoid the torrents that drummed on the roof, beating through the smoke-hole to land hissing on the stove-pipe.

We gratefully drank hot tea, trying not to think of the horses left outside in the rain. The one animal allowed the shelter of the ger was a grey and white cat, the first pet we had seen in Mongolia.

*

When the rain stopped, the usual evening round began of bringing in the horses, corralling the calves and milking the cattle. It was noticeable here that the women and children did all the work. Even chopping wood; we watched petrified as one of Tokhtbat's young nieces split logs, one wobbly hand wielding the axe while the other rested a couple of inches from the point where the blade fell. Meanwhile Erdenejav and Tokhtbat played cards, and the other men watched them and advised.

The two were an ill-assorted pair. One laughing and extrovert, the other unsmiling and self-contained; Tokhtbat - like his whole family - in del, boots and trilby, while Erdenejav wore western-style denim jacket and jeans, with a baseball cap - a cap which he sometimes wore back to front, in his one concession to frivolity.

The disparity, though, was more than skin-deep. For while Tokhtbat was pure herdsman, completely integrated with his way of life and surroundings, Erdenejav seemed an uneasy hybrid from two worlds.

Born in Ulaan Baatar, he had been brought up a city-dweller. He had been greatly influenced by his contact with the Soviet world, had respected the Russians, and obviously deeply regretted their departure. His time spent serving in Russia appeared to have given him fulfilment and left happy memories. His personality, naturally authoritarian, was in perfect harmony with the Soviet doctrines which had moulded him.

Yet somehow, whether by accident or design, he had landed up in a remote frontier-style town in Hovsgol aimag. He was as far as possible, both geographically and psychologically, from what seemed to be his natural city environment.

Could it be design? For there was that in Erdenejav which hinted of a yearning to return to his roots - even in the metropolis of UB, after all, few are more than a couple of generations away from the steppe. He seemed proud of his three horses, even if it was an impersonal, theoretical pride which left little scope to care for them practically, as we were to see. And he was clearly deeply attached to his friend Tokhtbat, constantly deferring to the latter's knowledge, resourcefulness and sheer endurance. "Tokhtbat," he was to say often in the days ahead, "is a man of iron!" Perhaps it was the attraction of an adventure in the wilderness with his friend which induced him to take us on. Somewhere in Erdenejav, however deeply buried, there may have lurked a romantic.

Yet for all the city and Soviet influences, his attitude to Carol and me was pure Hovsgol. Neither he nor Tokhtbat seemed to know what to make of two women entering their male-dominated world, viewing us as somewhere lower than the luggage they were to carry with us. "Perhaps," said Carol charitably, "he just doesn't know what to make of women who take their own decisions and know exactly where they're going." Carol was always more charitable than I about Erdenejav. But then, she didn't have to deal with him directly. Neither Tokhtbat, nor subsequently any of the Tsaatan, spoke Russian. The fact that only he and I shared a language meant that every conversation, every arrangement, every discussion about the least detail, had to be channelled through him and me. This exacerbated the friction which seemed to exist naturally between us.

It wasn't a comfortable situation, and it got a lot worse.

*

Tokhtbat's family lived on the very edge of their world. Beyond, the landscape changed dramatically.

This was the final boundary of the steppe, the point where it gave way to the taiga which, apart from the interruption of the Bolshoi Sayan mountains on the Russian border, stretched unbroken to the north until it gave way in its turn to arctic tundra.

It was more than just the meeting of two topographical features. It was the meeting of two worlds, two cultures, two histories: that of the mounted steppe nomads, which reaches south and west to Europe and the Middle East and back to the Scythian horsemen; and that of the forest dwellers of the north, from Scandinavia to Kamchatka.

Before we saddled up to leave, Tokhtbat's mum (Erdenejav couldn't remember her name, and wouldn't ask Tokhtbat for us; it was disrespectful, he said, for a young person to use an elderly person's name, so we referred to her throughout as Tokhtbat's mum) invited us into her ger for a ceremonial blessing on our journey.

She was herself Tsaatan and, like many of her kin, had given up her life with the reindeer to marry a Mongolian herdsman - and raise fifteen children. Her culture was shamanist, the age-old religion of steppe and forest alike. Shamanism is a form of animism, invoking local deities and numinous presences in wood, water and rock. Once the religion of all Mongolia, it had been relegated by Buddhism to an anachronism surviving only in remote corners - such as among the Reindeer People.

It came to her as naturally as breathing, then, when Tokhtbat's mum took a glass of arkhi and, using the third finger of the right hand, flicked

107

it to the four points of the compass to invoke the goodwill of the spirits along our way. We all in turn did the same, drinking a few sips before passing on the cup.

Unfortunately, the blessing did nothing to create harmony. Trouble began at once when I lengthened my stirrups a couple of holes. Erdenejav at once objected that this wasn't safe, reciting his usual litany of bad roads, bad horse, fall, stones, head...

"All the more reason to be comfortable," I answered, trying to smile at him. "This isn't like the horse you rode yesterday!" he retorted (I was now on the chestnut former baggage pony, since the Beetle was to be left behind). "This is a bad horse!" It sounded remarkably like the horse I rode yesterday, according to his earlier warnings about the Beetle.

He complained even more when Carol tried to level her own stirrups, having ridden lopsided throughout the day before, one knee under her chin.

"If you weren't women, you wouldn't be getting away with this fuss!" On the contrary; if we were men, there wouldn't have been any problem, we were now convinced.

But the worst came when we at last set off; for he decreed that I should be back on the leading rein for the duration of the journey. It was for my safety, he said piously (bad roads, bad horse, fall, stones, head), handing my tether to Tokhtbat, whose lack of Russian meant that there could be no disputing the case. Erdenejav's real concern for our safety was apparent throughout, as he kept Carol's horse on such a tight rein that it could barely see where it was going, and dragged it at breakneck speed through rivers and over marshy hollows so ruthlessly that it frequently nearly fell over. In fact he had another reason for ensuring that neither of us had any control over the journey, one which became clear to us only on the road home.

I gritted my teeth and bit my tongue. If I argued, he was capable of calling the trip off. It was an object lesson in humility. To find yourself riding a thirteen hand pony on a leading rein, supervised by a young man ten years your junior, is a bit deflating. It was also disorientating. I seemed to be hallucinating: once more I was a little girl in pigtails, short legs sticking out either side of a fat little pony. I constantly expected Tokhtbat to holler, in a rich Devon burr, "Use yer *'eels! Kick 'er in the stummick!*"

My dismay, though, went a bit deeper.

For six years of illness, I'd been unable to get about freely on my own legs, a restriction more frustrating than ever in this exciting country. At home, I could be independently mobile on wheels. Here, where I wanted to quarter every possible inch like a dog with my nose to the ground, I was without my own vehicle and could only follow routes laid down by other people. On the UB buses, in the truck, even with our "own" hired jeep, I was entirely subject to the will of the driver. I was moving, but not freely; running, as it were, on rails.

On a horse, everything was going to be different. I would have four good legs to replace my own two lousy ones, and could move according to my own will. Now, after just a brief glimpse, that freedom was denied to me. Here, at the most exciting part of our trip, I was again subject to the whim of a driver; back on a set of rails.

Tokhtbat, however, did his best to lighten the situation with his natural clownishness. At Erdenejav's dire warnings he rolled his eyes and lurched in his saddle with such high good humour that I could only laugh. Not for the first time, I wished we had a common language. Quite apart from the fact that it would make life easier, I wanted to ask all manner of things about this interesting man, and his herding life on the rim of the Mongolian steppe.

Instead, as we rode, I found myself constantly sparring with Erdenejav, as he continued to try and score off us. It was as well my Russian was limited, or I would have risen to the bait shamefully. When my leading rein caught on the saddle bags and I freed it with a slight jerk, making the pony shy, he berated me lengthily, and my patience snapped.

"Your friend," I said grimly to Tokhtbat, "is an old woman!" Tokhtbat couldn't understand, but Erdenejav was outraged. The resulting dressing down seemed to last forever.

Now he reverted to his earlier theme, telling us that Mongolian men were men of steel, Mongolian men were utterly straightforward. He added, with a sideways look at me, "not like women!" My answer was hollow and spherical, and he relapsed into a stony silence which was a blessed relief.

The journey was a miserable one in other ways. Almost at once we ploughed into hideous bog, through which the horses struggled and plunged. After a bit, a firmer path emerged, and we threaded a winding road through alternating patches of squelching heath and scrub into tree-covered mountains. Tokhtbat's mum was riding with us, taking the chance to visit her family. A few miles into the journey a lad on a grey horse appeared from nowhere to join our party; another of the Tsaatan. The rain closed in sullenly and pursued us all day, drenching us with periodic outbursts.

Erdenejav thawed enough to tell us something of the political and economic difficulties that beset present-day Mongolia. Despite his respect for the Russians, he didn't want them back. But he missed the predictability of the old regime. Like so many elsewhere, he blamed the collapse of the USSR, and its knock-on effect on Mongolia, squarely on Gorbachev. But was Yeltsin any more able to bring order out of chaos, we asked?

"Yeltsin," he said, "is a true and 'simple' Russian." Whether he meant straightforward or just dim wasn't clear.

But when the Russians left to sort out their own mess, most of the supply lines on which Mongolia had depended were shut off. Now there were no medicines, no fertilisers, not enough health care, unemployment. "Earlier," he continued, "there were at least some people who were moderately well off. Now everyone is just poor." If he had a large chip on his shoulder about the comparative wealth of tourists, we were beginning to understand that there was good reason.

By now we were all soaked from the relentless rain. I was the wettest, having opted to wear only trainers in the endless juggling over luggage weight versus mobility, and my waterproof wasn't. Erdenejav was driest. He took great satisfaction in pointing out both extremes.

"Why," he now asked for perhaps the fifth time, "do you want to make this journey?"

"Tell him we're on holiday!" answered Carol. "Tell him we want to enjoy ourselves!"

For an infrequent rider, Carol was performing heroically. But she was beginning to suffer from leg cramps, and her saddle sores were raw. And I was almost completely exhausted. We pressed for a halt, but it was an hour before we reached a spot where the dense scrub drew back from the narrow path to allow enough room to dismount and sit down.

Tokhtbat now produced a sack of biscuits: hard tack baked from flour and the inevitable mutton fat. He bid us dive in and fill our pockets. We did so greedily; the afternoon was well on and we had eaten nothing since our meagre breakfast.

We must have come some twenty miles, surely more than halfway. But among the trees, scrub and bog underneath, we had not passed a single spot where you could have pitched a tent. Where on earth was David's camping-place, where we were supposed to be spending the night?

Worse, there was no sign of Erdenejav and Tokhtbat having brought any sort of covering. They couldn't spend a night in the open in this weather. And with Tokhtbat's mum and the additional Tsaatan who had joined us, we were now six. Stop now, and we would be playing: How many Mongolians can you get in a two-man tent?

Like Tulgha at Ulaan Uul, Erdenejav made a show of deferring to us over what happened next. But we were over a barrel. There was no alternative but to hand the decision back to him. So we remounted and rode wearily on. Only days later did we realise that they had never, even before the monsoon, had the least intention of an overnight stop.

Now we plunged into the forest and arrived at the top of a precipitous slope. We dismounted and led the horses, slipping and sliding over the stones. I closed my mind to the problem of getting myself back up it on foot, on the way home.

At the bottom we came into a long valley between two ridges, which bent away at our point of entry and marched down endlessly to the south-east. At the meeting of the ways was a small obo. We stopped briefly, while Tokhtbat's mum brought strips of cloth from her pocket, and tied them on for the local deity.

As we rode soggily up the northern branch of the valley, not a bird or beast stirred on its forested slopes. It was as if evolution had passed it by. Towards the top was a sudden explosion of orange; a swathe of Siberian globeflowers, ravishing in the desolation. Above stretched a bank of melting snow. Suddenly the thought of reindeer seemed highly appropriate.

A large obo, surrounded by gentians, crowned the pass. We dismounted to make a clockwise circuit, and tied tufts of hair from our horses' tails to the central pole. Great mountain peaks now stood all around us.

Ahead, three valleys branched off. To the right, towering peaks at the end delineated the Russian border. To the left, a river of white water thundered down to join the distant Yenisei, gathering tributaries as it went. And in the centre valley, from which the torrent issued as a moderate stream, we could just make out in the distance a cluster of white dots: the tepees of the Tsaatan.

A few miles up the valley, we met a sudden commotion. Four hundred reindeer came crashing round the shoulder of the mountain, splashed through the stream and raced ahead of us towards the camp. Behind them galloped three mounted youths, whooping like cowboys. With an answering yell Tokhtbat was off, dragging my tottering pony in a headlong dash through peat hags and over rocks, lurching through the streams and hollows with scant regard for the life and limb of any of us. For the second time in two days we finished our march at the gallop. But as we approached I could think of only one thing: there was smoke issuing from the tops of the tepees. The promise of warmth and dry clothes beckoned.

Five minutes later we were under cover, drinking hot, salt tea and steaming gently by a glowing stove.

VI

VALLEY OF THE BURNT RIVER

A strange honking sound woke us. It came gradually nearer, and was followed by slurps, as rough, inquisitive tongues rasped on the side of the tent. When the imprint of cloven hooves began to dent the roof, we had to drag ourselves from exhausted sleep, and repel boarders.

Memories of the evening before were a blur. We had climbed off our horses barely able to stand. At once, friendly faces surrounded us, and swept us unto one of the tepees. Any fears we may have had about intruding vanished at once, for David's photographs made us welcome. In a moment, the small space was crammed with people. The prints flew from hand to hand, and small children crawled between the legs of grown-ups, trying to see themselves in the magazine pictures.

Having read the article many times, we could recognise our hosts. Bat was a tall, slight man, forty-ish, whose long face and lean features suggested northern or western origins. His wife Gerelmaa had a rounder face, marked with poise and serenity. Their ten-year-old son Pruvorj we also knew from David's magazine illustrations. His younger brother Prudow was a carbon copy, just a few inches shorter.

Not wanting to impose ourselves, we said our goodnights while only half-dry, somehow pitched the tent in what was now black darkness, and crawled into damp sleeping bags. "The next time you say you're planning a trip," commented Carol just this side of oblivion, "I'm going to Brighton!"

The rain was still falling today, although not so heavily. But it would take more than bad weather to diminish the surroundings.

Above the reindeer camp the valley divided in two. The main branch ran straight ahead to massive snow-covered ramparts encircling a couple

113

of corries. The other led off to the side, its enclosing slopes only just visible from higher up the valley. From the snowmelt in the corries two streams crashed down, merging noisily just above the camp into the Burnt River, as the Tsaatan named it. Along the summit ridges that were its source ran the Russian border, following the line of the Bolshoi Sayan mountains. The highest peak of this range, well over ten thousand feet, was just five miles away from our valley.

It was breathtaking scenery. Tantalising, too; once on those ridges you could have walked without losing height for a dozen miles, and seen for perhaps a hundred. With a decent pair of legs I wouldn't have been kept back by wild horses, border or not; and Erdenejav would have had a litter of kittens.

Today, though, he and everyone else were indoors, staying dry. The main reindeer herd had been taken out to pasture long before Carol and I were awake. Only the milch-deer were about the camp, and it was these who were now amiably climbing over our tent.

The milking system was the same as elsewhere: the calves tethered, in this case to wooden rectangular frames pegged to the ground, the does free to wander and graze. They were gentle and affectionate creatures, their trust testifying to the kindly nature of the Tsaatan. Following you about the camp, they would creep up behind and nudge you in the back. Even a loo-trip attracted an escort. Especially a loo-trip; for, obviously deficient in salt, they would wait to lick the resulting damp patch. Perhaps it was in the hope of weak bladders that they tracked us so remorselessly.

They were constantly vocal, making a noise somewhere between a honk, a burp and a bark. It always made us jump to hear such coarse grunts coming from these delicate, beautiful creatures.

But the reindeer were tough and hardy, for all their seeming delicacy. The camp occupied the only patch of open grass, long since grazed close, and the does had to search the valley for food among the rocks and scrub. It was perilous grazing. Between the clumps of wild rhubarb and yellow-flowered potentilla which formed the bulk of the vegetation, the dark-blue monkshood thrust its lethally poisonous spikes everywhere.

Yet the deer cropped dextrously all around, eating every shred of green without once touching its deadly leaves.

The Tsaatan children were equally wise. Wandering about the valley picking flowers, they would return with a bunch in each hand; but never a monkshood among them.

It was the children who gave us our first close contact with the people of the reindeer camp. They were less shy than their parents, and a couple of foreigners were good entertainment. For we were something of a rarity to them. Until David's visit the previous year, they had met no-one from the outside world; and we were the first western women they had seen.

While I was comatose most of the day, Carol went for a walk. She returned trailing a crowd of some twenty children. The youngest was Sa'alunkha, a little girl of perhaps four years, who was clutching Carol's hand in one small fist and an enormous bunch of flowers in the other. Her name, appropriately, meant "Rainbow".

The kids rampaged about the camp like a large, friendly street gang. Pruvorj, the eldest, was boss, with Prudow and Samburg, a tall lad in a striped jumper, his deputies. Unlike the adults, they were dressed almost entirely in western-style clothes; usually tracksuits and T-shirts, though Samburg's sister Unkhwayra, in primrose yellow dress and blue hair-scarf, might have just come from a party. Most went barefoot, despite the chilling rain.

When the weather let up, Carol produced the rubber balls she had bought in Mörön. They were a hit, instantly demolishing any barriers of language or culture. We started with polite games of catch; but they degenerated into a riot when Carol decided to introduce a game of "It", throwing the ball to hit individual players. She demonstrated on me; soon I became sole target for everyone, and had to retreat into the tent, begging for mercy.

Via the children, Bat and Gerelmaa sent us over bowls of tea. So did Tsindeli, a sweetly beautiful middle-aged lady whose tepee was nearest to our tent. It made us a good meal, mixed with instant soup from our sparse provisions, and we dunked in it the remaining stale heel of Alta's loaf. We sent the bowls back with "thank you" gifts of cigarettes from what Carol had designated the "goody-bag". Later, Gerelmaa followed up her earlier hospitality with a couple of reindeer ribs.

"It's a good thing they're ribs," remarked Carol as we gnawed on them like dogs in a kennel - our best meal in weeks. "The worms tend to end up in the hindquarters!" Never travel with a zoologist; you may learn more than you need to know.

In the evening, Gerelmaa and Bat invited us into their tepee, to enjoy again the comfort of their hot stove, and finish drying our wet things. As we sat drinking tea, a stranger came into the tent.

She was a tall woman in a green del, with unusual boots of variegated strips of leather. There was something familiar about those boots. In the shifting firelight, we took a closer look at her face. It was our companion of the jeep ride to Tsagaan Nuur.

Here, then, was the answer to the riddle, the sense of something elemental under the sophisticated exterior. No longer self-conscious in her city clothes, she blended into these surroundings so perfectly that we had almost failed to recognise her.

The sense of mystery persisted when she asked us to take her photograph. We each took a flash-lit shot of her, sitting in the darkness outside Bat's tepee. Yet both our cameras, faultless throughout the rest of the trip, simultaneously malfunctioned. On developing the pictures afterwards, we found that we had no record of her on film.

Her name, we discovered when she wrote down an Ulaan Baatar address for the prints, was Saranturyaa. Yet ever after we spoke of her, as if from the pages of Malory, as "The Lady in the Green Del".

*

The Tsaatan originated from the neighbouring Russian republic of Tuva, having crossed to Mongolia to escape the repressions of the thirties. But the way of life they brought with them was by no means new to these parts; the Urianghai, a tribe living in the north of Mongolia in the time of Genghis Khan, were described in contemporary records as "keepers of reindeer".

116

As well as their culture, they kept their own language. Tsaatan is a form of the Tuvan language, which itself is of Mongolian and Turkic derivation - the oldest form of Turkic in the world, some say. So the word for a dwelling, for example, is *yurtsia*, resembling the Turkic word "yurt" rather than the Mongolian "ger".

They may have escaped Stalin, but collectivisation pursued the Tsaatan. It finally caught up with them in 1959, commandeering their reindeer, clamping an unfriendly strait-jacket on their nomadic existence and reducing their wanderings to just four seasonal migrations.

Collectivisation wasn't all bad news. It brought benefits, too: along with Administration, Targets and Quotas came health care, education and subsidies. Although they may have mourned their independence, the Tsaatan, like so many on Mongolia's economic margins, had cause to welcome the Russian Bear. Cause, too, to regret its departure more keenly than most; for now that the old order is breaking down, it is the advantages that have crumbled, while, as we were to learn, the disadvantages remain.

Whatever the politics, life is hard for the Reindeer People. Their women, in particular, grow lined and worn at an early age. On first meeting Tsindeli we were taken aback when she began to suckle a child; we later learned that she was only forty-two.

Infant mortality here is comparatively high. Yet it seems that the Tsaatan thrive. Far from being, as we first guessed, under threat, they are actually increasing in number. Currently this group totals well over a hundred, as does the other Tsaatan group who live in the mountains west of Ulaan Uul; the "eastern" and "western" Tsaatan respectively.

The two groups intermarry now and then, but otherwise there is little traffic between them. Tsaatan-Mongolian marriages are more common, usually resulting in the Tsaatan partner leaving the mountains for the steppes, rather than the other way round. And there is still contact with Tuva. Tokhtbat's sister had married a Tuvan, and members of his family visit occasionally. Recently, however, such travel has been difficult as the border areas have become more sensitive. Three armed police, according to David, had been killed by smugglers in these parts not long ago. Perhaps Erdenejav's bandits weren't entirely a figment of his imagination.

The Tsaatan are a gentler people than the Mongolians. They are also astonishingly hardy, their toughness standing out in what is already a country of exceedingly tough people. They live the year round with just a thin strip of canvas between them and the elements, their only concession to winter being a camp at rather lower altitude, and within reach of the meagre luxuries of Tsagaan Nuur.

Some years ago, Alta told us, a Tsaatan delegation attended a conference in Mörön. They spurned their hotel rooms to sleep outside on the ground. It was a similar picture when the government tried to persuade them to live in houses in winter: they knocked out the windows to let the fresh air in. We asked Bat's sister Tsestik which was her favourite season. "Autumn" she replied. The summer, she added, was too hot. The snowline was just a few hundred feet above her yurtsia.

It was now that Erdenejav showed another side of himself. For none of the Tsaatan spoke Russian, and without Erdenejav to interpret for us, we couldn't have communicated in anything more than the most trivial way. With unexpected patience he took us round the camp, introducing us to every family and helping us to get to know them.

Life in the yurtsia was very similar to that of the ger, except for the scarcity of possessions. With only the reindeer (which can carry as much as a horse) and one or two ponies to move goods from camp to camp, there is little chance to gather moss, and anyway no money to spare for anything non-essential.

The positions for family and visitors were the same as we had become used to, as was the food. There was the usual tea, and the usual milky noodle stew, though made from reindeer meat rather than mutton. Tsindeli made an excellent reindeer sausage.

To my relief, airag was off the menu here - perhaps, at about a pint per milking twice a day, the deer don't give enough surplus milk - but clotted cream was definitely on. Once we were given a bowl of boiled reindeer milk, thick and creamy. And the reindeer milk cheese was the best we had tasted.

We watched as Gerelmaa made mouth-watering bread, without yeast or an oven. Mixing flour-water paste with some "starter" dough from the last batch, she bundled it into a plastic bag and tucked it under the poles of the tepee, near the fire, to prove overnight. Next day, when it was rising well, she transferred it to a large round pot on the stove, where it continued to rise at the top while cooking at the bottom. Halfway through it was knocked out, inverted and replaced. The result was a perfect loaf, light, moist, and better than anything from a supermarket.

Our own contribution to hospitality was mainly biscuits, which we had managed to hang on to when we threw out almost everything else. Also, cigarettes - the ideal gift for the circumstances, these, weighing almost nothing. Although both tobacco-phobic, we need feel no guilt about pushing the stuff here. The Tsaatan have little access to cigarettes, and enjoy a smoke all the more when the chance arises. Sometimes they would make a roll-up out of an empty piece of paper, once even from some pages of a book kept tucked under the spokes of the yurtsia.

As in the gers, these poles provided drying-room and storecupboard. Washing, haunches of meat, dried flowers, strips of reindeer sausage, juniper for kindling, nets of drying cheeses all jostled each other for space.

Bulkier goods like bedding were stored in the angle between tent canvas and ground. Here, too, lived the family rifle, used to supplement the meagre diet with anything that could be shot. Reindeer skins covered the floor. Together with cooking pots and stove, these usually made up a family's entire possessions.

Plus, of course, the hunting knives carried by the men. Bat's brother Ganghüyük, a drop-dead-gorgeous hunk whose purple del was set off by orange bus and trilby, would bring out a whetstone and sharpen the knife to his satisfaction before using it to shave. Meanwhile, the joints of meat in each yurtsia, and the fresh reindeer hides draped on the hitching rails about the camp, were a reminder that the knife wasn't just a fashion accessory.

There was one more item to be found in many of the tepees: an *ongghod*, or shrine to the family gods.

The most impressive of these belonged to Funtsal, a grandmother in her sixties. Her chosen god was Ariel, personified as a large, black eagle, and honoured with a hanging collection of charms and beads that included a pair of eagle's talons, a smaller set of claws - from a kite, perhaps - and the paws of something which had once been small and furry.

Funtsal was a herbalist, and told us something of the local plants and flowers she used. Most were for minor ailments; the little carmine-pink dianthus for something which Erdenejav translated as "women's problems".

It was perhaps no coincidence that Funtsal's ongghod was the biggest in the camp, nor that she was dressed in purple, the colour of the occult. "Do *not* mess with this woman!" David had said darkly. For Funtsal's father, now dead, had been the last camp shaman.

*

"Just as God has given the hand several fingers, so he has given mankind several paths. To you he has given the Scriptures... whereas to us he has given shamans." So spoke Möngke, Genghis' grandson, Great Khan of all the Mongols and thus the most powerful man on earth, to the Franciscan friar William of Rubruck.

William was a missionary and courier who in 1253 made the arduous journey from the Holy Land to Möngke's court at Karakorum. On returning he wrote a detailed account of the things he had seen on his journey. Among them is a description of the shamanism practised at the Mongol court.

This report gives one of the few glimpses afforded by history of Mongolian shamanism before, inevitably, it became diluted with lamaistic practices. Also giving a thumbnail sketch was William's fellow Franciscan, John of Plano Carpini, who beat him to the Mongol Khan by just seven years.

Both William and John were familiar with ongghon*, but those they saw were effigies made from wood, felt or silk, representing ancestors or

*plural of ongghod

120

living family members. Otherwise, John's account is brief and mostly limited to related superstitions, such as the many instances of purification by fire.

The Mongols worshipped a spiritual hierarchy headed by the Eternal Blue Sky or Tengri, and a female earth and fertility goddess named Itugen: the usual formula across the northern hemisphere in the ancient world. Ranked below these two, and more immediately accessible to humanity, was the world of spirits. A shaman was a holy man who acted as mediator, communing with the spirits and relaying their commands back to the mortal world. William of Rubruck thus graphically describes a seance:

"They gather in their dwelling at night those who want an answer from the demon, putting cooked meat in the centre of the dwelling. The shaman who issues the summons begins uttering his incantations and holds a tambourine which he bangs heavily on the ground. At length he falls into a frenzy and has himself tied up; and then the demon appears in the darkness and gives him the meat to eat, and he utters oracles."

His account matches those of the few travellers who have been lucky enough to witness the event in recent years. One thing William doesn't record, though, is the frequent use of hallucinogens to achieve the trance. In the past these would usually be hemp-seed vapour or "magic" mushrooms - probably the fly agaric, common throughout Siberian latitudes. The Vikings used this before raids to induce a state which they called "beserk"; red and white, it's the classic children's fairy-tale mushroom. (Often depicted with elves - another hallucination? - on top.) Nowadays, the trance is more likely to come out of a bottle, or several, of arkhi.

It was believed that in his trance the shaman would leave his body, quit the dwelling by rising through the smoke-hole, and fly through the air to visit the spirit world. He would be carried on his journey by a "familiar", the spirit of an animal, usually a horse or - especially hereabouts - a reindeer.

The idea of flying through the smoke-hole is common in pre-Buddhist sources. The *Secret History of the Mongols* is an account of the early life of Genghis Khan, commissioned by his son Ogodai and later transcribed into Chinese, in which form it survived. How much of it is pure history and how much embellished folk-lore is hotly debated, but its background details of everyday life can't be doubted.

It tells how Genghis Khan's shaman, Teb-Tenggeri, is killed after a disagreement with the Imperial family. His body is laid in a ger, and the door and roof-hole blocked. "But the roof-hole opened, and the body went out by it, of its own accord."

Imperial sleight of hand, more likely. But the explanation for the body's disappearance is presented as if quite plausible. Flying corpses were entirely credible - if the corpse in question happened to belong to a shaman.

Elsewhere in the *Secret History*, the idea of a sudden appearance is compared with jumping through the smoke-hole. On an expedition to rescue his wife from an enemy who had abducted her, Genghis proposes arriving by stealth "and then, as suddenly as though we had jumped down through the sky-hole of his tent, take him and his people prisoner..." The analogy with a modern fairy-tale is obvious. We might say, "as if we had arrived in a puff of smoke..."

Shamans were influential people at Möngke's court. The Great Khan would never, for example, have taken the decision to go to war without first consulting them. They took charge whenever the court moved camp, going ahead, says William, "as the pillar of cloud went before the Children of Israel", and moving where the omens directed. Their favourite divination tool was the scorched shoulder-blade of a sacrificed sheep. This must have been pretty effective, for its use continued until very recently; a twentieth century Mongolian shaman's handbook contains a diagram carefully explaining how to analyse burnt mutton.

Outsiders marvelled at the shaman's ability to influence the weather for good or ill. The Great Khan Kubilai, according to Marco Polo, kept at court "...wise charmers who go up on the roof of the palace, and... by their incantation dispose all the clouds and rain and all the bad weather to remove about his palace... so that everywhere else the bad weather went on; rain, storm and thunderbolts falling all about, while the palace was not touched by anything." The trick often involved use of a magic stone, suspended over water. These so-called "Zad" stones were made from "fallen stars" - meteorites, perhaps.

Such a skill, which in peace time was just a conjuring trick performed for the comfort of the Khan, could become a useful weapon in times of war. A sudden hailstorm falling on your enemy could soften him up nicely. But this sophisticated meteorological warfare sometimes turned out a loose cannon. It backfired on Genghis Khan's *anda*-turned-enemy Jamukha, says the *Secret History*, when the violent storm he summoned up to attack Genghis' army made a smart about-turn and hurled its thunderbolts on his own men instead. He lost the battle; and the war.

For all their reliance on shamans, the Mongol Khans showed a tolerance of other religions which was ahead of their time. Buddhists, Moslems and Nestorian Christians were allowed, indeed encouraged, to practise freely. The Nestorians, particularly, held some of the high positions at court. Many women of the royal family were Christian.

This liberality, much praised by later historians, may have been simple apathy; the Mongolians of this time don't seem to have been greatly inclined to religious fervour. It was also a matter of hedging their bets. Shamanism was by no means exclusive, and it was as well to have the gods of other religions on your side also. "The Mongols," drily observes David Morgan in his book of that name, "believed in taking out as much celestial insurance as possible."

Exclusivity, however, was on its way.

Buddhism took root in Mongolia at least as early as the end of the first millennium, and flourished at the court of the Khans. But it wasn't until the sixteenth century, through the enthusiasm of the newly converted prince Altan Khan, that it was first actively propagated, and its rivals suppressed.

Only a generation later the Mongolian people were embracing Buddhism with a fervour which they hadn't previously shown to any one faith. Though it wasn't always down to personal inclination. By the first half of the next century, draconian measures were being taken against any who sought to remain shamanist. Those found worshipping family ongghon were to have their sheep and horses confiscated, and the ongghon burnt. For shamans themselves there was an even more drastic penalty: "fumigation" with dog-filth. No wonder that shamanism retreated to the remotest parts of the country, to become a hole-and-corner affair.

Yet in the ensuing centuries it hung on to existence and eventually crept out again. There were shamans at the court of the Manchus, the last Chinese Imperial dynasty, a hundred years ago. And of course the Tsaatan, having come from Siberia, were never converted, forcibly or otherwise.

So nowadays Mongolian shamanism lives on mainly in northern Hovsgol. Every year the province holds an annual convocation of shamans, taking place place in a cave in the mountains and closing with a service of thanksgiving to Tengri, the Blue Sky.

A relic of the past, devoid of meaning in today's world? No way. Most of us have had more contact with Siberian shamanism than we know. The link began with the export of St. Nicholas to Siberia three hundred years ago.

Nicholas, a fourth century Turkish Christian associated early on with giving presents, became one of the most popular saints among the Russian Orthodox believers. Known as Nikolai Chudotvorets or the Miracle-worker, he was a fundamental part of the Christianity brought to Siberia by Orthodox missionaries of the seventeenth century.

Here, as elsewhere among primitive people, Christianity became loosely superimposed on the existing religion. And so Saint Nicholas, the Holy Man in communication with the world of the saints, became inevitably identified with a shaman; the giver of gifts began flying through the sky on a reindeer, and entering the world of man through the smoke-hole.

It is a picture familiar to every child. For thus St Nicholas, in his alter ego of Santa Claus or Father Christmas and dressed in the colours of fly agaric mushrooms, acquired two of his strangest and most definitive tricks.

*

Carol and I weren't the only western visitors to the Tsaatan this summer. On our arrival we had glimpsed a couple of flashy blue tents at the far end of the camp. We met the owners in Bat's tepee. They were two Frenchmen - or, possibly, French Canadians; at any rate, the fact that they conversed together in French was about the only point of reference we ever fixed on them.

One, at least, was typically Gallic. He was lean, hollow-cheeked and dark-haired, and seemed to be trying unsuccessfully to grow a beard. He sprawled at the far end of the yurtsia smoking roll-ups, long legs stretched towards the fire. I saw him later standing beside his diminutive piebald pony, and the stirrup irons reached below his knees. He never spoke a word to us throughout.

His companion was more close-cropped and, apart from an Arab head-cloth draped round his neck, less eccentric. He was also slightly more forthcoming, occasionally answering a "yes" or "no", or even "hallo", to our diffident approaches.

But they studiously avoided us. They walked away if we approached, or got up and moved if we sat too near in the yurtsia. Gradually it dawned on us that Erdenejav was steering us away from them as much as possible, although when we asked why, or if there was a problem, he simply shrugged his shoulders.

It was mystifying; and also intriguing. Their unfriendliness had the opposite effect of that intended, making us burst with curiosity about them and desperate to find out what they were doing here. From another point of view, it was irritating. They were travelling with quite a large entourage of interpreters and guides, and Uulchik, one of their party, spoke some Russian. That made him the only other person in the camp besides Erdenejav with whom we could talk directly, yet although he was as friendly towards us as the Frenchmen were hostile, it was only rarely that we could catch a word with him.

I was sure there was some misunderstanding that could be sorted out. Carol wasn't. She had tried to talk to them several times on the first day while I was still out cold, and reckoned that it was hopeless. Optimistically, I went looking for them to see if I could establish friendly relations.

I found them near the reindeer lines, heading back towards the camp, and walked straight up to say hallo. They saw me coming and exchanged glances; then simultaneously swivelled 180° about, bolted back to the deer and lost themselves among the herd.

That convinced me. I should have listened to Carol. She had the perfect explanation.

"I expect," she said dismissively, "they just don't like women."

No wonder Erdenejav was on their side.

*

It was Bad Form to go anywhere near our horses, which were tethered a little way down the valley. These were, as we were constantly reminded, Mongolian horses. They might learn bad habits from foreigners.

It was completely alien to me just to turn my back on the little chestnut who had carried me so bravely on the gruelling ride in. On a morning when Our Friend - for so we now referred to Erdenejav in private conversation, lest he hear himself being discussed - was safely out of sight inside Tsindeli's yurtsia, I sneaked down to get to know the pony better.

As if alerted by a tracking device, Erenejav was outside and on my heels before I was halfway there. I pretended not to notice him, and was making friends with my horse - and, even more impertinent, his own - when he caught up with me.

"Why do you sleep so much?" No polite "Hallo" from Erdenejav.

I went through my explanations again and then, to divert him before he could frogmarch me away from his horses, asked him to tell me about them.

He was proud of the horse he rode himself, a small but tough, stocky bay. He was, said Erdenejav, a "Khalkha" from central Mongolia, recognised as one of the best types. Khalkha was the name given to what roughly corresponds to present-day Mongolia in the centuries after Genghis Khan. It was interesting to hear that the name survives, although in a different context.

Interesting, too, to find Mongolian horses thus categorised; I had assumed that they were a pretty homogeneous lot. But this is far from the case, as I learned later from Mabel Waln Smith's book, *Land of Swift-Running Horses*.

"Chahar district? Those horses are small, weak and inferior. This is the district which borders on China, and was used for three centuries as the pasture land of the Manchus. The hired Mongolian keepers hustled all the superior colts farther inland to the Mongolian-owned herds.

"...Middle of Mongolia? This Gobi desert district has such a scarcity of food that only very hardy animals survive - extremely game little animals, excellent mounts on a long, hard trip, their weight-carrying ability, speed and endurance astonishing in comparison with their size.

"...North-western Mongolia? The snows here come early, giving a short grazing season which keeps animals insufficiently nourished. The tanghans of Tibet, raised under similar conditions, are given pigs' blood and raw liver to counteract this stunting..."

"...North-eastern Mongolia? Ah, now you're talking! *Ohai!* Splendid water, splendid grass is in the Kerulen valley... horses grow larger and stronger than in any other part of the country."

The Gobi and central Mongolia correspond most nearly with ancient Khalkha. Erdenejav's horse, it seemed, was typical of his kind.

"Why," I asked, "do you want to keep us away from the horses?"

Erdenejav was afraid, he said, that we would let them loose. Mongolia was a wide-open country, with no fences. If the horses escaped they could be in Tuva by nightfall.

"Why should we be that stupid?" I asked him. "We don't want to interfere, just get to know our horses better. Surely it's a good thing that a horse should be able to trust someone handling him, rather than be afraid of getting hurt?"

But this wasn't on. "There are too many horse thieves about," he explained, his upper lip riding up in the now familiar, unconscious grimace of concentration as he expanded on his theme. If horses became trusting and easy to handle, anyone could come along and take them without difficulty. Erdenejav wanted his horses to be afraid of strangers.

"But I'm not a stranger," I countered. "I've done a long day's journey with this horse. Now he's my friend."

The concept was quite foreign to him. We were never going to agree on this one. But maybe we gained something from the discussion: a better understanding of each other's point of view.

*

Pandemonium reigned in the valley each evening, when the main herd was brought in from pasture. Just before dark, several hundred reindeer would come crashing among the tepees, arriving at the same mad gallop that we had joined on the first night.

The whole camp turned out to meet them. The keepers shouldered their way through the milling deer looking for their own animals, marked with ear tags or scraps of coloured cloth tied about the antlers. The kids ran into the thick of the herd, leading or riding their deer home to tether them to the wooden frames for the night.

But for the children's clothing (and the intrusion of our synthetic tent) this picture might have seen little change for thousands, even tens of thousands, of years. It is likely that reindeer were the first large animals to be domesticated. Some anthropologists believe that, through earlier opportunity and their comparatively docile nature, they might have been routinely ridden long before men thought of climbing on to the less tractable horse.

Even before domestication, reindeer were the focus of existence for Cro-Magnon men, those north-west Europeans of 20-30,000 years ago, chiefly remembered for the refinement of their flint artefacts and the beginning of cave painting. For these people, the pattern of life was dictated by the seasonal migrations of the herds across the continent. They depended upon them for more than just food; for the reindeer provided both the incentive and the means for a highly advanced technology.

From reindeer antler, lighter and stronger than wood, the Cro-Magnons developed sophisticated weaponry. The main implement

Then and now: components of the Mongol war machine

Naadam archers prepare for competition

Through the finishing funnel after nineteen miles

Takhi mares and foals running free at Hustain Nuruu

Boarding the Shishhid ferry

Tokhtbat's mum nearing the Tsaatan camp

Evening muster in the Valley of the Burnt River

Shaman's daughter Funtsal, with grandchildren

Tokhtbat could raise a smile even from the dour Erdenejav

First of many breakdowns: Niamchuu's ger near Tsagaan Nuur

Worshipper and young lama at Shankh's temple

A small part of Erdenezu Hiid's treasures

New inhabitants of the first fence, Hustain Nuruu

Migrating herds pass under Hustain Nuruu mountain

An elderly arat prepares his pipe

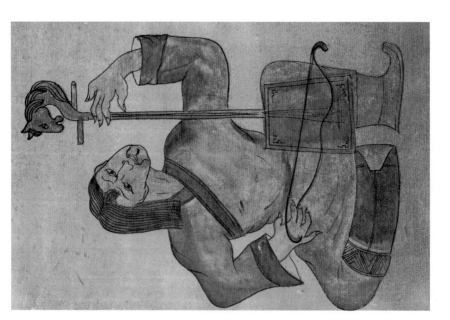

Morin Huur Player (painted by a monk of Erdenezu Hiid)

for hunting was a particularly efficient spear, with an antler shaft and flint tip. The Palaeolithic reindeer bore the means of its destruction upon its own head.

Nowadays, the antler is used to heal, not kill. Reindeer horn is a valuable export, prized by the Chinese and Japanese for medicinal purposes. Its sale at $1.50 a kilo is the principal source of income for the Tsaatan, enabling them to buy the few necessities which neither the deer nor their own surroundings can provide; for man shall not live by reindeer alone. Yet the Tsaatan themselves see only a small part of the profits, the majority going to the Collective.

Elsewhere, the collective farms of Mongolia have been dismantled, but for some reason this hadn't happened yet among the Tsaatan. Sadly, though, the fragile security of the Collective had disintegrated, and the system had degenerated into one benefiting few save administrators.

The head of each Tsaatan family is paid 5,000 tugrigs a year (less than ten pounds) for looking after the deer. He is allowed to retain only a small percentage of the profits from sale of the horn. Were it not for the few privately-owned animals he is permitted to keep - collectivisation in Mongolia was never absolute - his income would be negligible.

Worse, the keeper is financially responsible for any deer belonging to the Collective which dies while in his care. He must either replace it with one of his own, or pay its value in compensation. Formerly, a certificate signed by a veterinarian citing a natural cause of death meant the charge was waived. But now there is no money to provide a vet.

Kanzargan had a family of six children to keep. Together with his wife Irdenchimik, a fair-haired and blue-eyed girl with a gently wistful smile who looked too young to have produced such a brood, he ran over some housekeeping figures.

Flour, one tugrig a kilo in the days of Communist subsidies, now costs 108tg; his family gets through 50kg a month. A block of tea is 2,000tg. Canvas to repair the yurtsia costs 1,000tg a metre, and his annual need is 50m. Of his own deer, Kanzargan might sell four or five a year, at 10,000tg apiece. His books, it was painfully obvious, were never going to balance.

The system, we learnt, is about to be changed. A new proposal involves renting the deer to the Tsaatan, at an annual charge of 300tg per beast, and allowing them to keep all profits. This has met with approval from both sides, and is likely to be adopted. But, at the time of our visit, things were about as bad as they could be.

So we were reluctant, for fear of draining resources, when Erdenejav insisted that we move into Tsindeli's yurtsia. The rain had continued for two days and our tent, he said, was in danger of flooding. This wasn't true, as we'd foreseen the problem and pitched it on a slight rise. But it saved a lot of trouble to do what Our Friend told us. Besides, he had already arranged it, and to refuse would have been rude to Tsindeli. And, in all honesty, we were thrilled to be invited to share more closely in her way of life.

So we fetched our things and settled in, and tried not to suspect that Our Friend, himself staying with Tsindeli, simply wanted to keep a better eye on us - not even when he slept between us and the door flap.

Tsindeli herself welcomed us in like old friends. As in fact we were welcomed by all, according to the universal customs of nomadic society - and the warmth of the Tsaatan people. For our part, we tried to return the compliment wherever possible. Asking much of our hosts' lives, we told much of our own. And whenever we accepted hospitality we passed round our own things: cigarettes, nuts and nibbles, and packets of biscuits, which vanished with gratifying speed.

One evening in the tepee, we made English tea for Tsindeli and her friends. Into the wide tin bowl of boiling water went about twenty teabags and all our remaining dried milk. Mindful of the local salt brew, we handed sugar separately. It seemed to go down well; although you can't always tell enthusiasm from politeness.

The balloons, though, were a thumping success.

I had thrown a couple of packets into my baggage on impulse, for they were a novelty light and easy to fit in. We blew some up while we were visiting in a yurtsia with two toddlers, and batted them about a bit; and a moment later the tepee was full of children, lining up like a school dinner queue while we huffed and puffed desperately.

Half an hour later we came out of the tepee to a wonderful sight. All twenty or so of the camp children were closely grouped on a small stretch of flat grass; all the balloons were high in the air at once, all the faces simultaneously turned skywards. Five minutes later the game had changed, and the kids were charging round the camp, bellowing and waving balloons like vicious weapons.

For one family with small children, Carol told a story. Word quickly spread, and within minutes the tepee was packed with children - and several adults. All listened enthralled to her tale from *The Physicians of Myddfai*, heard at third hand after translations by me and Erdenejav. It must have been the first-ever rendering of a Welsh folk-tale, told in English and translated via Russian into Mongolian - and, certainly, ultimately into the Tsaatan language as well.

It was our turn to be fascinated when we visited a lady who shared with Bat's sister the name of Tsetsik (it means "Flower", and is a common name). Propped at the back of her yurtsia was a curved wooden cradleboard.

We had heard of these from David, as one of many similarities he had found between the Tsaatan and native Americans. On his visit last year he had brought photographs of Navaho Indians which caused a great stir among the Tsaatan. The similarity of facial features was astonishing, as were a number of cultural ties - not least, shamanism.

This should hardly be surprising, were it not for the time scale involved. For the whole of the Americas were populated by Siberian races, crossing the Bering Strait by the land bridge which existed during the last ice age. Blood-typing and DNA testing have enabled ethnographers to identify seven major waves of migration, going back as far as sixty thousand years. But ten thousand years ago Siberia and Alaska became separated. The two peoples are undoubtedly cousins; but many, many times removed.

Tsetsik was pleased at our interest in her cradle, but had more immediate concerns. Her baby was crying with earache. Had we any drugs with us that might help? Our travellers' pharmacopoeia, though, held nothing that we dared give to a small child, and we could offer only sympathy.

131

Access to regular health care was another casualty of the times. The headman of the camp, Gombo, kept a small stock of drugs, dressings and a hypodermic syringe. Otherwise the people relied on natural resistance, and Funtsal's herbal remedies. Generally, the children's robust good health thrived on the outdoor life. There were a few runny noses, but no more than might be expected from running around barefoot at seven thousand feet on the permafrost.

But serious illness, of another kind, was after all in the camp. A mystery plague, we began to learn, had struck the reindeer, decimating their numbers and threatening the entire Tsaatan way of life. About a hundred deer had died just in the last year, a fifth of the total herd.

Uugdorj, who had suffered heavy losses, told us of the signs. Onset usually in autumn, milky-white fungus on the tongue, abscesses on the feet to follow, intermittent fever. Foot and mouth disease? Apparently not, for there is damage also to internal organs. So far, except for a brief visit by a paramedic, there had been no help from the Collective, let alone the government - for this is too big a matter to be handled locally. But Mongolia's fragile democracy is besieged by financial problems, and the Reindeer People are small fry.

It is almost too grim to contemplate that this might be the final disaster, the tidal wave that could sink these people utterly.

Could there be a silver lining to their harsh existence? It seems strange, in this day and age, to think that anyone might choose to live such a hard life, to stay willingly so far beyond the reach of the modern world. Perhaps an enforced change, even a traumatic one, might ultimately be for the better?

I think not. For throughout our stay, Carol and I were continually aware of the contentment of the Tsaatan, of the sense of balance in their lives, of their completeness and self-sufficiency. Tens of thousands of years herding reindeer has given them a personal equilibrium and spiritual integrity that even such as Shakespeare, Michelangelo or Beethoven could not propagate so universally in the world of so-called "civilisation".

The last word belongs to Kanzargan. What, I asked him, did he like most about his life?

He gestured about him; to the high peaks, the tumbling stream, the valley heaving with gently grunting deer. "Living here with the reindeer" was his answer.

"And what do you dislike most?" He thought for a long while.

"Nothing!" he replied.

VII

OF HEAVEN, HELL AND HIGH WATER

We left just after dawn on a glorious morning. The line of sunlight was creeping slowly down the mountainside, too high yet to disperse the mist which drifted about the valley floor and curled itself around the smoke from the cooking fires.

Regretfully we said goodbye to Tsindeli, leaving gifts for her and others. They were mostly practical things: candles, matches, needles and thread, cigarettes and biscuits, a horse's halter, some T-shirts. There was a blue khadag, correctly presented draped across the forearms, which Tsindeli accepted with the same gesture. And all our remaining tea and sugar, "for English tea!" which raised a laugh to ease a sad moment.

In Bat's tepee we bumped into Uulchik, the French Lieutenant. With a conspiratorial wink he picked up a camera belonging to one of the Frenchmen and, before we could stop him, took a photograph of us with it. We all three fell about hysterically, to think of the surprise waiting for them when they got home and looked through their holiday snaps.

Funtsal and Batsor, a Tsaatan youth, rode with us. Today, through air sparkling like cut glass, we could fully appreciate the scenery as we jogged off down the long valley. We stopped briefly at the obo on the pass, gasping at the high jagged peaks which stabbed the sky in every direction. The long stretch down the other side was no longer deserted; pipits squeaked all around us, young snipe scuttled furtively from under the horses' feet and a single black kite searched the skies.

We stopped at the small obo beneath the bank to rest the horses, having first defeated the object by galloping up to it madly in usual Mongolian style. Now we dismounted and the horses were allowed to graze; all except for mine.

For some reason, Tokhtbat tied the reins around the front of my saddle, so that the pony couldn't lower his head. It was useless to argue. I simply looked blankly at Tokhtbat until he went back to his own horse; then, keeping the pony's bulk between me and the others, I began to pull grass and feed it to him.

At first the poor lad was bewildered. No-one had ever hand-fed him before. But he was hungry and it was no time to stand on ceremony; soon he was greedily devouring grass as fast as I could gather it. Once he'd got used to the idea, I tried to give him a Dextrasol tablet, the nearest thing I had to a sugar lump. No interest. I wrapped it up in some grass and tried again. This pony was going to have a small treat if I had to force-feed it.

He didn't agree. The taste was strange, and he cleverly manoeuvred it out between his teeth without dropping a single blade of grass. But some trust had been established at last. And when the men relaxed and lit cigarettes, I managed surreptitiously to unwind his reins and allow him to graze properly - without, for once, getting a bollocking from Erdenejav.

Later in the day, when the sun tempted out repugnant horseflies over an inch long, there was an interesting sequel. Suddenly the chestnut pony stopped in his tracks, and turned his head right round to my knee. I was mystified, until I saw the blood-sucking vampire attached to his nose. He was politely asking me to squash it. Coming from a Mongolian horse, it was a real vote of confidence, and almost brought a lump to my throat.

We remounted to ride up the steep bank which we had walked down on the way in. This was an intense relief. There was no way I could have got up on foot, and I had been dreading Erdenejav's withering contempt. It was only once this was safely past that I finally dared to tackle Our Friend about the leading rein. There had been enough nonsense; now I would ride alone.

Of course, he refused angrily and at some length. I stood quietly by while he got it out of his system and came round to my way of thinking. After a bit he abandoned the browbeating and started on the excuses. "I know," I pre-empted him. " 'Bad horses, bad roads, fall, stones, head...'." Then folded my arms, mentally crossed my fingers and prepared to bluff it out.

He was quite capable of riding off and leaving me standing there. But after a few pregnant moments he spoke sullenly to Tokhtbat, and the lead rope was relinquished to me. I took good care to hang on to it like grim death in case he changed his mind.

Halfway home, there was a diversion. With a shout, Batsor leapt off his horse and, barely stopping to tether it, charged off up the hillside. Erdenejav and Tokhtbat did likewise, closely followed, at a speed that belied their years, by Tokhtbat's mum and Funtsal. Afraid we were missing something, Carol and I scrambled up after them.

The Tsaatan boy disappeared up a tree: curiouser and curiouser. Then a shower of missiles hit us. They were red, knobbly and covered with sticky resin. Pine cones.

It was a fingernail job to strip the woody exterior and get down to the soft, unripe kernels. Tokhtbat and Erdenejav went at it like squirrels, demolishing several apiece. Carol soon got the knack; while I trailed hopelessly in the rear, eating more resin than anything else, and sticking to all I touched for the rest of the day.

Somewhere after this we diverged from our earlier route in, and found ourselves on a track that was new to us. We stopped for lunch at a lovely spot where a wide lawn of smooth grass spread itself under the trees. Gathering wood, we quickly got a raging fire ready to brew tea. The men took food from their saddlebags: Tokhtbat another bag of mutton-fat biscuits, and Erdenejav the loaf which Naran had given him as we left. Now that we were no longer scrounging off the Tsaatan, we ate uninhibitedly.

Finally Tokhtbat's mum added the *pièce de résistance*: a pouch of reindeer cream for the tea. Before we drank, Funtsal took a ladle and flicked a few drops to the four quarters, to honour the spirits of the place.

Half an hour later, when the pot was empty and the cigarettes were circulating, who should ride up... but the two Frenchmen. Alone, they would certainly have passed by on the other side; but their party, including Uulchik and three or four Tsaatan, came to join us without a thought. Among them was Tsindeli's son. His del was unfastened in the heat, to show one of our T-shirts underneath.

136

This was going to be interesting. We waited to see what would happen. With an ill grace the Frenchmen joined their company at our fire, on the side farthest from us. But they quickly gave terse instructions, and ten minutes later had their own fire going a dozen yards away - without lifting a finger to prepare it themselves.

Wasted effort. Within five minutes we had remounted and relieved them of our company. As we left Erdenejav forgot himself, and let slip that this was where David's party had camped the year before.

And now things began to fall into place: the unfamiliar spot, across the far side of the valley from the way we had come, the path vastly better here than the unremitting wetness of our route in. Not that there was a chance to discuss it, for Erdenejav - perhaps realising his gaffe - now set a scorching pace, racing off into the blue yonder at a fast jogtrot which he kept up for mile after mile with Carol in tow, while we became strung out behind and struggled to keep up.

It was by now a blazing hot day, far too hot for such speed. The little chestnut became desperately thirsty, for Tokhtbat wouldn't allow me to stop and let him drink even a mouthful at the frequent streams. Soon, though, my concerns turned totally selfish.

The grinding haste was purgatorial. For years I haven't had the leg strength to rise to the trot, the trick which should make the pace comfortable indefinitely, for more than a few dozen yards. What saved me was the pony's short legs, which made it possible to relax into the stride and absorb the bounce, while a taller horse would have rattled the very teeth from my head. That, and the long rest at Mörön. At the time I had cursed the unfairness of a week laid up after only two days' stress. The disproportionate crash, however, had been balanced by an equally disproportionate swing back of the pendulum; a head of steam, just when I needed it most. That had lasted me much better than I could have dared to hope; that, and the utter impossibility of admitting defeat to Erdenejav. But I couldn't stand this much longer without cracking up completely.

It was even worse for Carol. Her saddle sores from riding in had barely skinned over, and must have been excruciating. But it was the punishing heat that nearly finished her. Fair-skinned for all her Celtic dark eyes and hair, she was feeling the sun badly and beginning to suffer from heat-stroke. When the pursuing party came over a hillock and we found her sitting on the ground beside her horse, having almost passed out, my first thought - to my shame - was not sympathy for her but a litany of thanksgiving for myself. Now, at last, we must stop this lunatic pace.

So far in dealing with Erdenejav, I had made a bad tactical blunder. Russian, like so many languages, has two forms of "you", the polite/plural and the familiar. Being English and therefore almost by definition an idle and incompetent linguist, I'd always made do with the first; why get used to two forms when one will cover everything? Our Friend, who always used the familiar, assumed that in doing otherwise I was just showing the proper deference from a female to a male.

From now on I took care to get this bit right. It was high time to show that we weren't prisoners and guard, but customers and guide, and thus equal. This looked likely to be our worst clash with Erdenejav so far, and we couldn't afford hostages to fortune. We would finish the route at a walk, I demanded, firmly backed up by Carol. Our Friend was impatient. "There's only a kilometre left to go," he argued. It was at least four times that, for we were still in the bog. But the untruth was half-hearted. Somewhere inside his complex personality he seemed genuinely abashed at the state to which he had reduced Carol.

It didn't last long. Within moments of restarting, the men were sneakily urging their horses first to a slow jog and then a faster one. Uncompromisingly, we reminded Erdenejav of our agreement, and grimly insisted on it. The same happened again. And again.

Carol and I conferred hastily, and decided. Enough was enough. We tackled him again.

"What happened to your 'slowly'?"

"It'll take us too much time to get back," he retorted.

"So what? After all," I added spitefully, "it's 'only a kilometre'!"

I didn't understand his sour reply, but it was obviously unprintable. It led me head-on into the confrontation which had been brewing for days. This time, I was taking no prisoners.

"You've done exactly what suited you from the start!" I said

138

furiously. "That's how you've come to ride us into the ground." Carol, I reminded him, was an inexperienced rider and I partly incapacitated. "You agreed to take three days over the journey in. What happened?" He protested feebly. "Why did you detour around the only possible camping site? So that we couldn't argue about stopping?"

For this, of course, was the reason for preferring the sodden path in over the better one by which we had returned. Also why we had both been put on the end of a string, so that we could barely talk to each other, couldn't even stop our own horses, or cause other trouble.

At my diatribe, Erdenejav was unusually silent. Probably he had never been handbagged by a woman before. He could easily have fudged a defence by pleading my poor Russian, and misunderstanding between us; instead, he didn't speak another word. There were no further attempts to push the pace. For probably the first time in their lives, the horses came home slowly, and cooling.

Even more surprising, both men went out of their way to be nice to us that evening. Down to one packet of noodles between us, we were staggered to find ourselves invited to supper - then positively pampered with extra hot water brewed for our tea. We accepted without hesitation, reckoning it fair enough; and saying thank you to Tokhtbat's mum with our last cigarettes, while studiously avoiding the men.

But Erdenejav had the last word that night.

Three hours later, the horses were still at the hitching rail. They hadn't even been unsaddled, although Carol and I had caught an unsupervised moment to loosen our own horses' girths. But my pony's desperate thirst throughout the day, still unsatisfied, was tormenting me with every mouthful of my own tea. Finally I filched a tin bucket and, with Carol's help, filled it from the river and brought it back to our tent. A quick recce to check the men were indoors, and we headed for the rail to water all the horses.

As we approached, the chestnut pulled back, rolling his eyes at the bucket. Being waited on was a new and confusing experience. We stood still for a moment, irresolute, talking to him gently. Almost at once there was a yell; Erdenejav, antennae at the ready as ever, had us nicked.

"What are you doing?" He came angrily striding over, closely followed by Tokhtbat. We instinctively cowered, schoolgirls caught at a midnight feast.

"What do you think? You should should be ashamed of yourself to leave your horses so long without water." We returned to the job in hand, only to have the little horse untied and jerked roughly away.

"He's been thirsty all day. Whyever can't he drink?"

The answer, anger for once robbing it of the least fig-leaf of excuse, was revealing.

"Because *I* don't wish it!" The pronoun bore the unnatural resonance of that in Edward VIII's abdication speech. Seeing our recoil, he belatedly tried to cover himself. It would rain tonight, he said, pointing at the sky. Eating wet grass, he meant, would be quite good enough for thirsty horses.

It was useless to argue. Tears of frustration blurred my sight as I looked with loathing after his retreating back, with the dispirited ponies plodding behind it. Well after midnight, when there had been no sound from the ger for an hour, I took Carol's dish - our largest container, as I couldn't carry the bucket - and crept down to the horse lines.

They were tethered as far away from us as Erdenejav could put them, over by the river. I cursed him afresh as I stumbled in the dark through puddles of water and soaked my shoes. I was prepared to refill the bowl as often as was necessary from the river, but it was no good. In the dark, the pony was nervous of my approach, and the white bowl spooked him hopelessly. The rapport of the afternoon was gone.

I sat beside him for a long time, but couldn't get close enough for him even to smell that I carried water; and eventually admitted defeat.

*

There remained a short day's ride back to Tsagaan Nuur. But Erdenejav came up with another idea.

He knew of a jeep, leaving from nearby and going straight to Mörön. He thought we should hitch a ride on this. The rivers, he said, were very high after all the rain, and the route back to his house and on to Mörön would likely be impassable; whereas the jeep was going a different way, right round Tsagaan Nuur lake to the north, thus altogether avoiding the town and most of its surrounding fords.

There were already, we discovered, six passengers in the four-seater jeep. Its occupants would hardly be thrilled to have two more. Anyway, the question was academic, as half our baggage was at Erdenejav's house. He was, we gathered, as disenchanted with us as we with him, and trying to get rid of us a day early. He was even more disenchanted when we said no.

Out of interest, we asked who owned the knees on which he was proposing that we should sit for two days?

It was the Frenchmen.

*

The rivers were certainly higher, but not much, and dropping visibly. Their depth made it easier to let the little chestnut stop for the occasional furtive drink, as I deliberately trailed at the back of our group through the fords. Not too much; a huge draught on a long ride could give him colic, or cause other damage. And it would give more time for Erdenejav to catch me out, and take preventive measures. So I allowed him only eight or ten swallows each time before hauling his head up again, with great reluctance on both our parts.

It was the most enjoyable day's ride by far. The weather was comfortably warm, and the atmosphere among us much less stormy; yesterday's thunderous row had done much to clear the air. Even Erdenejav exerted himself to be pleasant, and Tokhtbat broke into song again, Mongolian marching songs for the horses. It meant a lot to us to erase the bad memories of the earlier travelling, and finish on a good note.

On the far side of the ferry, while Erdenejav was preoccupied with unloading his own horse, I gave mine his sixth drink. This time there was the satisfaction of seeing him lift his head of his own accord, rehydrated at last.

141

Back in Tsagaan Nuur, Erdenejav's wife Naran (whom we now looked at with a new respect) gave us tea. She served her husband first, with a cup twice the size of everyone else's, and then produced fresh bread and clotted cream.

We remembered a jar of jam in our bags, and introduced the party to an English-style cream tea. It went down like a lead balloon with the men, but we had no complaints.

*

A week ago, we had looked forward to a few days camped in Erdenejav's garden while we waited for return transport to Mörön; lazy days of rest and refreshment to be spent idling by the lake, and looking across to those stupendous mountains in the north with the satisfaction of having been among them. Not to mention taking Erdenejav's dog for a walk. From this side of the expedition, though, things were looking a bit different.

Our Friend was as keen to see the back of us as we of him. With visible urgency he somehow conjured, as a rabbit from a hat, a truck leaving for Mörön within the hour.

It was open to the weather, and three-quarters full with a consignment of empty bottles. Ten people, their luggage, half a dozen woolsacks and a forty-gallon petrol drum occupied the small remaining space immediately behind the cab. It was now raining - more heavily by the minute - and we were already wet, with no dry clothes to change into. I, at least, was totally exhausted, and in no state to travel further than the nearest sleeping bag. So, sharing Erdenejav's urgency, and his reasons, we climbed on board without hesitation.

"This truck is unreliable," he informed us ghoulishly. "It might take some days." Then, with a characteristic change of mood, he broke off his private gloating at the thought of the cold, wet night ahead of us, to warn us anxiously to put on extra clothes.

The last of our baggage was handed up. We expressed our warmest gratitude to Erdenejav and stretched our mouths into smiles of sincere well-wishing, and were off before we knew it.

We sat in a puddle, knees round our chins, the other passengers heroically squeezing themselves even smaller in the four-foot by eight-foot space. The rain beat down relentlessly, soaking our feet almost at once, and evading the hoods of our waterproofs to drip down our necks.

Within the first five minutes, the truck slid sideways down a muddy incline, coming within an ace of overturning; and then broke down irretrievably, before even leaving the last straggling settlements of Tsagaan Nuur.

We were stuck there for two days. It was absolutely wonderful.

*

For a start, the lady outside whose ger we were stranded was, we rapidly agreed, the Best Cook in Outer Mongolia. Justifiably proud of her hospitality, she fed us fresh bread and thick clotted cream with sugar sprinkled on top; for afters came a bowl of the sweetest, creamiest yogurt we had ever tasted. Later, after we had retreated to the tent for fear of eating her larder empty, she pursued us with *hushans*, fresh, crisp pasties filled with meat and fried in mutton fat.

Niamchuu's family was obviously well-to-do. Her ger was beautifully furnished, and among the usual brightly coloured cupboards and chests stood a glass-fronted display cabinet with china and glass, and a dresser painted with Chinese dragons. There were mod cons, in the form of a sink with an ingenious push-button water supply. There was even a small portable TV, wired up to an enormous free-standing aerial outside. All was immaculate, including Niamchuu's young son in his crisply laundered white blouse. Even the dog was well cared-for, with a shelter to keep the sun off. One felt instinctively that all prospered who came within Niamchuu's sphere of influence. Not least, us.

The other delight was our situation, on a grassy hillside just high enough to look back to the town and across to the lake. A river wound lazily through the meadow below, leaving one or two oxbows in which a herd of yaks squelched contentedly. A little beyond was the lake itself, across a slope thick with edelweiss and crowned with a knot of pine trees.

The first day the rain poured down and we kept to the tent, glad of the rest. On the second, with the fickleness of mountain weather, the clouds cleared to give a beautiful, fine day. Now we could see for ever, or at least out to the northern tip of the Hordil Saridag range, whose ten-thousand-foot ridges separate Tsagaan Nuur from Lake Hovsgol.

I walked over to the lake and paddled in its clear water from a small beach, then sat among the flowers enjoying the glorious day. Behind in the woods a girl was singing; while twenty miles away over the mountains the weather changed from sun to storm and back again throughout the afternoon.

Around the gers was a hive of industry. One of the corrals was being dismantled. Cleverly designed to be portable, it consisted of six pairs of stakes, with a hexagon of rails slotted into them. Within an hour all had been taken down, and the stakes were being hammered into a clean piece of ground. It was the job of the younger boys to collect the yak dung for winter fuel, at which they took turns with a wooden shovel. Afterwards, they worked off their remaining energy in the usual way, with a wrestling match.

Meanwhile, work continued on the truck. Thumps and bangs reverberated all day from the workshop behind the ger; the gear-box, Carol reckoned, was being rebuilt. There was no shortage of advice. Half the neighbourhood wandered up to express its opinion, and once a cow strolled over and peered helpfully into the engine.

Later that afternoon, Niamchuu called us in again. Bathüyük, the truck driver, was waiting to talk to us. With a neighbour interpreting, he asked to buy our tent; and was bitterly disappointed when we replied that we needed it for the rest of the trip. We wondered what he wanted with it. At the time, that was. After a couple of days we realised that he spent rather more time camped beside the road than going anywhere on it.

A couple more neighbours, a Russian teacher and her husband, dropped in, and we began to have a very sociable time. Soon the company was joined by a local doctor. He was highly entertaining, especially as the arkhi began to flow; but not, we felt, quite the man to whip out your appendix in an emergency.

Carol and I discussed in urgent asides whether we had enough food to cook for the company: would our remaining packet of Pasta Choice, with the help of a few noodles, stretch to six? Probably not. We settled for English tea. Just as well, for triumphant shouts outside greeted the truck's revival. It was time to strike camp and pile in to continue the game of sardines.

This evening, the journey seemed an entirely different proposition. Open and cramped the truck may have been, but this one at least had springs. Better, the radiant day gave way to an even more radiant sunset. We bounced along enjoying the ever-changing view of lakes and mountains, all flooded in luminous pink light. When we stopped for a check on the new gear-box, we climbed out to find ourselves in a meadow full of wildflowers.

Within minutes one family of four had collected at least a dozen different flowers. With infinite care the father showed his small daughters how to press them between the leaves of a couple of books. A closer look revealed his sophisticated taste in literature. One was a volume of Sholokhov; the second none other than a modern version of the *Secret History of the Mongols*. He was a government official on his way back to Ulaan Baatar - and a Tsaatan. The two children, aged perhaps five and eight, were charmers. Their high spirits underlaid by a typically Mongolian endurance, they never stopped smiling once throughout what was to be a long, cold, arduous journey.

The first warning note sounded when we made a wide detour to cross a swollen stream. Thereafter we got slower and slower as the effects of the recent appalling weather on the road multiplied. It was well past midnight when we crawled into Ulaan Uul. The warmth of the day was long gone, and it was absolutely freezing. To our relief Bathüyük decided on an overnight halt, and we trooped off shivering to a ger near the petrol station which served as a motel.

From inside a light glowed, with the comforting suggestion of a hot stove, and tea perhaps. But the stove was long cold, and the glow came from a single guttering candle. The host lay in bed, deeply asleep. It felt as if we had walked into a Dickensian novel.

145

A bowl was passed round. Tea? But it held only cold airag, small cheer, and we continued to shiver.

Our sleeping bags were still on the truck, which had been taken away somewhere. We passed a long, cold night sharing a single bed under one blanket. The food was with our luggage as well. We became acutely conscious of this mistake as the next morning passed into afternoon and the truck still hadn't reappeared. At two, someone mentioned that it had been taken to bits again.

We finally hit the road at four, spending a further hour in a tour of downtown Ulaan Uul to pick up more passengers. Hereabouts were the homes of what were obviously the pioneers, ancient shacks mostly crumbling away. If your house falls down, move out and build a new one. Surprising, with the timber past reclaiming for building, that these hadn't been used for firewood.

Here, too, were the administrative buildings, and the enormous Dutch barn of the former Collective. In the latter a couple of tons of baled hay, the first we'd seen, huddled folornly in the middle of the huge space.

Our two new arrivals seemed scarcely truck fodder: a teenage girl in a multi-coloured shell suit, and an older sister wearing dazzling white boots and a purple scarf to match her lipstick. They brought the numbers up to fourteen in the back, plus three in the cab - Bathüyük, his wife and a thin teenager who was driver's mate and who Carol optimistically called "the Engineer".

While we were immobilised in Ulaan Uul, the best of the weather had passed. Now it began to rain again. We pulled a tarpaulin over, but the only effect was to concentrate the water through the multitude of holes. The sisters put up an umbrella, producing a further circle of drips on those of us outside. The roads were a sea of mud, the rivers high, progress funereal. A sad-faced little boy was sick down Carol's legs. And all over the pristine shell suit.

Worse, the truck continued to ail, and every few miles ground to a halt for first aid. The cab tilted forward to expose the engine beneath, and it wasn't a pretty sight: the air filter tied on with white plastic washing line, other strategic bits bundled up in polythene bags. There was a

146

terminal unconnected to the battery, possibly the cause of the trouble. Bossily we pointed it out to the Engineer, who picked it up with an air of abstraction and dropped it smartly, having got a shock. He then called Bathüyük, who did exactly the same. They discussed it a bit, then leaned forward as one, picked it up simultaneously, and yelped in stereo. After this something constructive must have happened, for soon we were crawling onward once more.

I was now wobbling from hunger. We had some instant nibbles handy, but couldn't eat properly while travelling; all the passengers generously shared their own sweets or nuts with us, and when we did the same we were left with only a handful each.

William of Rubruck knew how I felt. He repeatedly bemoaned his party's lack of food; "On occasions my colleague was so hungry that he would say to me, almost in tears, 'I feel as if I had never eaten!' " Of sharing what little he had with starving Mongols, he declared, "I experienced what a martyrdom it is, when destitute, to give bountifully!"

I wasn't, I decided, of the stuff of martyrs. At each halt I walked away from the lorry and secretly whacked down half a packet of glucose tablets, crunching them in my desperation like a horse eating sugar lumps.

We made it over the high watershed south of Ulaan Uul and turned eastwards towards the valley of the Scythian tombs. The road here was hair-raising for such a large vehicle. Although the truck wasn't articulated it twisted its body like a great beetle over rocky river beds and washed-away bits of road, often tipping at a frightening angle. I passed the time trying to calculate how quickly it would roll when it finally turned over, and what was the best direction to jump. As we climbed, a covering of fresh snow appeared on the mountains behind.

Nevertheless, we arrived safely in the valley and passed the kurgans without incident. After the S-shaped ford I dared to comment that the worst was over.

It was a fatal mistake. A hundred yards on, we stopped again. For good.

It looked like Pasta Choice for fourteen.

*

In the end, we only fed the driver. The rest of the party traipsed off to a ger a mile away; not an option for me.

While Bathüyük prepared to spend the night with my sleeping bag inner in the truck, we pitched the tent alongside. There was no choice of ground, as everywhere else was rocky hillside. The site was vulnerable to vehicles which might swerve off the existing track to avoid our extinct dinosaur; so before we could go to bed we draped the green tent with white plastic bags and blue towels to make it visible in the dark.

On the far side was dangerous ground. The track mounted a bank just above us, so that anything breasting the rise wouldn't see us until launched downhill. Gathering rocks we built two small cairns, a jeep's width apart, so that any vehicle approaching from that direction would be forced to turn aside.

As we finally crawled into our sleeping bags, headlights appeared a mile away across the river and coming our way. We watched the newcomer's progress with interest. At worst, he would test our defences, while at best he might be a potential lift back to Mörön. But crossing the river in the dark defeated him. The lights went back and forth for fifteen minutes, then went out altogether.

At least this time we were in control, with food and warmth for, it seemed, another long rest. But at nine-thirty next morning the Tsaatan official hauled us into semi-consciousness. Last night's jeep had reached us, and its driver had cast a benevolent spell over our engine. Now everyone was anxious to get moving, as we might make the afternoon plane to UB. It was an optimistic truckload. The two little girls were smiling and laughing more than ever, and even the thin little boy, who didn't seem to belong to anyone, looked a little less wan.

Urgency never lasts long in Mongolia. After just a quarter-hour we had a ger-stop for a lengthy breakfast. By one we were still only half-way and the plane was an impossibility. So we had a further two-hour break when we dropped off the first passenger.

She turned out to be the Second Best Cook in Outer Mongolia. She produced heaps of clotted cream, bread and cheese followed by a sort of cheesecake, which was new to us here. The ger was comfortably shabby, and buzzed with activity. "It reminds me of Dai Jones the Garage's house at home," said Carol. Bathüyük's wife Oyung rolled up her sleeves and got stuck into the noodles; while the little boy ate as if his life depended upon it, which after days of being sick it probably did.

It was after seven when we rolled up outside Mörön's hotel, and the water had just gone off.

It felt like coming home.

*

I didn't move for two days, while Carol caught up on the washing and raided the shops for anything edible. On the third day we took ourselves off to the airport. No threat on earth (or above it) would get us near another Mongolian truck; so we mentally tightened our parachutes, and prepared to brave MIAT.

At the airport we bumped into David's party. They had found the Western Tsaatan in the Ulaan Taiga west of Ulaan Uul, and had then ridden east, straight through the Hordil Saridag and down to Lake Hovsgol. The group included the widow of travel writer Bruce Chatwin; being his number one fan, Carol was thrilled to have the opportunity of a brief chat with her.

The bad news was that the flight was fully booked. With no modern instruments, MIAT navigate by sight. The recent bad weather had grounded all planes for days, and caused a log-jam. We bought tickets for the next morning and prepared to put our tent up outside.

But we were scooped almost literally off the tarmac by a young American who lived in Mörön. He pressed us to come home with him, and wouldn't take no for an answer. Within minutes we were entering one of the suburban wooden compounds, where his wife, completely unfazed by the arrival of a couple of tatty strangers picked up off the street like stray dogs, gave us a warm welcome and a wonderful supper.

Thomas and Gayle Shook were members of a missionary group named Professionals International. We had already come across other PI representatives. Roger, whom we met in UB on his way out to the aimag

149

centre of Tsetserleg, had told us something of their work, which Thomas and Gayle now expanded on.

So far, they explained, evangelism was subordinate to practicalities. Small groups or individuals were teaching English and helping to establish aid projects or small businesses. A related scheme was already running in UB, under the name of Emergency Resources, to give local training in setting up or improving emergency services and safety procedures. Its aim was to teach these skills to Mongolians, who would then carry out their own training projects in the provinces. The scheme had started well, Roger had told us, but had received a tragic setback when the Director, on his way out to Mongolia, had been killed in the recent notorious Aeroflot crash, when the pilot had fatally passed the controls to his fifteen-year-old son.

Another group with a very similar approach was Joint Christian Services, who were assisting various farming projects centred on the Gobi-Altai region. Now that the barriers were down, it seemed that missionaries were beginning to race each other to Mongolia.

Thomas and Gayle had been trying to get here for years. In 1986 they were inspired by meeting John Gibbons, who had translated the Bible into Mongolian. But it wasn't until after the birth of Mongolian democracy that they finally arrived, along with others of their group. They had been warmly welcomed, as religious freedom was an integral part of the new liberalism sweeping the country. Now, however, the official attitude was cooling a little. A new law had been promulgated favouring Buddhism as the state religion, followed by Islam and shamanism; churches must now be registered, congregations individually listed. It was, said Gayle, "kinda scary". They weren't deeply worried, though, seeing these developments as no more than a knee-jerk reaction to too much initial laxity, rather than Little Brother stirring in his grave.

They described their organisation as "para-church"; non-denominational, based in and funded from Florida. While Professionals International had no desire to "westernise" Mongolia either spiritually or practically, they felt that, in its inevitable backswing against years of compulsory atheism, it was as ripe for spiritual development as for every other kind. "Just now, the country doesn't fit into the outside world on any level." It needed help from benevolent but tactful outsiders to help it relate to developments of the twentieth century elsewhere.

Tom and Gayle were firmly committed to the prevailing view that this help should consist of widespread but deliberately small-scale activities. Besides distributing aid and medical supplies, they were carrying out market gardening trials in Mörön, looking for ways to defy the unpredictable weather and short growing season. Roger was starting up cottage industries in Tsetserleg, just down the road.

They were all, as Carol put it, "gentle missionaries". Not for them the Bible-bashing, tub-thumping fervour of some of their predecessors. They were content for the moment to learn the language, help out, and generally establish their integrity with the local people until they could see "where Christ fits in".

And their goal? "In twenty years," said Tom, "fifty per cent of Mongolia could be Christian."

*

Hundreds of years ago, the Nestorians had much the same idea.

Nestorius was a Patriarch of Constantinople who preached the duality of the nature of Christ - that is, human as well as divine. In 431 AD the Council of Ephesus declared him a heretic; so he set off for the east with his followers to find somewhere that would appreciate him.

The Nestorians established churches successfully in Iran, Central Asia and India, and in the eighth century reached China. By the end of the first millennium two leading Mongolian tribes, the Kereyits and the Naiman, were largely Christian.

Of all this, the Christian Church in the west knew nothing and cared less. When some awareness of the existence of their Brothers in Christ finally began to prod their apathy, it took a strange form.

The twelfth century saw the dawn of the Age of Chivalry. Troubadors and minnesingers told of brave knights, of heroic deeds in battle, of immortal kings such as Arthur who would return in time of dire

151

need to lead their people to victory and freedom. Of such glittering stuff was woven the legend of Prester John.

Its first echoes sounded in 1122 when an eastern, probably Nestorian, prelate visited the west. He spoke of a great Christian kingdom in the east ruled by descendants of the Magi. Western Christendom, recently engaged in self-righteous struggle to drive the heathen out of the Holy Land, was heartened by the knowledge that it had allies it hadn't even known about.

Twenty years later the rumours began in earnest. An eastern king named Prester John, people said, had heavily defeated a Moslem enemy, and was now on his way to Palestine to aid the Crusaders.

The Franks reckoned that any enemy of the Moslems was a friend of theirs. And they badly needed help, for the Saracens were beginning to fight back successfully. A new Crusade had just been proclaimed, and some helpful propaganda would help to boost recruitment among the Faithful.

But no Christian Hero appeared out of the east, and the stories faded to whispers. Someone obviously thought they were worth reviving, for in 1165 a letter was passed around the courts of Europe. Some sort of hoax, it was supposed to have come from Prester John, and announced his intention of leaving his vast eastern kingdom to come to the aid of the Crusaders and visit the holy Sepulchre. This time the echoes persisted, and the Pope dispatched an envoy in search of the fabled king. The poor man was never seen again.

This almost killed the legend. But it wasn't quite ready to die, and forty years later surfaced one last time.

A so-called "Report on King David" reached the west, describing how a Christian King David, "commonly called Prester John", had advanced out of India to defeat a Moslem kingdom. This was almost certainly a bowdlerised version of historical fact on the "any enemy of theirs..." theme; the year before, on the first leg of his dramatic sweep westwards, Genghis Khan had annihilated the Islamic Empire of Khoresmia. And once again, the Crusaders were having a very rough time. News of Moslem defeats could only presage their own good. No problem that Prester John must be over a hundred by now; age did not wither legendary Heroes.

This time hard truth, in the form of the Mongol armies, was on a headlong collision course with western Christendom. After a heavy defeat inflicted on the Christian princes of Rus, nobody mentioned Prester John any more. But the seeds of awareness had been sown, and were beginning to germinate. There was a world out there in the east, and some of it moreover was Christian. And if that Christian part could be mobilised - in an evangelical and political way even if its armies were so much hot air - then it might be possible to halt the Mongol killing machine from within.

In 1241, the Mongols made a brief, bloody incursion into central Europe, before trouble at home called them back. Now for the first time western leaders fully understood their peril. Their weapons had utterly failed to stem the Mongol tide; it was time for diplomacy, for political manoeuvre. So it was that the second half of the thirteenth century saw a string of Catholic monks travelling to visit the Mongols, with purposes ranging from ambassador to missionary to spy, and all shades in between.

First of them - discounting the envoy who vanished - were the Franciscans John of Plano Carpini and his companion Benedict the Pole. Dispatched by Pope Innocent IV in March, 1245, they reached Kiev, capital of Rus, the following February. Kiev had fallen to the Mongols in 1240, and John was horrified by the "innumerable multitude of dead men's bones" lying all around. From here on was occupied territory and, travelling with Mongol guides via the *Yam*, or relay system, they reached Mongolia in July, an astonishing feat for a man of Carpini's sixty-five years - and considerable girth. Arriving at the court of the Great Khan Güyük, they were subjected to the ritual of purification by fire.

"They said to us, 'Go without any fear, for we are making you pass between two fires for no other reason than this, that if you are planning to do any evil to our lord, or if you happen to be carrying poison, the fire may remove all that is harmful.' To this we replied, 'That being the reason, we will go through, so as not to be suspected of such things.' "

Their mission was hazardous in more ways than one, for the Papal Bull they carried didn't mince words.

153

"Seeing that not only men, but even irrational animals... are united by a certain innate law after the manner of the celestial spirits... we are driven to express in strong terms our amazement that you have invaded many countries... and are laying them waste in a horrible desolation... breaking the band of natural ties, sparing neither sex nor age, you rage against all indiscriminately.

"We therefore... do admonish, beg and beseech all of you that in the future you desist entirely from assaults of this kind... and that after so many and such grievous offences you conciliate with a fitting penance the wrath of Divine Majesty, which without doubt you have seriously aroused; nor should you be emboldened to commit further savagery..."

Brave words, uttered from the safety of the Vatican. But although the Mongols had many faults, shooting the messenger wasn't one of them. Despite almost perishing from hunger at the Mongol court - for they were allowed only near-starvation rations - the Franciscans survived to bring back Güyük's answer.

"That you wonder at so great a slaughter of men," this went, "we reply that this we do not understand." There followed threats of what would befall the western nations if they did not "accept peace... and surrender your fortresses." The letter exists to this day in the Vatican archives.

Not a very heartening reply; but not exactly unexpected. The real value of Carpini's journey, of course, was the wealth of information he brought back about the Mongols themselves.

At times he appears to be credulous to the point of naïvety. There are tales, for example, of "monsters who had the likeness of women... every male had the shape of a dog." Then there were the "cyclopeds", living in a desert near Armenia, who had one arm and one leg. These, reported a wide-eyed Carpini, could hop faster than a horse could run; when they got tired of this they turned cartwheels on their single hand and foot.

But it is a very different matter where he describes what he has seen for himself. There is a wealth of accurate detail about Mongol warfare, armour and weapons, treatment of subject peoples, customs and beliefs - pure gold to western leaders, allowing them to flesh out with reality a threat whose true substance had until now been unknown, and therefore all the more terrifying.

It was autumn 1247 when Carpini returned - now, presumably, with much reduced circumference - to present his report to the Pope. He and Benedict were welcomed as "men who had risen from death to life".

The ice was now broken, and two further missions were sent in quick succession. Neither went further than Central Asia, and the leader of the first, a Dominican named Ascelin, nearly lost his head through overbearing behaviour. They brought back the news - wrongly, in fact - that a leading Mongol prince was Christian. When this reached the court of the Crusading King Louis IX of France, it sharpened the interest of a certain Franciscan friar among his entourage... William of Rubruck.

William, described by Christopher Dawson in his commentary to *Missions to Asia* as "an exceptionally observant man with the temperament and eye of an artist", is variously cited as the messenger of Louis or the Byzantine Emperor, Baldwin. But although he carried letters from both, these seem to have been no more than letters of introduction. William had his own agenda, a divine mission. He maintained throughout that he wished to preach the Catholic faith to the Mongols, and appeared to be genuinely disappointed when the Khan sent him home as an envoy.

After a rather less forced journey than poor Carpini, William was well received at Möngke's court. Invited into the Presence, he entered singing a Latin hymn and then prayed for the health of the Khan - who appeared to be drunk. Very soon, as the airag circulated, so was his interpreter, and the interview degenerated into an alcoholic stupor.

There was much that William disapproved of. He was scathing of the Nestorians, who were, he observed, "completely corrupt... userers and drunkards... some have several wives, just as the Tatars." Most of all, he was outraged by the general assumption that he had come to offer terms of surrender to the Mongols, who took it for granted that their subjection of Europe was just a matter of time. "On this as on many other occasions I have had to exercise great self-control in order to conceal my indignation and fury."

The climax of William's visit was a theological debate between Nestorian Christians, Moslems and Buddhists, and "umpired" by one of each. William captained the Christian team and, if his account is unbiased, effectively demolished the opposition. Afterwards, he comments gloomily, "everyone drank heavily."

With his secret ambition, the conversion of Möngke himself, unfulfilled, William returned home after a total of three years' absence. He had baptised just six converts.

One more notable mediaeval evangelist travelled east: John of Monte Corvino, who went to Kubilai Khan's new capital of Peking. He founded an Archbishopric there, and a cathedral at the mediaeval port of Zaytun. A subsequent mission to this church was accompanied by an unusual gift for the Emperor: a monstrous war horse "11 feet long and 6'8" high", as reported by a goggling Chinese scribe. When the Mongol dynasty came to an end, however, the missionaries were promptly expelled.

As for Mongolia, it took nearly five centuries before they returned. The Russian government allowed the London Missionary Society to build a Mission on the Siberian border in 1817, before changing its mind and throwing them out again a few years later. They left behind seven lonely graves and several hundred New Testaments in Mongolian; some of those, it's said, may still be seen on the family altar in gers here and there.

By the end of the century various groups were operating in Mongolia, particularly the Swedish-Mongolian Mission. And then the Communists came.

*

The Shooks and their three children, Ryan, Joy and James, lived in a home which combined all the typical elements of Mongolian and American lifestyles.

Like all the others in the street, their house was a wooden building in a wooden compound with a wooden privy in the corner. Inside, it was

156

furnished with painted local furniture like Niamchuu's or Naran's. The iron stove was a close relative of those which had burned in the Tsaatan yurtsias. The thick double glazing was packed with wool which, explained Tom, blocked draughts and reduced condensation.

Books lined the walls; Gayle home-schooled the children herself. In the corner lay a dartboard and a mountain bike, and other various gear of American teenagers. The house swarmed with children, Mongolian as well as the three Shooks. Upstairs was a microcosmic US household, with Gayle's laptop computer and a TV for the kids, several of whom were sprawled on the bed watching a video.

The varnished pine was brand-new. They had finished building the upper floor last year, only to have the children burn it down again while searching for birds' nests with a candle. The entire contents of the big attic room had gone up in smoke, but the family was fortunate in that all the irreplaceable stuff was in the lower storey, which escaped unscathed. "God was looking after us then," said Gayle.

Over dinner we met some newcomers to the ex-pat group. Mark, Karen and their nine-month child had arrived just a week ago, and planned to make a new life here. They discussed Mongolian lessons with Gayle, while Tom and Joy argued about who was to go for water; it was gone seven, the stand-pipe down the street would soon be off, and there were three *batongs* - a sort of truncated milk-churn - to be filled.

The Shooks, anchored by their faith, seemed to have transplanted themselves contentedly between two of the world's most widely differing societies. Were there times, we asked, when they regretted more than fleetingly the amenities of home?

"We did have one glitch last winter," Gayle replied.

They had been short of fuel, so that the water in the batongs used to freeze overnight. In midwinter, Tom found an excellent source of dry wood in the planks that had survived the upstairs fire. "He sawed the planks into smaller chunks, but grew lax, and broke some up with his leg. With one whack too many, Tom broke a rib!"

"Thanks a lot!" he said. "I refuse to accept that, because it might show my lack of common sense. So let's just say I was working endless hours so my family wouldn't freeze to death this last winter. Yeah, let's say that - it sounds better."

It was time to try out the Mongolian Health Service. Tom went to Mörön Hospital.

"It was quite an experience. One of our neighbours, who is a nurse, offered to assist me. She introduced me to the doctor, who promptly took off my shirt and asked me where it hurt. I showed her the approximate location and she began to examine me.

"After a few questions and a lot of poking she walked over to her medicine cupboard, and retrieved something that they call *botag*, which means paint in Mongolian. She then began to paint the right side of my upper body with this stuff, that smelled like formaldehyde.

"Now, I'm not a doctor, but I did watch my fair share of Marcus Welby MD when I was a boy. And one thing I remember is that when the doctor painted a patient, it meant he was going to have an operation. All sorts of things started to race through my mind, like, maybe they were going to cut me open right there on the spot. I was so scared I started hyperventilating.

"She must have seen the fear in my eyes, because she assured me that they would not cut into me, and that the paint was merely for the doctor in the X-ray department. After I'd regained my composure, they escorted me down to the X-ray room.

"I waited in line with about six Mongols. When my time finally came, I entered into this very large and intimidating machine that looked about fifty years old. The doctor was a short, chubby man also about fifty years old. He had one peculiar feature, though, that helped me identify him as the X-ray man. You see, he was wearing space goggles. The same kind that I saw on TV once. I think it was a documentary on the detonation of the first atomic bomb.

"As you might guess, I was a little concerned. I vacillated for a moment or two as to whether I should run for the door, but it was dark in the room, and my side hurt too bad. So I took my chance and let them nuke me. After the doctor took my X-ray he said I was *guygue*. Mongol doctors have three answers that they offer their patients. The first answer is *sine*, which means good. The second is *guygue*, which means, not too bad. And the third is *oohenn*, which means that you are going to die. I was somewhere between not bad and dead. How reassuring!

"After my trip to the X-ray lab I was politely escorted to the Heat Room. In this room they take a heat lamp and fix it on the area where someone feels sick. It doesn't matter what ails you, the heat lamp is supposed to fix you right up. I lay down on a bed, and the doctor very kindly put the heat lamp right up close to my skin and left the room.

"After about two minutes I was burning up so bad that I began to squirm around like a fish out of water. Fifteen minutes later the doctor returned, and said that that should do it, and I could go home now. As you might have already guessed I made a beeline for the front door and never looked back.

"Wow!" he finished. "What an experience! I sure am glad things like this don't happen every day."

VIII

BRAVE NEW WORLD

The skies had cleared, the sun shone and the flight prospects looked good. Tom conjured up a jeep from somewhere and we left early. On the airport road a lad riding a yak hurriedly shooed his sheep from our path. Looking back we saw the early sun ricocheting off the wet rooftops with dazzling light, as if Mörön was trying to persuade us that it wasn't such a drab place after all.

We had an eight-hour wait while our plane flew in from Ulaan Baatar then made two shuttles to Hatgal, on Lake Hovsgol, and back. Unpacking the stove, we filled the time with cups of tea, entertained meanwhile by a MIAT pilot who was at first sober and kindly helpful, later drunk and troublesome, finally hung-over and bolshy with deliberate disinformation.

At last it was our turn to fly, and Carol led the sprint across the tarmac for seats. For there was no fussing over reservations, and it was first come, first seated. The laggards wouldn't get off the ground until tomorrow.

The tiny seventeen-seater plane had an unexpectedly sharp turn of foot, and at only half the runway's length the undercarriage wheel directly below the window was off the ground and dangling in the air, faintly ridiculous. Mörön was below us, the houses in their regimented grid of suburbs looking like the car-lines at a county show. We straightened up and set off flying visually along the track by which we had entered a lifetime ago. Our hearts went out to the poor wretches setting off by truck for the two-day journey along that route. We thanked our stars that this time we weren't with them.

160

From twelve thousand feet, the surface of the steppe might have been a synthetic sports surface: dry, dull green and scratchy. Gers sat at intervals like abandoned golf balls. Even the individual sheep were distinguishable, small white wriggling ovals as tightly packed together as an outbreak of maggots on a piece of rotten meat. So close to the mountain tops, the north-south divide of the forestation was striking. As we flew east the hills on our right were densely covered, those on the left bare; each window showed a different country. In a wide patch of plain Carol spotted a fumarole, a miniature, perfectly formed volcano.

Poor Carol wasn't having a comfortable flight. For the lady next to her was even less comfortable. Ominously, she had brought with a her a large plastic bag, and soon began to use it frequently. Before long her friend, two seats ahead and less well prepared, was feeling the same need. The bag passed rapidly back and forth between them, its contents slopping about revoltingly in the turbulence. We watched with compulsive fascination as each lady became progressively greener, and wondered what would happen if both needed relief at once.

The flight path followed the Selenge Mörön River, which later gathers in the Tuul and the Orhon to flow through Siberia into Lake Baikal. When the line of the river drifted too far north we left it to cut across to Bulghan, over the mountains whose beautiful scenery had been so refreshing on the second day of our truck odyssey. The pilot, noticing my aviation map (in his rear-view mirror?), came back to consult it, which was disconcerting. But he found his way back to UB all right, and we landed in a cloudburst that had spray shearing up and back from the wheels as the plane braked to a halt on a runway covered by a good inch of water.

*

The Steppe Inne was the social centre of UB. The sign went up every Friday evening over the door of a Terrapin in the grounds of the British Embassy, and ex-pats of every nationality gathered to share drinks and the latest gossip.

161

There were teachers, oil men, even the occasional diplomat. The Mongolian Biodiversity Project was usually well represented; in fact it was Chris, he of the Przewalski horses, who had first sent me along here. This week, he was accompanied by Tom McCarthy, who was working for the International Snow Leopard Trust.

The snow leopard is dangerously high on the list of the world's endangered species. Some survive in Mongolia's Altai Mountains, but numbers are dwindling; although they are officially protected, it is said that, given the right contacts and waving a wad of dollars with enough noughts, foreigners can still go and shoot them. Tom was tracking the leopards with radio collars, learning their habits and estimating their numbers. He hoped that ultimately the information he was gathering would help to safeguard the rare and beautiful creatures.

The men we were hunting tonight, though, were the vets.

Nick Honhold and Alastair Grieve were here under the flag of the European Union, working on the project "Strengthening Veterinary Services in Mongolia". We had met them before leaving for Mörön, and they were, we thought, just the people to tackle the reindeer sickness. This was why we had taken such detailed notes from Uugdorj and Erdenejav. To our great relief and satisfaction, Nick and Alastair were deeply interested. It was, they said, the very sort of thing that their organisation was here for. They took some contact addresses, and promised to investigate.

Mongolia's veterinary services were in considerably more robust shape than its medical science could offer the human population. The principal reason for this, Nick explained, was the emphasis laid on vaccination and preventive medicine. Our own Ministry might learn a thing or two here; for many diseases which strike terror into the average British farmer, including foot and mouth disease and bovine TB, have been eradicated altogether, and brucellosis is in sharp decline.

An essential factor in the equation is that Mongolia produces all its own high quality, specifically developed animal vaccines at the excellent "Biokombinat" vaccine factory. This means that Mongolian vets have less need than doctors for imported pharmaceutical goods, that need which has had such dire effects on the human population - as we had learned from Erdenejav - when the subsidised supply from the USSR dried up so suddenly.

Low stock density has also played a part; as has the well organised and widely distributed field service. The latter includes a vet in every sumoin and a veterinary technician in every bag. There are also diagnostic and food hygiene labs at aimag level. Unlike, for example, the education services, this structure has remained intact throughout the post-democracy traumas.

Inevitably, it is in question whether it will remain thus. So much in the new Mongolia is being privatised - including, with the demise of the collectives, 95% of the animals themselves. At the moment, the veterinary system is almost staggeringly cost-effective: 42tg per head of livestock per year, about six pence. But already costs are rising. Animals once kept together at the collective are now far more widely distributed in private ownership, increasing the travelling time for a largely horse-borne staff; while labs which were once over-stocked with technical equipment from abroad have seen their sources dry up while their hardware ages. No wonder that privatisation of the veterinary service is under serious discussion.

Can the state afford to go on paying for the service? But can it afford not to? Livestock is the backbone of the Mongolian economy, and its needs must be well served.

On one point Nick was adamant: "Complete cover for vaccinations and other preventive treatments must be maintained." If impoverished herdsmen weren't able to safeguard the immunity of their stock, the long-term results for the country could be disastrous.

To privatise or not to privatise, and to what extent? This is just one of the many dilemmas facing Mongolia at a cross-roads of her history.

*

A couple of miles from the Steppe Inne, at the far end of town, a spot of *perestroika* was going on. Gandaan Hiid, the largest monastery in Ulaan.

163

Baatar, was being stripped and rebuilt to accommodate the resurgence of Buddhism sweeping the country.

The fifteen-foot, solid oak doors to the main temple stood open, and the workmen raised no objection as we stepped tentatively through them. Inside, ornate pillars and scaffolding poles raced each other skywards, ultimately lost in the heights of the roof.

All smelled of fresh paint. It covered the latticework bannisters and intricate honeycomb carvings; it turned the ceiling blue and red; it decorated the four central pillars with images of green earth and mountains, rising through blue sea and sky to reach gaudy dragons levitating among white clouds. High on the walls, stylised paintings imitated fringed hangings. Tibetan characters trailed spiders' footsteps along the beams and down some of the columns, while up others twined ferocious-looking serpents with technicolour scales, mouths open to threaten with pointed fangs.

Beside such brilliance, the workmen's ladders scattered around the building were rough-hewn and clumsy. You felt that if anything as frivolous as a game were allowed here, it should be *up* the snakes and *down* the ladders.

Taking a chance that might never come again, we climbed flimsy stairs to the first floor gallery. Here you could get out on to the roof and walk right round, past the great bronze bell at the corner, to where the traditional emblem of a wheel flanked by two deer stood above the door.

We peered between the spokes, enjoying a spectacular view over the monastery compound, down the main allée to the entrance gate, across the city and out to the hills behind. The lamasery had obviously once commanded extensive grounds, although some of its buildings were long given over to secular use. Two temple compounds remained as such, standing either side of the central cross-roads with its two great *stupas* - domed Buddhist shrines. Directly before us was a large open space, while to one side stood the smaller temple which had once been the monastery library.

Even at this level, as yet untouched by the restoration, the painted woodwork was astonishing. The curved, frilled eaves bore flower patterns, fish and monster heads, while Tibetan writing spoke its prayers along every beam. There was more than a hint here of former glory.

Founded in 1840, Gandaan suffered heavily in the lamasery purges of the thirties. But it survived after a fashion, "preserved" as a sort of museum. A few monks were kept on as living exhibits, allowed to say the offices but encouraged to set up a craft co-operative to justify their existence. When Ivor Montague visited in 1954, he found only a few aged monks in residence. "Not", he was told piously by his Communist guide, "from any government prohibition, but because there was no longer sufficient public interest."

"A congregation... was composed of no more than three or four withered crones, with one or two infant grandchildren.... All save the infants were so old, old... that I ventured to ask a plump lama a question, rather shyly and shamefully because the question was so cruel and we had been well received. 'Where will you all be in twenty years time? I mean - how will this go on?' indicating the prayers. He bared his teeth in a grin. 'We hope - the Lord will provide.' "

The Lord did provide. The larger temple complex now throbbed with life, even though prayers for today were over.

Entering its yard by a postern in an ornamental gate, we found ourselves in a courtyard with two temples. An open-air shrine, consisting of an altar in painted stone with a Buddha figure, occupied one corner. People pressed round it to leave offerings and turn the prayer wheels, or sat quietly on prayer benches.

Two white lions guarded the door of the larger temple. The smaller, yellow and gold, bore the same deer and wheel motif that was repeated all over the monastery. Outside, a brazier burned fragrantly with juniper, and wind-chimes chattered inside a great urn. Pigeons scratched contentedly in the dust, under the shade of poplar, larch and acacia. By the main, arched gateway - also watched by lions - a concrete flowerbed was designed with interlocking squares, the same type of pattern as that used to hook up the trailing ropes of gers.

We tried to turn the colossal prayer wheels in the street outside, but it took our combined strength to shift them. Smaller wheels, tied with strips of cloth, stood in the corners for the faint-hearted. Messages in Mongolian or Cyrillic script were stuck to them. "Jesus loves you" said the only one in English.

*

Although the leading monastery in UB, Gandaan was by no means the oldest.

It was only when the earliest monasteries were built here in the eighteenth century that the site of the city became fixed. Until then it had been a migrating camp defined by the presence of the Khutuktu, as a swarm of bees settles around the queen.

When Nikolai Przewalski visited in the 1870s, it was still known to the nomads as Bogd-Kuren, or Sacred Camp; the Russians called it Urga. The settlement was then in two parts. The Mongolian half, grouped about the Khutuktu's Palace and various temples, was a ger city. Three miles to the east lay the Chinese quarter, the preserve of Manchu officials and traders who, forbidden by law to settle abroad with their families, comforted themselves in the arms of Mongolian concubines. Between the two halves was the Russian Consulate, then the only secular building of any size to be seen in Urga.

"The population of the Mongolian part," wrote Przewalski, "is chiefly composed of lamas." He estimated the lama population at one third of all Mongolian males, and around ten thousand in Urga. They didn't, apparently, rate cleanliness next to godliness.

"Outwardly the Mongol part of Urga is disgustingly filthy. All the filth is thrown into the streets, and the habits of the people are loathsome. To add to all this, crowds of starving beggars assemble on the market-place; some of them (mostly poor old women) make it their final resting place... The decrepit or crippled hag lies on the ground in the centre of the bazaar with a covering of old pieces of felt thrown to her by way of charity. Here she will remain, too weak to move, covered with vermin and filth, imploring alms from the passer-by. In winter the cold winds cover her den with the snow-drift, beneath which she drags out her miserable existence. Her very death is of an awful nature; eye-witnesses have told us how, when her last moments are approaching, a pack of dogs gather round and wait patiently for their victim to breathe her last, when they devour her corpse..."

There were two main reasons for Mongolia's poverty at this time: the enormous burden of debt to Chinese traders, at crippling interest rates, which had become a way of life for most Mongolians; and the onerous duty of supporting the church, which held a large proportion of the country's wealth but tied up perhaps as many as half (estimates vary) of all adult males in non-productive occupation.

As well as for rapacity, the Chinese were hated for the increasing brutality of their rule. When rebellion at home in China toppled the Manchu dynasty, the princes of the old Mongolian royal houses saw their chance. On December 1st 1911, they made a unilateral declaration of independence, naming the Khutuktu as Head of State.

Mongolia could not stand alone in such a step. For some years she had sought an increasing degree of rapprochement with her northern Russian neighbours, and now requested their active help to give legal backing to the move. China, still in turmoil within, became a reluctant signatory to the tripartite Treaty of Khiakta in 1915, granting autonomy to Outer Mongolia.

But revolution was in the air. Two years later it was Russia's turn to descend into chaos. China, now sailing downwind again, reneged on Khiakta. In 1919 General Hsu Shu Teng marched back into Mongolia to install a more repressive regime than ever.

Within months, a revolutionary movement was drawing its first breaths. It took the form of two small groups, headed respectively by Sukhbaatar and Choibalsan, two names which were to resound throughout the century in Mongolia. They quickly pooled their resources, and jointly approached Russia for military backup to throw out the Chinese once and for all. Before the Russians would commit themselves, however, they demanded the sanction of the Khutuktu who, though now a blind and shambling old man little more than a figurehead, alone possessed the power to unite the country by expressing his will.

167

A letter from the Khutuktu requesting Russian intervention was duly obtained, and entrusted to Sukhbaatar. His ensuing flight from the country, with the letter concealed in the handle of his whip, has become the stuff of Mongolian legend. With the certainty now of Russian support, Sukhbaatar, Choibalsan and five associates set about forming a government in exile and laying plans for invasion.

Before these plans reached fruition, though, a new and wholly unexpected player had entered the stage.

*

"A tall, red-haired, white-faced, Imperial Russian Cavalry officer in his early thirties, of part-Baltic and part-Hungarian extraction, by religion a Buddhist, with long, thin fingers, a small head set on broad shoulders, a high-pitched, hysterical voice, piercing, watery-blue eyes, one set lower than the other, pale lips above a narrow chin, a straggling, reddish moustache, a fearful sabre-cut across his forehead and manifestly paranoiac tendencies, usually believing himself to be a re-incarnation of Genghis Khan or, in his less lucid moments, the God of War in person. Such was His Excellency Chang Chun Major-General Baron Fyodorovich von Ungern-Sternberg, the descendant of a long line of Baltic barons, Crusaders, pirates and freebooters by sea and by land, carrying in their veins, their descendant proudly claimed, the blood of Attila's Huns, which gave him, or so he believed, a special affinity for Mongols and Mongolia." Thus Fitzroy Maclean describes Baron von Ungern-Sternberg in *To The Back of Beyond.*

The Mad Baron was looking for a stage suited to his special calling. His career so far hadn't done him justice: an officer in the Trans-Baikal Cossacks, he had been twice thrown out of the army for duelling and other scandals. His third attempt saw him on the German front, where he distinguished himself for repeatedly "dashing into battle like a lunatic", collecting decorations for gallantry - and a sabre-cut to the head which relieved him of his few remaining marbles.

168

On the wrong side after the Russian Revolution, he kept one step ahead of the Bolsheviks with his band of White Russians and assorted desperadoes. In the autumn of 1920 he crossed into Mongolia, where he believed lay his destiny: to re-establish the empire he had personally conquered in his earlier incarnation as Genghis Khan.

He extended his small troop into an army by an unusual conscription process. Rounding up groups of peasants, he would stride down the line assessing the talent like a knacker at a low-class horse fair, before screaming his verdict on each man: "To the army!" "Back to the cattle!" or "Liquidate!" The last instruction, freely applied to any with a disability or defect, also embraced wholesale Jews and Bolsheviks, to whom the Baron had a particular aversion.

He marched on Urga with a sizeable force. Attacking according to the advice of his soothsayers and the portents of sheep's shoulder blades, he was twice repulsed by the Chinese before taking the city at the third attempt. He almost lost this time, too; for the omens said he was two days early, and he temporarily called off the assault just as he was beginning to win.

Victorious at last, his men swept into the city like savages, killing, pillaging and raping with all the blood-lust of their early Mongol idols. The Mongolian people locked up their daughters and nervously welcomed him as a liberator. But the Baron was barely into his stride.

His first task was to free the Khutuktu, who had been imprisoned by the Chinese, and declare him Emperor of all Mongolia. The Baron himself would be Military Adviser; by the way, he announced, he was also the incarnation of Tzagaan Burkhan, the God of War.

The self-proclaimed God of War now embarked on a reign of terror. With the enthusiastic support of his officers, an exceptionally nasty bunch of cut-throats, he set about liquidating a great many of his new subjects. Chief targets were all those who had done business with Chinese or Bolsheviks, which gave him a wide field of choice; and he and his men proceeded from one atrocity to another, rarely repeating themselves in ever more inventive acts of sadism.

But already his enemies were mobilising. In the border town of Khiakta the Mongolian Government in Exile was busy making plans with the Red Army for invasion. Hoping to get in the first blow, the Baron gave instructions to his thugs in Urga to keep up the good work, and marched north.

He missed the first act; one of his divisions had already attacked and been defeated. Pausing just long enough to beat his only Medical Officer to a pulp and have one of his generals buried alive - and, of course, consult a dead sheep - he warmed up by attacking a village, slaughtering its inhabitants, and then engaged the Red Army. Despite odds of two to one in his favour, he was soundly routed.

Licking its wounds, the decimated army retreated into central Mongolia. Meanwhile, the Mongolian Army, tiny but growing daily, and its all-powerful Red escort, moved south, mopping up as it went bands of Chinese soldiers who had survived the Baron. By July 1921 it was in possession of Urga.

After receiving spiritual refreshment and, no doubt, heavenly guidance at Erdenezu monastery, the Baron regrouped. Marching north once more, he managed to defeat a couple of Soviet units.

But the writing was on the mutton bones. Now surrounded on all sides by crack Soviet troops and even attacked from the air, his men began to desert in droves. Those that remained mutinied, turning on their leader. Bleeding from numerous bullet holes, the Baron escaped on horseback, eventually falling to the ground unconscious to be found by local herdsmen. Fitzroy Maclean describes the denouement.

"Their belief that he was indeed Tzagaan Burkhan, the God of War, and consequently immortal, had been reinforced by the events of the night. Had not everyone tried to shoot him? And was he not still alive? After much deliberation a number of their bravest men were sent with ropes to bind him hand and foot. When they had done this they galloped off, each in a different direction, before the divine wrath could overtake them.

"Next day a Red patrol, happening to pass through the valley, came upon a solitary, helpless, shackled figure, lying in the grass with the ants running over him. 'Who are you, stranger,' they asked. 'I' came the angry answer in the famous high-pitched tenor, 'am Baron Ungern-Sternberg.'

170

"Such was the terror the Baron inspired that the first impulse of the Red soldiers who had found him was to turn tail and run. But then, pulling themselves together, they picked him up, brushed the ants off him, gave him a drink and took him back with them to their headquarters."

He was taken to Verkhneudinsk, put on trial, and shot.

*

The Mad Baron was a hard act to follow. For its first twenty years, though, the Party rose heroically to the challenge.

The full horrors of these years will probably never be known. Official reports routinely shrouded in self-righteous propaganda the reality of the show trials, the executions, the power struggles; as they may, perhaps, have inflated the enormities of the Baron. It is always the winners who write the history books.

But it is hard to see what course Mongolia might have taken other than to become a Soviet client. Economically, politically and culturally, the Mongolia of 1921 had reached rock bottom. "To put it at its bluntest," says C.R. Bawden in his *Modern History of Mongolia*, "the Mongol race was dying of inanition and syphilis. Every traveller noted the apathy of the people, their enslavement to a church... which, where it impinged on daily life, held the people at large in ignorant dependence on itself and on its outdated and corrupt ideals. Filth, disease and ignorance marked the Mongol... the outward expression of the essential rot within."

The impetus for fundamental change couldn't come from inside. A few individuals, however inspired, simply couldn't provide the necessary momentum - even if Mongolia had been at liberty to act independently from her neighbours, which she emphatically was not. Clamped between two powerful countries, she could only choose to trim her sails to the wind of one of them. And Mongolia had had enough of China.

Within three years of the Revolution, three leading figures were dead: the Khutuktu, Sukhbaatar and the first premier, Bodo. The Khutuktu, though only fifty-five, may be reasonably assumed to have been carried off by disease. Sukhbaatar was believed to have died from

171

natural causes. His demise was most convenient for his colleague Choibalsan - too convenient, some think - since he was probably the only person with the power and prestige to have hindered Choibalsan's ultimate rise to dictatorship. But there was no doubt over Bodo. Having expressed reservations over the degree of Soviet influence, he was accused of plotting against the government, and executed. The charges were very similar to those brought a couple of years later to remove Danzan, another worthy, card-carrying revolutionary.

With the Khutuktu's death Outer Mongolia, until now formally a theocracy, was declared as the Mongolian People's Republic. As yet Party policies remained fairly moderate. But things were about to change radically.

By the end of 1928, Stalin had consolidated his grip on Russia, and was ready to begin his campaigns of collectivisation, stamping out religious practices and generally removing anyone who disagreed with him. "Advisers" representing the USSR at the Mongolian Party Congress almost certainly backed their advice with the threat of Soviet military intervention, and Mongolia embarked on a violent swing to the left, in slavish imitation of Stalin's path.

A crash programme followed of industrialisation, nationalisation, collectivisation and just about every -isation in the Communist handbook. Private enterprise was banned, although as yet very few state shops were up and running, so that trade of all description ground to a halt. Incentives were given to monks to leave the church, punitive taxes were imposed on those who remained and the monasteries were stripped of their herds.

Collectivisation, forcibly imposed and clumsily carried through, was particularly disastrous. Herdsmen often slaughtered their livestock rather than deliver them up to the state. Many opted for the devil they knew and fled en masse to China, the ultimate Mongol thumbs-down. The experiment cost the lives of an estimated seven million animals, one-third of the total stock. Based almost entirely on herding, and expecting Soviet help which never materialised, the Mongolian economy - such as it was - collapsed completely.

In 1932 the five-year-plan was abandoned. A monumental cock-up was of necessity publicly admitted, but laid at the door of incompetent individuals; Party ideology could not possibly be at fault. The entire Presidium and Secretariat of the Central Committee were sacked, and the New Turn Policy, in reality an urgent back-pedalling, began.

Under the new programme, collectivisation was reversed and most livestock redistributed into private ownership. An amnesty persuaded many emigrants to return home. Private enterprise was reinstated, and freedom of religion declared. But the damage was done. Disillusion was widespread; and on the march.

From 1930 a number of uprisings broke out, often instigated by the lamaseries. These were effectively suppressed, sometimes with terrible atrocities; and frequently, now, with the help of Soviet troops.

Meanwhile, a bigger and better excuse arose for the Soviet Army to penetrate the country. For in 1931 Japan had seized Manchuria. By 1937 it was in possession of Inner Mongolia and knocking on the gates of Peking. Stalin, fearful for his own borders and wanting to keep the Mongolian buffer intact, prepared for the Japanese to attack eastern Mongolia. In 1939 the attack came, but a joint Mongolian-Russian force repulsed it, finally defusing the Japanese threat.

The Japanese bogeyman had been useful for Choibalsan, making a convenient gibbet on which to hang his opponents. For, taking a lead as ever from Stalin, he was now systematically eliminating all threats to his leadership. "To judge by the reports of trials in the 1930s," says Bawden, "Mongolia was penetrated from top to bottom by Japanese intelligence. Every ministry and public office was a hotbed of sedition, and the whole of the Presidium of the Central Committee of the Party, more or less, with the exception of Choibalsan, were Japanese agents."

Along with political manoeuvrings there now came a full frontal assault on the monasteries. With the church often implicated in rebellion, these too might now be universally considered potential schools of counter-Revolutionaries. Thousands of lamas were arrested, sent to concentration camps or executed. By 1939 most of the lamaseries had been closed. Besides Prime Minister, Choibalsan was now

Commander-in-Chief, Minister of War, Minister of Foreign and of Internal Affairs. An estimated twenty-seven thousand people had died, seventeen thousand of them monks.

Choibalsan now went in for another great Stalinist institution: the personality cult. Statues of him were erected all over the country, and Mongolia's fourth largest city was renamed after him.

Was Choibalsan a monster, or simply Stalin's Mongolian stooge? Stalin's power over Mongolia was complete, and his constant exercise of it painfully obvious. Worship of the lesser god was implicitly also worship of the greater. And the constant need to lick Big Brother's boots was evident in the cringe-making invocation from the Party Congress in 1941:

"Thanks to Stalin's concern, in the country where the Living Buddha was worshipped there appeared the industrial combinat; into an uncultured land there penetrated the light of culture; black-eyed children made friends with paper and pencil; rosy cheeked girls went to school. The high sky - our father; the vast world - our mother; the father of the people - Stalin; the mother - the native soil."

As yet, though, only 11% of black-eyed children were making friends with pencil and paper, and the industrial combinat employed less than 2% of the population. The destruction of the old order was complete, but construction of the new had hardly begun.

The truth was that Mongolia was more heavily strapped for cash than ever. Arming against the Japanese threat had accounted for half the national budget in the thirties, with very little Soviet aid except for military training. And now that Russia was fighting its Great Patriotic War, supplies - mainly horses, wool and furs - poured into it out of Mongolia, further beggaring the economy. It wasn't until the following decade that real progress could begin.

In 1952 Choibalsan died, thus for the first and last time pre-empting his Soviet mentor by a full nine months. He was succeeded by Tsedenbal, who publicly denounced him a few years later - just as Kruschev denounced Stalin - for the atrocities of the thirties, and for his personality cult. Even in his grave, Choibalsan was still imitating his boss.

Now Mongolia's new society was picking up speed. China, which had hitherto asserted its continuing territorial claims, grudgingly recognised Mongolia, subsequently even giving economic aid and help with building the country's new infrastructure. Collectivisation was tried again, this time cautiously and with reference to the grim lessons of the earlier attempt, and successfully carried through. Mongolia entered a period of high economic growth. As affairs stabilised, so the degree of ideological control relaxed, and the people enjoyed greater freedom. Periodically, minor purges occurred, but now it was usually careers rather than heads that rolled. And in 1961 came UN recognition, long denied because of objections by Taiwan, which still considered itself guardian of China's integrity and thus suzerain of Mongolia.

In the late sixties, the USSR fell out with China, and the ensuing Sinophobia brought Soviet troops flooding into Mongolia again. Once more, the Russian grip tightened on all aspects of government: the Party, the economy, the army - even the legal system. This time, though, there were real economic benefits to sweeten the pill. Throughout the next decade, the USSR poured even more money into Mongolia than it did into Cuba. The UB intelligentsia may have resented their Russian bosses, may have wished to see development along with the subsidies; but they had to admit that living standards had never been higher.

But the certainties that sustained them were beginning to crumble. Across the world, *glasnost* and *perestroika* became household words; not only symbols of real change, but also fig leaves to obscure the imminent collapse of the Soviet economy.

When the Russians began to retrench, the possibilities were obvious. In March 1990 the whiff of freedom brought thousands to pro-democracy rallies before the Parliament building in Sukhbaatar Square. The cry of "Mongols! To your horses!" went up. Hunger strikes began, and the demonstrations grew daily. The government was called on to resign.

Events were poised between those of Mongolia's two long-term controllers: radical change or another Tian-an-Men Square? The government actually passed a resolution calling the tanks in, but Tsedenbal's successor, President Batman, didn't sign the order. The will

175

of the people prevailed, and the constitution was amended to permit multi-party elections.

The political and social barriers of totalitarianism had crashed. The old problems were gone. The new ones were only just beginning.

*

On our return to UB after a few weeks' absence, we had found meat prices doubled, bus fares trebled. Whinge as we do about inflation, we soft-living westerners, we can't even begin to guess at the pressures of changing overnight to a market economy, one from which the rug of foreign subsidies has been pulled.

The meat rise was inevitable. The arats may be nearly self-sufficient, but they must have funds to buy their few necessities, and just now had no slack in their belts; meat and hides are their only product, and they must receive a fair price. Public transport was even more of a problem. Already deeply in debt to Russia (echoes here of the earlier relationship with China?) and lacking hard currency to buy her fuel, Mongolia has difficulty keeping her buses on the road - let alone her planes in the air, as we had already discovered.

There is plenty of oil to be found. But the fields so far developed give poor quality, to which lead must be added before a vehicle can even be persuaded to choke on it; so it is used only for heating. Yet the survey work already completed by foreign companies indicates that there is enough of the good stuff for Mongolia to become an oil exporting country. First, though, it must be brought above ground, refined, piped elsewhere. And all that takes money. Back to square one.

The problem is that, with a small population and narrow industrial base, Mongolia doesn't fit the usual pattern for large-scale private investment from abroad. And without hard cash, industry remains restricted: a self-perpetuating problem. So for now her planes continue to spend much of their time on the tarmac; and her power stations still burn lignite, heavily polluting brown coal; while in the north-west huge seams of coal sit in the ground waiting for their time to come - coal which "burns so clean," said geologist Mike Kulchisky, another Steppe Inne regular, "one could inhale the combustion without any effects."

Always in the background are those difficulties which have become so sadly familiar as the West has watched with mixed feelings the social fall-out written into the obituary of Communism. A fifth of people living below the poverty line; average wage around twenty pounds a month; degradation of health services; rising child mortality and falling life expectancy; children running away from alcohol-driven abuse to live on the streets - or in the sewers, their only warm refuge; corruption in high places; even the death from starvation of prisoners in some jails - the last the result usually of economic pressures and incompetent administration, although, as befits an ex-totalitarian state, Mongolia's Human Rights record isn't yet squeaky clean.

The outlook isn't all bleak. For although the private developer may keep his distance, there is much support from the international community at large. From the very small NGOs consisting of a few people like Tom and Gayle, via the larger organisations like Save the Children (working on poverty alleviation, training and early childhood care) and Amnesty International (arranging Human Rights seminars and tackling the prisons) to the really big players on the international stage: the World Health Organisation (currently mostly administrative development) and, of course, the United Nations, widely active in Mongolia. And, perhaps most importantly, the World Bank.

Mongolia was accepted for membership with the establishment of democracy. Since then the World Bank's International Development Organisation has disbursed $114 million in loans, at a current rate of $25-30 million annually, to reduce poverty, build better infrastructure and - primarily - aid the transition to a market economy.

Foreign goodwill is helping the Mongolians with the slow rebuilding of their country. But it cannot prevent the immediate hardships, nor the turbulence that occasionally erupts about such radical political change. The new structure is a fragile creature; 1998, a year in which total foreign aid exceeded $200 million, saw three changes of government - and a cabinet minister assassinated with an axe.

As Russia and many of her former satellites know only too well, you cannot buy a prosperous, stable outcome to traumatic and fundamental economic reorganisation. But foreign investment could perhaps help to promote conditions in which prosperity and stability are better able to take root and, ultimately, thrive.

*

One afternoon I wandered into the Drama Theatre opposite Nairamdal Park, and found a traditional folk music concert in full swing.

Brilliant in Sunday best national costume, a group of seven musicians sang to instrumental accompaniment. Among the peripheral drums, cymbals and horns was the focal point of the music, as the string section to a modern orchestra: three morin huur, the beautiful little two-stringed instrument with a horse-head scroll, played vertically like a cello.

There was something self-conscious in the presentation: Mongolian tradition as preserved by the Russians, now trying to regain its spontaneity. Banned for some years following the Revolution, folk music was brought out of the closet after a safe interval, dusted off, and formally presented mostly for the pleasure of foreign visitors. There was still a slight whiff of the artificial about this show. But the performance gave me a chance to hear the famous Mongolian "throat singing", an extraordinary process in which the singer produces two notes simultaneously - a rather nasal, tuneless top line backed up by a sort of drone from the depths of the larynx.

The earliest music and drama in Mongolian tradition came together in the so-called "conversation song", a kind of ballad-cum-opera performed with voice and accompaniment by one or more players. Around the time of the Revolution, a number of local drama groups were beginning to appear, producing old Mongolian and Chinese plays. Under the paranoia of the new regime, however, all such activities were condemned. The actors were guided, it was said, by "rightist

178

deviationists", the folk singers represented "illicit continuation of feudal traditions". The huge, echoing theatres hastily thrown up in the central squares of Mongolian towns were not for the benefit of bona fide Mongolian drama. In future all music or plays, the Party decreed, should have a political message, all literature must be compatible with "socialist realism".

Thus proscribed, the old Mongolian performing arts might have perished. In fact, the enthusiasm of private collectors ensured that many early manuscripts, much folk literature, were preserved. Often, these were first published in western Europe.

With the rather more liberal attitudes of the sixties, Mongolia's ancient literature began to see the light of day once again in its native country; ironically, not for its own merit but because it was now deemed to show "democratic tendencies". Still, authors and publishers on the one hand, and the works themselves on the other, often rode a switchback alternating between condemnation and rehabilitation, according to the whims of varying political imperatives. It was tough that there were writers for whom rehabilitation was posthumous; you can only be purged once.

Much of present-day Mongolian culture, then, is developing from a standing start. But it seems to be emerging from the Communist strait-jacket like a sprinter.

For instance, the resurgence of the old Mongolian script. Running vertically down the page with the curves and sweeps of a down-turned arabesque, this was first adapted for Mongolian from the thirteenth century Uighur script, by order of Genghis Khan. Soon after the Revolution it was thrown out (illicit continuation of feudal traditions, do we hear?) and replaced by the Roman script universally imposed also on the non Russian-speaking peoples of the Soviet Union; then, after another decree, by Cyrillic. After such a shambles, it is no wonder that the old script has been so joyfully resurrected. Already it is being taught in every school, appears in paint or even neon above banks and businesses, and is taking over in the media.

So, too, Mongolian art.

Zanabazar is reckoned the first artist here worthy of the name. Born in 1635, he was Mongolia's Renaissance Man: painter, sculptor, religious leader, linguist and politician. Some of his works are at Gandaan Hiid, although - unfortunately for us - currently in mothballs.

Zanabazar's paintings were *tankas*: Buddhist themes depicted on fabric, usually cotton or silk. Most art in past centuries was religious, although later another subject emerged, that of life on the steppe. This has now become very popular for the tourist trade. The top floor of UB's department store had whole cases devoted to paintings of gers, horses and camels.

Steppe scenes predominated, too, at the exhibition in the gallery just off Sukhbaatar Square. Here they assumed their proper form; not small, trivial daubs for foreigners with a few spare dollars, but huge, compelling canvasses, often in fierce primary colours, over which herdsmen strode among their gers or tended their herds, sometimes sparse in number against the immensity of the steppe, sometimes packed in with Breughel-like density.

An exuberant clash of other styles covered the walls. Some were Chinese influenced, some Persian with mail-clad, scimitar-armed knights on mail-clad, caparisoned horses, their enemies painted upside-down to represent defeat. Some might have come straight from the pages of Tolkien, while others, of hunters in capuchins and feathered hats, were pure mediaeval Europe - but for the leopard riding on the rump of one horse.

Religious paintings filled one end of the room. Among tankas and paintings of the Buddha stood the Eighth Jetsundamba Khutuktu, accompanied by two scowling giants. Were they minders - or doorkeepers barring him from Nirvana for his depravity?

The underlying style of these works continued into secular themes on the adjacent wall. A goggle-eyed man broke in a goggle-eyed horse, surrounded on four sides of the canvas by caricature faces; alongside, two wrestlers and an acrobat had a similar audience.

Star of the exhibition, for me, was Yadamsuren's Folk Story Teller. An ancient, richly-clad bard played a morin huur, while behind him, seen through the window, swirled an infinity of intricately-painted clouds. Balancing the beauty of human achievement against the breadth of the world outside, it gave the best of Mongolia in microcosm.

IX

ACTS OF FAITH

On the way to Hujirt we flew straight over Hustain Nuruu. Twelve thousand feet below us lay the unmistakeable arrowhead layout of its six gers, with the blockhouse at the point, and the intricate mesh of its valleys was clearly reognisable. The wardens' herds stood out plainly, but although I strained my eyes to see the takhi, there wasn't so much as a hoofprint. I'd already thought them well camouflaged against the pink granite. It seemed that natural selection had even considered their visibility from the air.

This time, it was Carol who almost needed a plastic bag. "I never want to see or smell another hushan!" Nick and Alastair, more familiar than us with the amenities of UB, had taken us out of town to the old Russian quarter, where the classier restaurateurs were now strutting their stuff among ordinary Mongolians and producing a much better meal than you got downtown with not a muttonburger in sight. Grabbing the chance of some decent junk food, I had opted boringly for pizza and chips. Carol, with fond memories of Niamchuu, had gone for the local cuisine. But these hushans were stuffed with tired offal, not fresh meat, and she was now feeling very ill.

That made two of us; I was still paying off my bills from the Tsaatan excursion, and was almost catatonic. But flights to Hujirt left only once a week, and we couldn't afford the luxury of lying up any longer to recover.

Soon we were circling over the town, and floating down in a gentle spiral while the pilot checked the airstrip for stray yaks. Then came a feather-light touchdown on a field carpeted with alpine flowers. We taxied to a stop near a dilapidated airport building, sad with peeling paint and sagging window frames. Nearby waited the only person to meet the plane, an arat who had come with a spare horse to pick up his wife.

182

With the other passengers, we hid from the sun in a pagoda-type shelter until the "airport bus" arrived. The old army van packed us in two deep, and dropped us in Hujirt by the tourist camp and hotel. Both were quite deserted, even though it was the day for the plane.

So we brazenly camped in the neglected park opposite, setting up the tent on a thick bed of chamomile (and, we soon discovered, an ant-heap), brewed a gallon or so of tea, and went to bed for two days.

*

Tourist camp and hotel? But this is Mongolia's Visitor Centre, the only spot that tempts the casual tourist outside the metropolis. For Hujirt is the nearest airfield to the town of Harhorin, site of the country's two main historical attractions: Karakorum, sometime capital of the Mongol Empire, and Erdenezu Hiid, the Buddhist monastery later built from the stones of the deserted city.

There wasn't a lot to see in Hujirt itself. Until recently it had been a health resort almost exclusively used by the Russians, who had come here to take the waters from its hot springs or simply for holidays. With their departure it had become something of a ghost town, its buildings mostly empty and some only half-finished. A series of metal posters once depicting healthy-looking families and local wildlife were almost obliterated by rust. A beautifully ornate restaurant at the centre of the town imitated a Buddhist temple with its frilled eaves, elaborate paintwork and even the deer and wheel motif; but now stood locked, empty and crumbling, like so much around it. There was no housing shortage here - if you weren't too fussy about the general state of repair.

The sanatorium was still going strong, though, and now the Mongolians themselves got to use it. The state health service refers them to Hujirt to take the cure for various ailments, particularly heart complaints and arthritis. The process is simple: immersion in mud, concocted from the mineral waters and lovingly matured in a special hut over four months - or six, for the five-star treatment.

For outpatients like us, the only access to the famous water was a pipe, which poked from the bottom of a mysterious tall wooden tower behind the sanatorium and led down the hill to the hut. Both tower and hut were securely locked, but the pipe leaked generously. The water was invitingly warm. I tried a symbolic teaspoonful and spat it out at once: sulphurous and vile. Better out than in; I used it instead for a good hot scrub.

Back on the airport road, in a wide meadow under a craggy outcrop, we found some strange tombs. They were barrows, jumbles of collapsed stones around a burial chamber framed with large blocks, like the thousands along the western coasts and islands of Britain from the Scillies to the Hebrides. A wide circle of stones enclosed each one.

They seemed extraordinarily out of place in east Asia. When I got home I searched out their origin. They belonged, I found, to one of the oldest settled peoples of Asia: those of the Andronovo culture of the second millennium BC. Originating from much further west and racially Indo-European, they lived by raising horses and camels, tending their crops with stone hoes and copper sickles.

They were one of the few sedentary societies in Mongolian history. A thousand years later, these north-eastern steppes were home to the Hsiung-Nu, fierce nomadic horsemen who for centuries terrorised the settled lands of China. At the peak of their powers, in the third century BC, the Hsiung-Nu held sway from Manchuria to the Pamirs. A similar people to the Scythians, they were indistinguishable from the latter in many respects: their culture, lifestyle, burials, battle tactics - also the grisly habit of using their defeated enemies' skulls, gold or silver plated, as drinking cups, an art which the Mongolians preserved into our own century.*

Eventually the building of the Great Wall checked the incursions of the Hsiung-Nu, if not their ill intentions. They continued to be a thorn in China's side until finally crushed in 52 BC, and broken into smaller groups. One of these drifted west into Central Asia, and may be

*Not just the Mongolians. In a letter to the Daily Telegraph, Frank R. Long describes how "Col. Maurice Willoughby used to recall meeting one of Kitchener's officers in 1941. This chap, name of Wingate, had been responsible for tracking down the Khalifa, the Mahdi's nephew. When Willoughby met Wingate, this officer proudly produced a gold mounted skull from his desk. To Willoughby's horror, he declared cheerfully that this was what was left of the Khalifa. 'Every year, on the anniversary of Ondurman,' he said, 'I always drink a bottle of Veuve Cliquot out of this thing!' "

184

reasonably identified with the Huns who, four hundred years later, exploded upon Europe as viciously as their ancestors had so often overwhelmed the Chinese.

Heirs to them in geography and a similar European destiny were a people from the Altai whom the Chinese historians called the T'u Chueh. This is the first appearance in the history books of the Turks, who in the mid-sixth century AD spread across the whole of Central Asia, parts of Siberia and - after a thousand-year odyssey - right into central Europe.

In Mongolia, the Altai Turks were succeeded in their turn by a branch of their descendants, the Uighurs. These laid aside the violence of their steppe heritage to rule with a gentle hand, under the new and unlikely influence of Manichaeism, an early Persian religion. "This land of barbarous customs," they said of themselves, "smoking with blood, was transformed into a vegetarian state, and this land of slaughter became a land devoted to good works." They were the type of nomads whom the Chinese would have described as "cooked" - that is, near to China and comparatively civilised.

"Uncooked", on the other hand, were the Khitans*, who in the tenth century erupted out of the steppes to conquer China and Mongolia and, becoming settled in their turn, founded a new Chinese Imperial dynasty. They ruled both countries firmly; but the Jurchens of the Chin dynasty who ousted them had little interest outside their Chinese dominions. Until Genghis Khan burst on the scene, Mongolia broke up again into a miscellaneous collection of small tribes.

The blood of all of these peoples must have been in the shepherd who now rounded the hillside with some hundred sheep and goats. As the sun went down behind the hill, he dismounted and leaned on his saddle, while his animals browsed among the tombs of his ancestors. Just so must they have stood in their turn, leaning on their own saddles and watching their own herds, simple people getting on with their quiet lives while the tides of history parted and flowed around them.

*

*the same people as the Kara Kitai of Genghis Khan's time

Ten-thirty meant, of course, Mongolian Time. After one hour sitting on our bags and twiddling our thumbs, and another desperately casting around for other transport, we were so grateful when our jeep actually turned up that we forgot to be cross.

It took us on the Harhorin road as far as the village of Shankh, where a small renaissant monastery lies at the top of a hill above a cluster of wooden houses, looking across the valley to a low mountain ridge. We climbed off the laps of our fellow-passengers and stood in the open space below the monastery gates, watching the jeep bump off over the ruts to rejoin the main road. After its brief intrusion, silence descended like a blanket. The streets were empty.

Up at the monastery, though, life stirred. A few townspeople came and went, seeming to pass freely in and out. The heavy oak doors under the ceremonial archway were firmly barred, so we peered tentatively through a side gate. Getting an encouraging smile from someone inside, we drew a deep breath and entered.

Three temples stood in a row. The largest, in the centre, was stripped to bare ribs of wood for rebuilding. A low hum coming from the right-hand one indicated a service in progress. So we went left, past a big ger, to the third, and smallest. A young monk beckoned us to enter.

At first we thought this to be sleeping quarters. Rows of bed-sized benches filled the hall, placed end to end and laid with mats. Hangings and fringes covered the walls, and a painted wooden horse's head in a corner carried votive offerings of twists of cloth, with banknotes pushed into the mouth. We added our own donation. It seemed to be an Open Sesame; for the young monk instantly opened a pair of doors at the far end of the room, and led us into an inner sanctuary.

The narrow back room was windowless. As our eyes adjusted to the light, we slowly began to make things out.

Wonderful things. It was a Tutankhamun's tomb crammed with treasures of religious art; some sparkling richly, some faded and cobwebbed. Golden statues stood on the altar, beside a figure of the last Bogd Khan. Butter candles surrounded them, with incense and handfuls of wheat placed as symbolic gifts. A huge pair of brass cymbals leant at the front. To either side of the altar were wooden chests, gilded and carved, with more statuettes, and a photograph of the Dalai Lama displayed prominently. Gilded wooden tablets carried Tibetan inscriptions. Silken paintings covered the walls and drooped from the ceilings; hangings embroidered with prayers, or tankas depicting Buddha figures and devils.

And this was just a tiny monastery in a tiny town.

They say that only 5% of Shankh's treasures survived the purges; most were carried off to distant - mostly Soviet - museums, or destroyed. The local faithful saved what they could, spiriting away pieces of priceless history and religious artefacts to the safety of caves or holes under floorboards and entrusting the secrets of their whereabouts to succeeding generations. Five monks maintained the sanctity of the site, quietly reciting the litany behind closed doors. When Shankh Hiid officially reopened, its temples quickly filled with its former possessions. The local devotees had done their work well, and now joyfully brought it to completion.

Afraid to disturb the service, we sat discreetly on the steps of the other temple to listen. To the monks and townspeople continuously passing in and out, we stuck out like sore thumbs. Word soon got round that a couple of oddballs had arrived, and the local children came in hordes to look us over. Soon we were causing more disruption outside than in, so cautiously asked if we might enter.

Inside, this temple was more elegant than the first; more carefully cherished, as befitted the active place of worship. Fresher paintwork, enriched with scrolled or geometric patterns, and flowers covering the ceiling; a stand with three peacock headdresses; and, over all, a central, many-layered circular fringe, a chandelier crafted in silk and illuminated by the brilliance of its fabric.

Now we understood that the benches were not for sleeping but served as pews, the monks sitting cross-legged on them while they intoned the litany. The lamas themselves were either very old - at least one over eighty - or very young, with nothing in between. One ancient was on crutches, his heavy gutuls making no concessions to his disability.

Distribution of airag accompanied the devotions. Two finely-dressed ladies acted as servers to the lay worshippers. One motioned us to a seat by the door and handed us a huge wooden bowl filled to the brim from a central vat; we quickly shared it before a second could follow. A few moments later the vat was replenished from a great tin drum which had just arrived at the gate by truck. Airag splashed everywhere, and lay undisturbed in puddles on the floor.

As the service continued we were led deeper into the temple, passing clockwise behind the chanting monks into the inner sanctum. Here, besides the wide variety of artefacts we had seen before, were the most priceless possessions: four great prayer horns inlaid with silver, and a pile of boxes for prayer scrolls wrapped in silk. Returning, we were presented to the head lama, a venerable figure of many years and little hair, seated in cathedra amid the congregation. We made our offering of some money and a blue silk khadag, which he formally accepted; then gave us a blessing, tapping us each on the forehead with a tiny bronze statuette. Soon afterwards the offices were over for the day, and the monks departed to their homes in the village, the senior ones splendid in their ceremonial hats.

It was while we were leisurely debating where to set up camp that Carol made the awful discovery. Her camera was gone.

Instantly all the sense of peace and serenity, which had gradually enfolded us during the service, was shattered. Our surroundings seemed ugly and threatening. The monastery gate was now locked against us; we persuaded its keeper to let us back in, and searched the grounds in the vain hope that Carol might have dropped the camera accidentally. No luck. There was no doubt that it had been neatly lifted from her bag while we sat inside the temple.

We had by now attracted a small group of sympathisers, the more persistent core of a larger crowd who had come to gawp at Carol's misfortune and then, bored, drifted away. They included a young lama and Tserenkhand, a lady from the house at the bottom of the hill, who had very hospitably come to bring us a batong of water. Both were distressed at the theft, and with their help we circulated the news as widely as possible; then pitched our tent slap outside the monastery gate, the most conspicuous place in the village. Perhaps the sight of us there, a constant reminder of the crime that had desecrated the temple, might crack the thief's nerve. After that there was nothing more we could do but cook a gloomy meal and eat it in silence.

Our depression contrasted sharply with the glorious evening. The grassland sloped gently down to Tserenkhand's house, beyond which animals grazed about the river. The soft green outline of the far mountains glowed vibrantly with the last of the sun, now setting behind the monastery. I was abysmally unreceptive as I sat on the hillside, trying to clear my mind of the oppressive sense of unpleasantness.

And now the young monk was back, bearing a purposeful air in his gentle brown eyes - and a promising bulge in his del. With triumph he reached inside and pulled out the camera. A small child, he explained, had pinched it for a lark. I yelled for Carol, who burst out of the tent to give him a decidedly un-monastic kiss. The last few shots on the film had been finished. At least, unlike our French pal, Carol was ready for the unexpected when the prints came back from the lab.

We went and told Tserenkhand the good news, then brewed a celebratory cup of tea and sat enjoying the evening for real. The sunset had deepened for our benefit, edging the mountains with bronze, and there was a timeless quality in the to-and-fro of the village preparing for night. Herds of sheep and cattle were coming in, children played a last game before bedtime, the odd villager passed with a batong on the way to the spring for water. It took little imagination to picture Genghis Khan's squadrons riding out from Karakorum along the valley, yak's-tail banners before and clouds of dust behind, with the dull thud of unshod hooves and the clatter of bits and stirrups, on their way to conquer distant lands.

*

At ten the next morning we were woken by a sound like a rather melodious factory siren. Sticking our heads cautiously between the tent flaps, we saw two lamas perched on a high platform, blowing conch

189

shells to summon the monks to prayer. Soon young and old were streaming in from all directions, and before we had packed up to leave the first service was under way.

We had heard in Hujirt that it was possible to hire horses in Shankh, and had arrived with high expectations of continuing our journey on the hoof. But the best four-legged offer we could find was a yak cart. With polite excuses we made for the main road to grab the first set of wheels that came along. It was half a mile away, half a mile that seemed to go on for ever. Fortunately it was mostly downhill; my little trolley earned its keep many times over, bouncing merrily over the ruts and making its own way much of the time. Soon we were overtaken by Tserenkhand and her young son, who took a bag from each of us to hurry things along a bit.

At the junction we said our goodbyes and settled down in the grass under a hot sun. A long time passed, and still the only sounds and signs of life came from the ever-active crickets. At last we resigned ourselves to a lengthy wait, putting up the tent flysheet for shade and preparing a second breakfast. It worked like a charm. Literally as we put the spoons to our mouths no fewer than four vehicles appeared over the skyline.

Just as well, for the first three were full. But the fourth - coming, just to spite us, through the centre of the village and right past our overnight campsite - had space. It was a truck (how we groaned inwardly at the prospect of another Mongolian truck) with even fewer springs than the Bouncing Bomb and going at double the speed, which made the rest of the muesli rather fun. At least it was only a dozen miles; almost before we had spluttered on the last mouthful we were at Harhorin.

We had had enough of the tent for now. When we spotted a block of gers, laid out in regular rows like a Boy Scout Camp as at Hujirt, we smelt soft living for tourists and made a beeline for it. A fussy little man, in western clothing incongruously topped by a Mongolian pointed hat, showed us to a ger. He brought us hot water and - indescribable luxury! - filled and lit the stove, all the while pointedly listing a number of extra services by which he could relieve us of further cash. For three dollars, for example, we might receive a tour of his own ger, an extravagance we managed to resist.

But we found a transaction rather more to our liking when we discovered that he owned a couple of horses. Yes, he would hire them to us the next day. He took us to see them, and their good condition and virtual absence of saddle galls were above all expectations. It was a marvellous find, for the nearby ruins of Karakorum are vast, and I hadn't a prayer of getting round them properly on foot.

For the rest of the day we lazed, did our washing, lazed, drank copious tea and lazed some more. I boiled my socks in a tin bucket on the stove and got them clean for the first time in weeks. There were just two slight glitches: supper, promised, hot, for seven arrived, cold, at five; luckily we were going nowhere that day, and were there to eat it. And Pointy Hat decided he wanted to keep an eye on his horses, and "had arranged" a third so that he could come with us. It was, we reckoned at the time, understandable; but in retrospect represented the first symptoms of changing his mind.

Day two, and things were definitely going downhill. For a start, there wasn't any breakfast. We weren't pleased, as we had actually done the unthinkable and set an alarm clock to be ready for it. Next, there were no horses. We still weren't pleased, if not yet worried; after all, didn't ten-thirty Mongolian Time mean around mid-day? At twelve, Pointy Hat came to cheer us up: horse number one (his transport to work) had arrived, and numbers two and three were on their way. At one, it began to rain. Naturally, said Pointy Hat, this was why we still hadn't started.

We gave it until four, by which time the rain had stopped and the sun had been streaming down for an hour. Pointy Hat had prudently vanished. He had taken horse number one with him. It was Shanks's Pony or nothing.

*

The wall, a quarter-mile long, seemed to fill the plain. Stupas placed at intervals gave it a castellated effect; their whitewashed surfaces, wet with the recent rain, threw back the sun so fiercely that you couldn't look directly at them. In the centre stood a monumental gateway, dwarfing the two ponies tethered beneath.

191

Erdenezu Hiid, Mongolia's leading monastery, was built with devoted care from the stones of old Karakorum in 1586, and largely destroyed with malice and dynamite in 1938. The great square of its walls once held, by varying accounts, between seventy and a hundred temples, and housed a thousand monks. Today it is an echoing void, scattered with debris and broken stones, in which just a few temples were permitted to remain as museums. But life is beginning to creep back to the void, and the echoes of liturgical chant are driving out those of the screaming kites.

Too late now for Karakorum's ruins, we had opted today for the monastery. We entered through a little slot in one of the massive doors, to find ourselves in a windswept, grassy field. No need to hesitate here, for the tourist is a familiar visitor, pays an entrance fee - and even hires a guide. So did we, for without her we couldn't have seen the three locked temples in a little compound on the west side.

A monk preceded us into each of these, pausing in the doorway to strike a gong. Its brassy throb reverberated for a long moment, clothing the occasion in suitable gravity. As we followed him in he prayed silently; before we left, after admiring the holy relics, he led us clockwise round the prayer corridor, a narrow passage running right round each temple within its double wall.

In the single temple of the other remaining compound a service was in progress. We took a glimpse inside, but the furnishing was richer and the proceedings more formal than at Shankh, so we listened from behind the door. Here the beating of drums and the occasional dramatic clash of cymbals punctuated the low rhythmical chant of the lamas, and from time to time grains of corn were sprinkled on the floor. Lay servers sold incense in long twists of paper, while others dispensed airag. The two smells mingled pungently.

A brazier in the compound burned juniper, giving off yet another scent. A line of prayer wheels nearby squeaked and rattled sporadically, as people walked up and down the row to turn them and send unspoken prayers heavenwards. On the steps beside them sat an old man, his head bowed over a wooden bowl of airag in silent and drowsy contemplation.

The resurgence of faith since the removal of the Communist veto would have astonished many earlier observers, not least Montague. "To the young Mongolian," he wrote in 1956, "Lamaism has... become something absurd... of which it is hard to remember that in it their parents, and even some of their own number, once believed."

Buddhism, for all the grip it once exerted here, took a long time to establish itself in Mongolia. It was two millennia after Siddhartha first preached in India before his teaching became firmly rooted in the steppes.

Though Buddhists, like Nestorian Christians and Jews, had been around for some time by then. Genghis Khan's grandson Kubilai, who moved the seat of empire from Karakorum to Peking, adopted it as part of his fascination with Chinese culture, enhancing its prestige by appointing the Tibetan lama Phags-pa as "Imperial Preceptor". Ironically a secret Buddhist society, the White Lotus, helped to foment the revolt that toppled his dynasty a century later.

It was the sixteenth century ruler Altan Khan who enforced Tibetan Buddhism as Mongolia's state religion. His enthusiasm was no doubt fired by the discovery of a happy coincidence: that not only was his chief lama, Sonam Gyatsu, the reincarnation of Phags-pa - a healthy leg-up to the career of Sonam, who was to become the third Dalai Lama - but also that Altan himself was the reincarnation of Kubilai.

But Buddhism, embraced at first with a fervour that blew through Mongolia like a gale, gradually settled over the land like a heavy blanket of fog. From its very beginnings, it was diluted by the persisting undercurrent of shamanism, which had been suppressed by decree and sent spiritually underground. Shamanistic practices crept into the forms of worship; shamanistic gods or devils were "converted" and absorbed into the Mongolian pantheon. By degrees, Mongolian Buddhism became degenerate - and dragged the people down with it.

As the establishment of monasteries attracted local settlement, the old tribal society based on universal nomadism began to break apart. A feudal system grew up, based on grazing rights controlled by an increasing number of petty khans, or by the lamaseries themselves. More and more young men forsook the saddle for the cloth. They learned how to pray in Tibetan, and forgot how to make war. Before long Mongolia fell once again into the hands of the Chinese Emperors, this time the Ch'ing dynasty from Manchuria. The Manchus quickly recognised the sedative effect of the lamas on the once-warlike Mongols. "Where (the early khans) brought in hundreds, it was left to the Manchu victors to bring in thousands - rigidly excluding Lamaism from their own home territory of Manchuria," commented Montague. And the Manchus didn't hesitate to manipulate the system. More than one Khutuktu was bumped off for failing to toe the Chinese line on Lamaism - and its political applications.

"Lamaism" - the word smacks of Papism, the derogatory term once used by Protestants to describe Catholicism, full of the hatred engendered by fear and suspicion; conveying contempt by replacing the object of worship by its medium. It is a word that crops up over and over again in the writings of travellers of a hundred years ago, who found a world where a third or maybe even a half of the male population was either a lama or a *shabinari* - monastery serf; where the lamaseries exacted enormous taxes from the remainder of the population; where lamas openly flouted the rule of celibacy to consort freely with their own (or other people's) wives, and contributed freely to the raging spread of syphilis throughout the land; where all knowledge - legal, medical, educational or social - came from the pages of the sacred encyclopaedias, the *Kangur* and *Tangur* of fifth century Tibet. When the Revolution swept away the Old Order, the writing was on the wall.

Not that the new government needed such specific charges to bring against the church. It was already, according to the Communist manifesto, doubly damned. Firstly, because religion in any form was anathema. Secondly, in a country without a natural proletariat and with only a few ruling nobles, Marxist-Leninism found itself rather disorientated, for it was lamentably short of *bourgeoisie* or other natural targets. The church, which had long drawn its Khutuktus and High Lamas from the elite families, embodied and exemplified the feudal tradition. It was pretty well the only candidate for the hit list. Nothing, therefore, could save it.

But Choibalsan had a fight on his hands. Initial moves to close the monasteries met with a huge popular backlash that almost derailed the Revolution, and had to be replaced by more subtle measures. Church privileges were curbed, the shabinari system abolished. Lamas were offered rewards for returning to secular life, while those who remained found their tax bill rising. They drifted away in large numbers. But the loss of the uncommitted only left the church leaner and fitter. It began to get its act together, and introduce long overdue reforms from within. Soon it posed more of a threat than ever.

Now the pressure was building on both sides. The violent Soviet campaign against religion from 1929 onwards found, as ever, its echo in Mongolia; while some among the lamas thought it was their turn to take the initiative by instigating revolt.

They had no chance of success, and only hastened their own destruction. A rebellion centred on Bandid Gegen monastery in Hovsgol was put down with terrible atrocities. After this further plots, or fabrications of supposed plots, gave Choibalsan the excuse to send in the cavalry. The ensuing scene resembled, far exceeded, that of Reformation England. Monasteries were destroyed wholesale; lamas thrown on the streets, put to forced labour in concentration camps or simply massacred; head lamas summarily executed. By 1939 the job was done, with only a handful of lamaseries preserved as living museums, and held up to ridicule as caricatures of superstition. The Soviet moguls pointed approvingly to Mongolia as a text-book example of how to deal with "the problem of religion".

*

They would have gnashed their teeth to see the problem of religion reasserting itself today. The service over, scores of worshippers streamed out from Erdenezu Hiid on their way back to Harhorin. Tens of monks were among them, early shoots of a tree pruned back to its roots to endure a long hard winter, but now bursting with spring growth and the promise of a fertile summer.

We followed them, hoping for fleshpots or at least food. But we found neither. The few dingy shops were long closed; while the hotel, at the far end of a long street between vile, crumbling factories, had no functioning restaurant. In fact it lacked any attractions, inside or out. Huge puddles filled the undulating mud of the square alongside. Nearby the bracing statue of a tractor flanked by wheatsheaves, braying the virtues of work and plenty while disintegrating with rust, failed dismally to inspire us.

Worse, a vicious thunderstorm was brewing over the mountains beyond the Orhon River. For some time we had pessimistically watched the clouds gather and swell, and as we emerged still hungry from the hotel the first drops of rain, carried ahead of the storm by a freshening wind, were beginning to hit us with the force of lead pellets.

Searching desperately for transport, we commandeered a petrol tanker as a taxi home for the outrageous sum of three dollars. We were just in time. As we stumbled into the ger, lightning tore the sky, and rain began to descend in bucketfuls.

But there were no luxuries for us tonight. Pointy Hat had a new guest to impress, a sleek Israeli travel-agent who was a better bet for baksheesh than a couple of raggle-taggle gypsies. So there was no supper, no fire to cook our own, no heat to dry the rest of the washing.

At least we got breakfast next morning; only to find that it wasn't, as Pointy Hat had told us, included in the price we had already paid him for bed and board. His treachery pained the chef, a splendidly bosomed Mrs. Beeton figure in a tall white hat. With an air of tragedy, she declared that the restaurant business was her own, separate from that of the ger camp, and that Pointy Hat had injured her personally.

Making ourselves promises to deal with him later - if the cook didn't get to him first - we followed her back to her HQ to settle up. We arrived to find the manager with her, and were baffled when she refused our money with some embarrassment. The manager seemed surprised as well. When we explained why we thought ourselves in debt to her, the truth came out. The manager ran and financed the whole show, gers, restaurant and all, and was most interested to hear about Pointy Hat and the chef's extra-curricular tariff. As he listened, Mrs. Beeton seemed to shrink a good six inches, and her bosom to deflate slightly like a punctured tyre; while the manager gained a corresponding six inches and began to change colour. Over his rising shoulder, we could just see Pointy Hat swanning into work at eleven, unaware of the gathering stormclouds.

We left them to enjoy their domestic spat, and prepared to travel back seven centuries.

*

Karakorum - for thus the mediaeval monks rendered Harhorin with its guttural h's - is popularly called Genghis Khan's capital. But he was little more than a link in a chain, the temporary occupant of a place which had intermittently been the centre of gravity of other empires and which was to become great again only briefly, and that after his death.

Here, where the Orhon River divides the sharp escarpments of the Hangai Mountains from fertile grassy plains, a convergence of natural routes and an abundance of good grazing made for an obvious centre of rule. The Altai Turks thought so, making their settlements here and burying their dead in family necropolises whose stone stelae recorded their life and times. The Uighur Turks who deposed them governed their vast empire from Karabalgaun in the Orhon valley. They were at Karakorum, too, leaving behind them a number of stone tortoises which the Mongols were later to recycle. Genghis Khan's ally-turned-enemy Toghrul, according to the *Secret History*, had his main camp hereabouts. Genghis himself made Karakorum his headquarters, and it was from here that he set off to conquer Turkestan.

During his lifetime it was no more than a mustering-place, a tent city; it was left to others to build something enduring. But there can be no doubt that Genghis conceived the ideas that his successors were to realise. Although his primary impulse towards the great cities of Khoresmia was to destroy them, he cannot have failed to be impressed by, secretly to envy perhaps, the objects of his devouring fury. It was no coincidence that those few who survived the slaughter were artisans, craftsmen, builders; Genghis had plans for them. Not for him the second-hand, plundered cities of collapsed empires. It was proper that the ruler of all the world should have his own capital, grander than any other, in his own country.

But this one ambition failed. He died before his city had progressed from his imagination into stone and brick. It was Ogodai, his third son and heir as *Khakhan* - Khan of Khans - who in 1235 walled Karakorum, made it his administrative centre and built the first imperial palace. He seems to have done little else there but drink; on his death in 1241 there were whispers of "poison", but if so it was certainly of the alcoholic sort.

By the time William of Rubruck reached Karakorum a few years later, it was a thriving city. Even now, though, thriving more in its cosmopolitan population than its works of architecture. The two main streets carried most of the permanent structures, while the corners - as in UB today - were filled with ger camps. Moslems, Buddhists, Nestorian Christians and Chinese traders mingled with Mongolians, together with captive Russians, Georgians, Armenians and Hungarians; churches, mosques and temples had sprung up among government buildings and palaces. Möngke had spurned Ogodai's palace for something of grander style, built in a large compound by the city walls and surrounded by storehouses for supplies and treasure. William describes it with awe:

"The palace resembles a church, with a middle nave and two sides beyond two rows of pillars and three doors on the south side. The tree stands inside, opposite the middle door, and the Khan sits at the north end in an elevated position so that he is visible to all. There are two stairways leading up to him, and the man who brings him his cup goes up the one and comes down the other. The space in the middle, between the tree and the stairways that give access to him, is clear; there stands the cup-bearer, and also envoys bringing gifts, while he sits up above like some god. To the right, namely on the west side, are the men, to the left the women; for the palace extends from north to south. Near the pillars on the right there are raised pens rather like a balcony, where his son and his brothers are seated; and there is a corresponding arrangement on the left, occupied by his wives and daughters. Only one wife is seated up there by his side, though not at such a high level as he is himself..."

Obviously, Möngke revelled in the trappings and outward show of power; yet the arrangements and orientation of his palace were essentially those of his simple steppe forefathers. The "tree", though, was something else. Although William's description punctiliously avoids comment, across the space of seven centuries you can almost sense his lip curl.

It was, he reports, a glorified bar in the form of a silver fountain, its four branches standing on four silver lions and twined with gilded serpents, dispensing respectively wine, refined airag, mead and rice ale. At the top an angel cavorted like a Christmas tree fairy; the sound of its trumpet, blown at a signal from the butler by a man hidden inside, was the cue for stewards to pour drink into the various conduits. Möngke apparently intended to go the way of his uncle Ogodai. Certainly William, to his despair, rarely found him sober.

Three years after William's visit, Möngke transferred his capital to Shangtu, on the other side of the Great Wall. His brother and successor Kubilai, admirer of all things Chinese, settled in Peking. Although Kubilai now went native in many respects - including founding a new Chinese dynasty, the Yüan, after the best traditions of conquering steppe nomads - he stuck to his Mongolian roots on the subject of drink. It wasn't just to remind him of home that he pastured a herd of ten thousand white mares on the parkland surrounding his summer palace. Chinese tea would have offered little to tempt the robust palate of a Mongol.*

But Kubilai had no more time for Karakorum, which now went rapidly downhill. The Mongols remaining there must have been thankful to abandon their unaccustomed city life, probably enforced, and drift back to wandering the steppe. By the time Marco Polo visited in the 1280s, he found a city of mainly timber and earth. Sacked by the Ming Chinese in the following century, Karakorum effectively ceased to exist. An archaeological expedition in 1946 found triple walls, a moat nearly six feet deep and four gates; otherwise, the city yielded little more than a few glazed tiles. The sites of the Khan's palaces were never found.

*Something forgotten by those who accuse Marco Polo of inventing his stories of Kubilai's court - because he doesn't mention tea!

Perhaps there isn't much to find. Karakorum was the centre of the Mongol empire for barely sixty years, passing swiftly thereafter into nonentity. So there isn't the usual situation of layer within layer, like an onion, as at, for example, Troy or Jericho. Sixty years is a short time in the history of man, little enough to build up an accumulation of lost coins, discarded artefacts or other debris of human occupation. But surely there must be further secrets for the soil to give up to the archaeologist; and it is astonishing that there has been so little excavation here.

Nevertheless, there was more to Karakorum than timber, earth, gers and a few palaces. Even though its stone was looted to build Erdenezu Hiid, the plains around remain littered with worked granite. On our limited, two-legged exploration (earlier, in Harhorin, I had spotted two boys riding ponies; I had waved one hand full of dollars and the other of tugrigs under their noses for the use of their horses for a couple of hours, but they just exchanged jittery glances and fled) we found recognisable masonry; here the base of a column, there a huge cistern hollowed out of solid rock. Not far from the monastery walls we came on the prize exhibit: a Uighur tortoise, one of four which guarded the gates of the city. Of the other three, one is said to be far out on the plain, one high up in the surrounding hills and one - turned turtle, perhaps - at the bottom of the Orhon.

This one turned its face towards the Hangai mountains. Though blackened by the prevailing winds, it still clearly showed flaring nostrils, snapping teeth and fiercely narrowed eyes, with never a wrinkle after thirteen hundred years; stones heaped on its flat back turned it into a symbolic obo, changing its menace to something more friendly. Otherwise we might not have dared to perch on its neck for tourist snapshots.

Hard to imagine this desert place as the centre of the world's largest empire. Yet as we sat, backs to Harhorin and faces to the steppe, straining our imagination and listening for ghosts, we gradually discovered that it was not, after all, quite deserted. Far from it. It was still a thriving city.

Holes pock-marked the grass, holes linked by a network of arrow-straight paths, well-marked as if the locals had a hectic social life.

When we sat very still, we realised that we were the latest subject for gossip. Cautiously a perfect circle of tiny heads emerged, at a radius of about ten yards. They regarded us fixedly, ready to bolt if we twitched a muscle.

They were hamsters. Siberian hamsters, little bigger than a mouse. Thousands of them. Strange to think of the stones under which they burrowed, of the potsherds and other oddments, the detritus of empires, which must lie in and around their homes. Perhaps their living rooms were carelessly furnished with Khoresmian coin, fragments of Chinese jade, lapis lazuli mined from deep underneath the Hindu Kush.

They were an eloquent comment on Karakorum's decline and fall: a city once the preserve of the most feared, the most terror-inspiring people on earth, perhaps long haunted by its shades, now populated entirely by hamsters. Sic transit gloria mundi.

*

Why did the Mongol Empire last such a short time? The question is often asked. But it is an unfair question, for the Empire lasted, in various forms, remarkably long.

That it didn't survive the century as a complete entity was surely due to its vast extent. When Genghis Khan, like Lear, divided his lands among his heirs, he must have foreseen the difficulties attendant on long-term continuing cohesion. Yet, although the Khanates thus created were immediately autonomous, cohere they did, giving their allegiance to each successive Great Khan as head of the family.* Despite occasional squabbles over this succession, the Empire remained unified for two more generations. Kubilai Khan's permanent defection to China, leaving a political and psychological vacuum in Mongolia itself, was perhaps the death-blow.

Yet Kubilai - son of Genghis' fourth son Tolui - was a true Mongol in his grandfather's image, for he had his own ambitions for extending the Empire. Having subjugated Korea, he used its navy to send an expedition against Java; and another - disastrously unsuccessful - to Japan. The

*see the Genealogical Tree on page 238

201

dynasty he founded, the Yüan, was to last another century before being toppled by the Ming Chinese in 1368.

His brother's line was shorter lived, but typically Mongol in its ferocity. Hulagu had been sent to destroy the Assassins, the fanatical Moslem sect of northern Persia. Having summarily dealt with them he continued west to sack Baghdad, where he claimed two hundred thousand victims; the Caliph, last of a long line, was trampled to death under a carpet, the inventive method of execution traditionally reserved by the Mongols for those of high birth. Hulagu now pressed on into Syria, where the terrified Crusaders found themselves pinned between the devil they knew and the devil they didn't. They flirted with the Mongols for an alliance against their old enemy, the Egyptian Sultan; then, recognising their Faustian pact, switched sides to the Sultan. The Egyptians soundly defeated Hulagu's generals in 1260, thus finally cracking the myth of Mongol invincibility. Hulagu retired to Persia, where he ceased to destroy and began learning to build. His heirs, the so-called Ilkhans of Persia, embraced Islam and ruled until 1335.

Truest to their roots were the Mongols of the Khanate of Chagatai, Genghis' second son. Holding the lands roughly corresponding to western Turkestan, they ruled their captive cities from their felt tents on the steppe. From their line came another great empire, that of the Turko-Mongol Timur-i-Lenk*, who claimed descent from Genghis Khan. As well as sharing his blood, Timur shared the precarious path to power of his illustrious ancestor, progressing through penury and captivity to warlord and finally conqueror of lands stretching to the Mediterranean. His descendants drowned in a bloodbath of patricide, fratricide and indiscriminate homicide; the last survivor, Babur, fled to India, where he founded the Moghul Empire.**

Perhaps the most influential on western civilisation were the Mongols of the Golden Horde (*Altan Orda*, or Golden - Royal - Clan), heirs through Genghis' eldest son Jochi to the lands north-west of the Caspian Sea. Having taken Kiev, ancient capital of the Rus, their Khan Batu swept west into central Europe in 1241, wasting large parts of Romania, Poland and Hungary - and threatening the Baltic states so that

*Timur Leng, Timur the Lame, or Tamerlane
**Moghul, Mogul, Mo'gul are alternative transcriptions of Mongol

202

their seamen stayed at home, disrupting trade and producing the bizarre effect of depressing the English herring market. Only the death of Batu's uncle, the Great Khan Ogodai, saved Europe, drawing Batu - now approaching Vienna - hotfoot back to Mongolia with hopes for the succession, a far greater prize than a few miscellaneous countries on the far edge of his world. Indirectly, though, the Golden Horde was to initiate a greater holocaust than any they had inflicted by war. While besieging the Black Sea port of Kaffa in 1345 they were struck by an outbreak of bubonic plague. Ever loth to waste an opportunity, the Mongols lobbed diseased corpses into the town, whence refugees brought the Black Death to the West.

Not until 1502 did the Rus, from their new capital of Moscow, break free of Tatar rule, and it was a further half-century before Ivan the Terrible turned the tables and made them a subject people - a defeat still bitterly resented today by their descendants the Chechens.

Not such a short-lived empire, then; more than three centuries before the Mongols were finally broken. And - if Timur truly knew his fathers - not until the British deposed the last Moghul Emperor in 1857 did the line of Genghis Khan cease to rule.

*

The best, in fact the only, amenity of the Harhorin hotel was its ample windowsill, on which we cooked supper while thunder and lightning crashed and crackled outside.

After a bit the storm huffed and puffed and blew itself out. We still hadn't seen the Orhon, the river which through its ample water supply and the easy passage of its valley had spawned so much history here. Armed with waterproofs, we set out to take a look at it.

The kindest thing that could be said about this end of Harhorin was that there wasn't much of it. Some Soviet boffin had designed a causeway for three roads meeting in a triangle, but had forgotten the drains, so that a cheerless swamp oozed slime into the centre. On the far side a shanty town, deprived of its natural drainage to the river, rotted greasily amid a wasteland of foetid puddles.

203

But the watermeadow beside the river was unspoiled. Turning our backs on Mongolia's ugliest town, we made our way through peacefully grazing yaks to where a string of willows marked the line of the river, hard up against the hills that were the outriders of the Hangai Nuruu.

The Orhon is prettier than most Mongolian rivers, but otherwise very ordinary. There is nothing to suggest its importance in earlier days. Yet seven or eight centuries ago these banks must have seethed with people, watering their animals and drawing supplies to satisfy the needs of six square miles of busy metropolis. Carefully; severe penalties awaited those who polluted running water - especially by washing in it.

Again, we stretched our minds to picture the *tumans* riding out to war: rank upon rank of swarthy riders in iron helmets and mail of boiled oxhide fastened with leather; bearing wicker shields, quivers with arrows and sharpening file, sometimes a hooked lance. Small, hairy horses jogging tirelessly under them, four or five remounts to each warrior following behind. In narrow file, surely, along the opposite stony bank, as thousands of hooves would have churned up the soft grass of the watermeadow in no time. Though perhaps the Mongols wouldn't have worried about such a minor inconvenience.

Thunder brought our minds abruptly back to the present. The sky over the mountains was viciously black, throwing flashes of lightning into sharp relief; and the gale which had suddenly sprung up was blowing the whole lot our way. Carol ran for home; while I, holding my coat out like a sail, was blown effortlessly along at high speed, getting back only a few minutes behind her and still relatively dry.

The next morning, ticketless but forewarned of the problems that might cause, we were at the bus before the bus itself. Early sun drenched Harhorin in forgiving yellow light, making it look almost friendly.

Head of the queue, we had no difficulty getting seats in a vehicle consisting of a bus-like body mounted on a truck base. We were lucky, for within an hour fifty people were crammed into the small interior, sitting on baggage stowed down the centre or standing precariously in the aisles thus created. Almost the last to get a seat was an elderly gentleman, an old arat in his best, though well-worn, clothing. A pity it happened to be his winter gear. The green del was of thick felt, sleeves hanging well over the hands for winter warmth and bound with red and gold braid. His pointed gutuls, gorgeously tooled and sewn, were thickly lined with cotton-covered, embroidered felt. It was clothing fit to keep out snow-laden winds at forty below, and at the same time to show that he was, or had been, a wealthy man. It was a hot day, and when he later yielded to the heat so far as to loosen the neck of his del, it fell open to show a woollen knitted sweater beneath. The outfit was finished by a herdsman's trilby, worn over a shaven head and a face deeply scored by surely eighty years. His bright, darting eyes picked up everything of interest, which he pointed out to the grandson travelling with him. We soon learned to watch him carefully, to follow his gaze or his gesturing finger.

A world away from the cursing, elbowing passengers on UB's buses, this human cargo sat quietly, or squeezed courteously closer to make room for others. Mothers soothed fretful children, or told them stories to pass the time. Put to such use, the Mongolian language sounded utterly different from that we had heard bellowed gutturally across the steppe: soft, sibilant, liberally punctuated with aspirates, each sentence fading gently into a sort of chattering whisper.

At last the bus started to move; but the first miles were agonisingly slow. Despite the new tarmac road presently being laid eastwards out of Harhorin, the driver clung from habit to the old tracks through the cornfields, horribly rutted and heavily puddled by all the recent rains. At least this truck was exceptionally well-sprung, and each time we hit a particularly bad bump the company performed a Mexican Wave, beginning with those sitting over the front wheels and rippling through to the back.

These cornfields were the most extensive we had seen anywhere. Watered by canals from the Orhon, they stretched several miles in all directions, and must be the country's main breadbasket. Now, in early August, the wheat was still green; it must be an annual race to get in the harvest in Mongolia's short summer. I thought of the wheatfields at home, which would by now be mostly yellow stubble.

It was progress at snail's-pace. An hour and a half out of Harhorin, when the truck circled to negotiate a herd of forty camels, we could look out sideways and see the squat, ugly town still visible under the mountains, still make out the gleaming white walls of Erdenezu Hiid. But at last a good asphalt road appeared, and we ate up the miles to UB through countryside in the familiar pattern of steppe edged and broken up by low mountains. In this hot weather herds of cattle and horses clustered thickly at water holes, standing up to their bellies in soothing mud or streams; while the gers showed their versatility, lifting their skirts cheekily to expose their latticed ankles to cooling breezes.

It was six by the time we finally made it back to the Altai, and Dr. Tserendeleg and all at MACNE had long since gone home.

X

MAGIC MOUNTAIN

Svenzhal and Gambaatar were cheerful and chatty lads, though Svenzhal frayed Carol's nerves with his tendency to approach a blind summit at seventy in the middle of the road. For myself, after the grinding, bone-rattling miles of truck travel I was content to sit back in the luxury of a car, watch the miles pass at unaccustomed speed and trust to Svenzhal's instincts of self-preservation.

Having contacted Dr. Tserendeleg and been given clearance for a return visit to Hustain Nuruu, we were leaving UB courtesy of the Toshiba Taxi Company. It was a dreamy, misty morning, with the sun diffusing through already yellowing leaves as in an English October, reminding us that already winter wasn't far away from Mongolia.

It was more than comfort which distracted me from Svenzhal's driving. For neither of the lads had heard of Hustain Nuruu, and I was navigating - in theory. Eyes bulging for familiar landmarks, I cursed the small window of the jeep I had travelled in before, and Baigal's pleasant but distracting conversation. Already I had almost made a major blunder, directing Svenzhal the wrong way at the first junction out of UB before some instinct made me ask him to turn round. A good job it was the only junction. There aren't many pluses driving in a country with less than seven hundred miles in total of surfaced roads; but lack of opportunities to get lost is one of them.

We had been travelling for nearly an hour and I was getting jumpy when I recognised the long cornfield stretching up the hill. Now all I had to do was watch for the left turn with its line of telegraph poles. We had already passed one such; had we overshot? Several more minutes, and I was just beginning to sweat when another row of poles appeared, this time leading to the familiar patch of dunes.

Svenzhal attacked the rough track like a rally driver, barely slowing even for the worst bits. We stopped at the obo in high good humour, and five minutes later were gratefully waving the two lads goodbye.

A frosty reception was waiting. Dr. Gala had made his once-daily radio contact with Dr. Tserendeleg only a few minutes before we had telephoned the latter, so he didn't know we were coming. Permission, we were made to understand, shouldn't have been given without first consulting him. Our names, it was clear, were mud. There was no-one to take our side. Jan was on leave, Lee had completed her research and gone home, Sukh was on holiday; only Hans was here, and we had spotted his back view disappearing over the hill on his pony as we arrived.

So we grovelled duly, explained that we had our own tent and provisions and would be no trouble, and took ourselves off to camp unobtrusively behind the gers. Just in time, for black clouds had chased us down the track. As we hustled the last of our gear under cover the first rain fell, shortly followed by vicious thunder and lightning and then fierce hail that drummed on the tent like gravel, severely and successfully testing its mettle.

By the time the sun was out and the tent beginning to steam Hans was back. He gave us a hearty welcome and then spoke music to my ears.

"If you like, you can borrow my horse."

I could have turned cartwheels. I was working up to the subject, but had decided to wait until after we had broached the bottle of arkhi.

Further conversation could wait. On a glorious evening we set out up the valley, Carol generously letting me take first turn with the chestnut pony. The first fence, Khaan's old enclosure, had new occupants, for the next consignment of mares had recently arrived from Holland. Alert and glossy-coated, they outshone their new husband, a small and rather poor specimen from Askania Nova chosen for his genes rather than his beauty.

From here we went our separate ways. Carol made for the ridge above the camp in the hope of finding Khaan and his mares; while I, freely mobile at last, turned the pony towards the hilltops which I had so yearned after on my first visit. The sturdy little chestnut willingly lent me his four strong legs, climbing northwards to where the long U of Hustain Nuruu mountain came to a sudden and spectacular end at a pair of granite outcrops overlooking the main valley.

Down below the gers had shrunk to white blobs, the takhi browsing in the enclosure to brown-pink dots merging into the earth and boulders. Above, the bare ridges of the mountain irregularly blossomed into pink tors. As I gained height the Tuul valley appeared to the south, with its backdrop of line upon line of mountains running into immeasurable distance. To the left, the sun was dropping towards the shoulder of the mountain. The four generously busy feet picked their way among daisies, dianthus, gentian and edelweiss; and released the heavy fragrance of bruised chamomile. Higher still came the true alpines: stonecrop, roseroot and many, many tiny flowers I couldn't name.

At the top I dismounted, slackened the girth and let my friend relax and graze. The shadow of the mountain reached the camp and crept slowly up the far wall of the valley, while the sunset turned the tor above my head from pink to brick-red. When this, too, began to fade, I climbed back into the saddle and headed for home, deeply content.

This was the freedom I had longed for: the chance to wander at will over a small part of this intriguing country, to savour its most intimate taste at leisure. This was the Mongolia which I had dreamed of, fantasised about. That my small experience of it should be here, in these incomparable surroundings, on this most lovely of evenings, and within reach of the first takhi to return to the wild, was more than I could have dared to hope for.

I was singing like a drunkard all the way back down the hill.

*

Carol hadn't found Khaan's mob. The next day we went searching in earnest, retracing the path which Lee had taken a month before, over the hill behind the camp.

No luck. We caught the clucking reproof of several wheatears and a few marmot wolf-whistles, but no sight or sound of the takhi. But the day wasn't wasted. We spent long, pleasant hours lazing on a low tor and watching the movement of the camp below - and following the antics of a family of hobbies, using the rocks as a launching-pad to try out new wings.

In the evening Carol set off down the main valley on Hans' pony, passing the salt-lick in the river bank and heading for Davadorj's gers and the Tuul valley. I took a look in the canyon of the lower side valley, thinking that the herd might have come down at evening for water. Still no joy. What rotten luck that there was no-one to ask for help but Hans, who was not personally working with the takhi and didn't know their movements as intimately as, say, Lee or Jan.

We each gave up our search and hurried back so as not to be late for supper. Up until now we had cooked our own food, and were looking forward to a change. But there wasn't any supper. Evidently we were still officially personae non gratae, for the cook said firmly that she hadn't enough food for us. It was Supernoodles again.

As we were forcing down the last of them Hans came over, bringing his own meal with him.

"Best off cooking your own." He shook his head in revulsion. "How can anyone eat this rubbish?"

It was meat dumplings, another variation on the theme of flour and minced mutton. Carol and I weren't too proud to eat his leavings, and appreciate them. We swapped them for strong black coffee and conversation. Interspersed with blues music - Hans was delighted to find a knowledgeable enthusiast in Carol - we discussed the takhi, their prospects for the coming winter, their future here.

It was generally accepted that the biggest threat to them in their first winter of freedom would come from the wolves. Mature horses were pretty well able to take care of themselves, but the youngstock, no longer secure behind electric fences, were a different matter. Immediately, one of the fundamental dilemmas of conservation had reared its head. Do you allow the Reserve to find its own balance, or do you control the predators of the species you consider its most important inhabitant? How far should you interfere, how far let nature take its course?

Patron's group had already had a trial run with the Hustain Nuruu wolves. The outcome raised jubilation all round. Their genetic programming undiluted by a century of soft living, the adult mares had encircled the foals in wagon train formation, while the stallion took the offensive against four attackers. One kick from Patron, and the show was over. So far, so good.

Hans, in any case, felt the wolf problem was exaggerated. "Livestock losses to wolves in Mongolia are reckoned to be under ½ %. OK, the supposed all-time USSR 'expert' came up with 2 - 7%; but that was at the other end of Siberia!"

Certainly, he believed, the locals, when asked what they thought of the situation, were piling on the agony a bit. "They love a good yarn. But how can you take people seriously, when they tell you that a kangaroo rat will steal a cow's milk by jumping up and down to get to her udder - or a badger will climb on an animal's back and lick dung from its rear end!" We were quite glad we'd already polished off the last of his dumplings.

No, he went on; the biggest threat to the future of the takhi was the old one, the threat that had been around for thousands of years and nearly eliminated them altogether: competition with domestic livestock, and particularly with other horses; that is, with Man. But, as we had already discovered, the Dutch Federation was already way ahead of that game.

The crucial question was: how would the local herdsmen react to such an ambitious project, one which would take over some of their traditional pasture, compete with their needs, interfere even with their own herds? Here, in and around Hustain Nuruu, the answer was: enthusiastically. Both sections of the population, the local arats and the townspeople of the nearest sum, Altan Bulag, were thrilled to have the takhi returned to Mongolia, and installed in their vicinity. *Their* takhi. For so they instinctively felt; and, through sensitive consultation and involvement, feel ever more strongly.

So the statue of a takh stands in Altan Bulag's main square. The locals compose songs about the horses, and demand news of the latest arrivals and foalings. The recent shipment from Holland was celebrated with racing and wrestling - and a lot of arkhi (and "Takhi" brand of beer) - at a party in the Tuul valley. And if there are problems the nearby herdsmen, far from being irritated or resentful, are only too generous with their help. Like the time when Dzun, a harem stallion newly arrived from Holland, burrowed under his fence like a tarbagan and made off to the northern borders of the Reserve. Despite the best efforts of Jan and Dr. Gala to find him, it was a couple of young arats who brought him home, as the Federation newsletter described.

"...there is Dzun only twenty-five metres away from the gers. Two young men on horseback dismount and tell us that they drove Dzun with their two geldings back to the Reserve. Dzun had visited their family... they immediately knew that it was the lost Przewalski stallion. The grandmother of the two men was so impressed by the takhi, that she waited until he excreted some dung to sacrifice it at the Lama altar in her ger..."

It's a fringe benefit, then, rather than a necessary carrot, that the Reserve provides employment for local people, and healthcare beyond its own boundaries; that the Federation has set up a cheese dairy in Altan Bulag to promote local business; that future plans for eco-tourism should generate further jobs. Schoolchildren eagerly look forward to their visits to Hustain Nuruu, while the few remaining herdsmen (most have willingly moved out to alternative pastures arranged by the mayor of Altan Bulag) keep geldings rather than stallions in their domestic herds, and look out for poachers - like the two who had just been jailed for hunting the red deer of the Reserve.

And so the takhi have truly come home. In Hustain Nuruu they will never be driven out, or hunted once more to extinction.

*

The Federation wasn't alone in bringing Przewalski horses back to Mongolia. Far to the south, another programme was under way.

The official Government Report on re-introduction of the takhi wasn't too sure about Hustain Nuruu as a suitable site. It preferred the

Jungarian Gobi region, on Mongolia's southern borders, the area on the edge of the Altai Mountains where the last wild populations existed. Hustain Nuruu, with its more severe winter conditions, was "not the best place to attempt the establishment of a free-ranging, self-sustaining population". Nevertheless, it recognised the quality and breadth of the MACNE/Federation schedule to integrate the needs of the Reserve with those of the local people.

But when an international sponsor group had come forward with a proposal to bring takhi back to Takhiin Tal in the Jungarian Gobi, it had seemed the perfect plan. Takhiin Tal, named for the takhi, the last place on earth that they existed without - rather, in spite of - man's intervention.

There were a lot of hard-headed reasons to back Takhiin Tal, besides romantic inclination. The Report groaned with favourable statistics about the Jungarian Gobi, the sort of statistics beloved by Soviet scientists, for whom the power of numbers was infinitely superior to gut feeling. Statistics on forage per hectare, temperature, water tables, average height above sea level, numbers of poisonous plants, parasite levels. Best of all, the low human population meant little competition, save with other wild animals, the animals - gazelles, Argali sheep, *kulan* (wild asses) - with which the takhi had historically and successfully cohabited.

Somehow, it didn't quite add up. If the forage and climate were so good, where were all the herdsmen? And did it really make sense to choose the spot where the horses had died out? Had they not finished up at Takhiin Tal because it was the very last place on earth that anybody else wanted? Surely, however ideal the Jungarian Gobi might be in general, it had better sites to offer.

Takhiin Tal wasn't a success. The first groups brought here fared poorly. Two of the horses had lost weight rapidly and died. The remainder were now reported to be in poor condition; there were fears that they wouldn't survive the coming winter. And this while they were still penned and supervised. Their ultimate release was looking more and more of a pipedream.

What, specifically, went wrong? Did they find poisonous plants? Did they perhaps bring with them parasites or infections which lowered their resistance? They came from Askania Nova, where the bugs are bad; post-mortems on the dead horses confirmed a high level of parasites. Lack of genetic variation, the perpetual spectre haunting Przewalski breeders (and particularly so at Askania Nova, so long isolated within the USSR), may have made them degenerate.

The questions have to be asked. If there are solutions, Takhiin Tal may yet be made viable. But, for all its enthusiasm for the Jungarian Gobi, the Report was pessimistic. "It is highly unlikely," it reluctantly admitted, "that takhi will ever be released from this site to become a free-ranging, self-sustaining population."

*

Our last full day in Hustain Nuruu. Our last therefore, apart from travelling, in Mongolia. It was now or never to find the takhi.

We woke to cloudless skies, with a fresh wind to offset the scorching sun. It was a day for ambition to run sky-high. That suited me very nicely; mine did. With no further need to hoard the last of my resources, I was going for broke. For the top of the mountain.

The southern rib of the Hustain Nuruu horseshoe rose from the ridge above the camp, the ridge we had searched yesterday for Khaan's group. Its summit was perhaps a mile away, and a thousand feet above. Having found a Russian-speaking warden who had some idea of the horses' movements, I now understood that we had concentrated our efforts too far to the south. Since a month ago, Khaan had begun to range farther north, towards the corrie enclosed by the mountain; that is, above the valley leading past the two fences and ultimately down to the camp.

The shortest route to the top was on to the ridge and straight up the rocky spine leading off it. If I made the summit I would descend right-handed into the corrie, contour round above the second fence and drop into the valley to return. It would be pretty unlucky if I didn't run into the herd somewhere along the way.

While Carol, mindful of her earlier problems with the sun, decided to sit out the hottest hours of the day in the camp, I picked my way alone through the dense flowers beside the stream. The crickets seemed to fence me in with a wall of sound, broken only by the occasional shriek of a marmot. I surprised one of these a good hundred yards from its burrow; the ungainly, lumping run as it gallumphed to safety was very like a badger's. Near the first fence I bumped into Dr. Sharhun, a parasitologist from UB out for a few days' research. His young son kept up a constant, noisy chatter, and my heart sank; this was no way to creep up on wild horses. But they were bound for the new arrivals in the enclosure, and I was alone again as I made my slow way up to the plateau from which the real mountain began to rise.

At the top I found fresh droppings, and followed them blindly in the wrong direction to a spot with a commanding view. Not a horse to be seen.

This was no time to learn tracking skills by trial and error. Today of all days I mustn't waste my legs. Anyway, if the ranger was right, there was a much better chance of success on the way down. I abandoned the search for now, and made a beeline for the shoulder of the mountain.

The best things in life come when you're not expecting them. Eyes riveted to the sky while I watched a group of hobbies, I almost walked slap into Khaan's herd. Under the sharp rib of Hustain Nuruu one of the pink boulders stamped and snorted; I was just in time to drop to my knees before it saw me. Crawling now, I worked round until the curve of the hill hid me from sight. Looking back, I could still make out the gers. I hoped desperately that Carol didn't have her binoculars on me, watching this idiotic Davy Crockett performance.

Now I could stand again, and circle round crosswind to some rocks which would shield my approach. I was getting quite close and feeling ridiculously pleased with myself, when I realised that I'd cocked it up.

Brisk hooves sounded suddenly behind me. Turning, I saw a lone horse trotting across the open hillside straight at me. Caught with egg on my face. Even if there had been anywhere to hide, it was too late; the horse must have seen me a full half-minute before I had heard its approach. All the faffing about on my tummy was wasted. My language was unprintable, though I managed to keep it to a whisper.

Another few seconds, and I could see that it was Khaan himself. That was the best of a bad job, as he would be less worried than any of the mares. Come to think of it, a mare would hardly have detached herself from the group in that way; only Khaan, laid-back and independent as he was, would have been so casual. He must have been down to the stream to drink, and was now hurrying back to find the others.

He regarded me with interest but unconcern; his only concession to my intrusion was to make a slight detour around me. But my cover was at least partially blown. When he rejoined the mares, they would sense from him that something was up. Sure enough, when I crept among the rocks for a closer look, one of the mares - Svetlaya, probably - was alert, head up, doing sentinel duty for the others. Manoeuvre as I might, whenever and wherever I stuck my head up all I could see was the same red-brown face, seeming to look straight into my eyes. I cursed my bright scarlet necktie, protection against the sun, and took it off; then settled down for a long rest behind the rocks, waiting until the takhi forgot about me.

At last my patience was rewarded. From a perfect vantage point between two rocks I watched them at my leisure. Only fifty yards away they idled comfortably, mares dozing in the mid-day sun, foals fidgeting in boredom or scratching lazily on a favourite rock.

It was all too brief an idyll. Still essentially wary, or simply restless as ever, they were soon ready to get moving. Khaan for once dictating the action, they made off purposefully in single file along a narrow track. One after another the foals left their scratching post and trotted in pursuit until only one, blissfully rubbing his back against the rough granite and forgetting his brothers and sisters, looked about suddenly to find himself alone. He ran here and there, whinnying in panic; then caught sight of them and went into overdrive, galloping full-tilt along the rough path and catching up just as they all disappeared round the massive shoulder of Hustain Nuruu.

There was nothing to be gained by following. I sat for a bit refuelling from my pocketful of nibbles; then took a deep breath and prepared to tackle the steep arête rising directly ahead.

It was tough going; no path, just a case of finding the easiest route among the boulders which defined the backbone of the mountain. Higher up, though, the deer had worn a track - and used it recently, judging by the fresh hoofmarks. The return of the *maral*, or red deer, is another of the successes of the Reserve. Herds of forty plus are becoming quite common, as are sightings of Argali sheep and goitered gazelles. Moving carefully, I kept my eyes peeled; but whatever it was that owned the hooves was moving rather faster than I was, and would by now be well hidden among the trees lying just below the ridge. Birch trees, of course - the *hustain* that give the mountain, and the Reserve, their name. Invisible and unguessed at from the bare southern slopes, they were another case of the north-south divide of mountain vegetation, that had been so obvious from twelve thousand feet up.

From the penultimate tor I could see an eagle sitting dramatically on the summit, just a hundred yards away. Another second, and he saw me too and was gone, gliding effortlessly down the rib which had taken me the last two hours to get up. Naismith would have written me off; over four times his reckoning.*

He wouldn't have thought much, either, of the long time I spent recharging on the top. But then, Naismith never had the view that I had that day. It was worth lingering over. I had worked hard enough to gain it.

To the south, the Tuul was a long ribbon stretching east-west, framed by wave after wave of mountain ridges beyond. In the middle distance the pink tors of Hustain Nuruu's satellites rose irregularly along a series of parallel horseshoe ripples, falling away gently to the river. Turning, I looked down into the combe of Hustain Nuruu itself. Both the first and second fence were invisible under the mountain, but I could pick out Khaan's mob on the track far below. A good mile from where I had left them, they were well up the valley. No wonder we had failed to find them on the first two days.

One last long look, and I was on my way back down by an easy north-west gully, exchanging the bright but attenuated flowers of the peak for the lushness of thigh-deep technicolour by the rill that drained into the corrie from the summit ridge. Even after weeks in Mongolia, this profusion of flowers still took my breath away, especially after a few

*Naismith's rule for estimating ascent times: one hour for every three miles plus a half-hour for every thousand feet.

217

hours' comparison with the sparser vegetation of the mountain-top. It had its disadvantages, though, for a tick crawled suddenly over my shoe, and - having been walking in shorts - I nearly strangled myself in my leggings in my panic to cover up. Every Eden has its serpents; a few weeks ago, a foreign Reserve worker had been flown home and hospitalised by a very nasty disease carried by the ticks here. In fact, not a hundred miles away is a particularly bad area for bubonic plague, endemic among the marmots. Both, I reckoned, were complications I could do without.

The little stream, growing now, came out at the corner of the second fence. Its occupants were up at the top end, a few barely visible dots. I wasn't going to see them from any closer, for by now my legs felt as though they had been filleted. Stumbling slowly down, though, I once more bumped into Khaan's group, which had come even further up the valley.

Again I stalked them on hands and knees. This time it was through deep grass and vicious nettles. Bugger the ticks, I thought recklessly; after all, I was starting for home tomorrow, and priorities had their place.

As before, it was Khaan who saw me first. He raised his head above the long grass to look straight at me, and it was obvious that I was rumbled. But he remained relaxed and unperturbed, so I slowly straightened my cramped limbs, took a rapid tick-check, and stood openly and frankly admiring him; while he seemed to sense my admiration and bask in it. For long moments we gazed at each other; then one of the mares, much further off, saw me and became edgy. So I retreated before I disturbed them any more, to sit on the hillside and enjoy watching them from a distance they were happy with.

A low whistle came from above me. I turned to see Carol, and again hoped she hadn't seen me playing Boy Scouts. I'd had more than my fair share of takhi-watching, so I left them for her to enjoy, and set off back home.

It was a very long way. It was about a mile, but felt like ten. I drank every time the track crossed and re-crossed the stream, for at six in the evening the sun was still baking hot. A family of orange-legged kestrels travelling down the valley with me were doing their own bit of wildlife-watching, perching on the telegraph wires that had come to meet the path, and peering down enquiringly at the slow, earthbound oddity below them. At the first fence I stopped for my last, long look at Mongolian takhi.

At last I was stretched out in the tent, my body in bits but my mind completely whole at last. Meanwhile Carol, to my eternal gratitude, poured gallons of tea down my throat and cooked the supper.

*

The largest ger in the camp was designated the "disco ger". We thought it was a joke; but that night there was a disco.

Everyone in Hustain Nuruu was invited. The keepers came, with their families. The cook's daughter turned up in short black skirt and bovver boots, looking for all the world like an alien from a Western shopping precinct on a Saturday afternoon; her sister outshone her in purple lycra leggings. The herdsmen from all around arrived in their best dels.

It was one hell of a bash. Interpersed with ear-banging disco music was more of the glorious Mongolian unison singing. The noise must have been heard in Altan Bulag; if, that is, there was anyone left there to hear it, anyone who wasn't already at the party.

Only we, obvious and unforgettable in our tent directly behind the ger, didn't get to go to the ball. For Dr. Gala was host, and we still weren't forgiven for arriving without his prior knowledge. Our disgrace persisted, and was to be rubbed in.

Poor Carol. Very much a party animal and ready to bop till dawn, she itched and fretted. As for me, I couldn't give a monkey's. My head was still high on the summit of Hustain Nuruu, my body was better not mentioned. I heard the first two numbers hazily, then slept like a dormouse through every last decibel.

*

Little moved the next morning. That included us, for once again the rain drummed down while we waited for our transport back to UB. We fidgeted uneasily, for our departure the following day on the Trans-Siberian Railway was in the lap of the gods, or rather, the devil - that's to say, Sanjaa was responsible for having bought our tickets. We had even gone so far as to forsake the Altai and book our final night's accommodation back at Mongol Tour Rules OK, all the better for breathing down his neck.

At lunchtime the sun dispersed the rainclouds, and a few bleary figures began to totter about. We found Hans sifting wolf-dung, washing it through a fine sieve with a trickling hose-pipe. This messy analysis was an important part of his work, giving a fair idea as to who ate what, or whom, on the Reserve. ("Dung!" Jan had said, raising his eyes heavenward in mock despair. "He's crazy about dung!") He pointed out the various clues, while we watched and learned. Too late, I realised that I was crouched slightly downhill from him; intent on his explanations, I had failed to spot my shoes insidiously filling with dilute wolf-turd.

As the afternoon wore on, the hot air stirred under the bleating of many sheep. Round the corner and up the central valley appeared a flock of several hundred. A score of cattle, a few horses and four mounted arats followed. Hustain Nuruu's main valley is a major migration route, a sort of nomadic Great North Road. We had the good luck to be seeing a family moving from summer to autumn pastures. They had set out from somewhere about the Tuul valley, perhaps, before turning north through the great cleft in the hills, among the fifty or so Turkic graves clustered hereabouts, past the ruins of the old lamasery, until they reached our few gers, spartan traces of the valley's latest civilisation. We wondered where they would be at nightfall; and the nightfall after that?

They came on slowly, sacrificing speed to order. A truck followed, piled high with the family possessions, including the dismantled ger. One hundred years ago, or three thousand, they would have travelled exactly so, but for a wooden ox-cart in place of the truck.

Half a mile up the valley they stopped for a cigarette and general breather. We found them there when we finally got moving, and had to plough a careful furrow through the sheep, spread-eagled across the road. We hoped our driver wouldn't fall asleep before he had passed them all. But he made it without so much as a yawn, and after paying our final respects to the obo we said goodbye to Hustain Nuruu.

We sped back to UB on a beautiful afternoon, past fields in which a few haycocks had mysteriously appeared where no hay had been cut a few days before. Perhaps in the short, wet Mongolian summer it's best to cut the grass and pile it up, silage fashion, after just wilting a little. Haymaking certainly isn't a major part of Mongolian agriculture. But then, agriculture isn't a major part of Mongolian agriculture. A lamaistic (as opposed to Buddhist) superstition prohibits disturbing the earth's surface, a superstition probably worth observing if you think digging is a waste of space and would rather eat old mutton than fresh vegetables anyway.

Congratulating ourselves on immaculate planning, we picked up our spare luggage from the Altai while we still had the vehicle, and carried straight on to the Sanjaa flophouse - to find that somebody had been playing with magic wands.

Gone was the shell, the pile of building rubble, the echoing corridors. Instead, a pretentious entrance hall now boasted a plush carpet, leather armchairs, and a ridiculously large reception desk complete with decorative bimbo. Mongol Tour OK stickers stuck to everything stickable on, and a rack bore dels priced at four times the rate of the UB department store, and twice that of the Bayangol - UB's priciest hotel. Sanjaa was mobilising upwards.

But he wasn't taking us with him. He'd forgotten all about our reservation, and there was no room at the inn.

XI

THE GINGERBREAD HOUSE

The staff stared at us with blank faces. No, Sanjaa hadn't entered our booking. No, they didn't have a room for us. The hotel was full.

When it became clear that we were prepared, if necessary, to doss down in the foyer, blankness turned to consternation. The bimbo's Russian was, if anything, worse than mine. We argued in circles. In desperation she phoned Argizuu, Sanjaa's personal secretary, who spoke English. For some twenty minutes they discussed us, until I snatched the phone.

"I want to speak to Sanjaa."

"That is not possible. Sanjaa has gone to the country."

"Where in the country? When will he be back?"

"He has gone to China. He will not be back until eight. He will go straight home."

"Where does he live?" This at a perceptibly higher volume.

"He will be late. Not until ten o'clock."

"That doesn't matter. *Where does he live?*"

"He will be very late. Not until at least eleven. In fact, he probably won't be home at all tonight." Thumbscrews weren't going to drag the address out of her. As ever, Sanjaa's loyal employees were closing ranks. No doubt, I reflected grimly, they'd had a lot of practice.

"We are waiting for some Japanese tourists who don't seem to have arrived. Maybe they're not coming. If so there will be a room. Meanwhile, why don't you go to the Guesthouse restaurant and have a nice meal?"

The thought of food was suddenly very appealing, and quite took the wind out of my sails. Pacified, I rang off. Maybe they would give us a decent meal on the house as compensation for the shambles. It was a pleasant surprise to find that MTROK now had a restaurant on the premises.

Unfortunately, it was a surprise to the staff as well. The restaurant wasn't even built yet. The nice doorman, who had been following the pantomime with sympathy, confided that there wasn't a restaurant for miles. The quaking receptionist refused to divulge Argizuu's phone number or ring her back.

At this point my knees literally collapsed. It was carbohydrate or bust. I made for the food bag, and was sitting like a hippy in the middle of the foyer's deep-pile carpet surrounded by a makeshift picnic, eating jam butties, scattering crumbs and generally lowering the tone of the joint, when the busload of Japanese walked in. Bang went our hope of a bed.

"We will find you a place at another hotel. Of course, it will be more expensive. Maybe, fifty dollars."

"No problem. We have arranged a price with Sanjaa. He can pay the difference."

They suddenly remembered a much cheaper pad. Carol went off to inspect it, and returned grim-faced. Filthy, no hot water.

"There is no hot water at all in the city tonight." Oh, sure. Except, of a different kind, for them; and us.

At least we were in the right place to deal with the really serious problem. For it was painfully obvious that Sanjaa hadn't remembered to get our train tickets.

"Of course he has bought them. They are here at the hotel."

"Show them to us."

"I meant - Argizuu has them." Argizuu, of course, said that the receptionist had them. Then that Sanjaa had them with him. He would bring them that night.

"But you just said he wouldn't be back till tomorrow." It was almost child's play to tie them in knots with their own contradictions.

"You must give us your passports, so that he can bring them." This meant, of course, "so that he can buy them." No cross-border tickets would be issued without such documentation.

"But he doesn't need our passports, as he has bought them already." This wasn't just playing games; to give up our passports would have been the ultimate folly. Anyway, Sanjaa had photocopies, specifically for getting the tickets. If there were a cat in hell's chance of buying them at the last minute - something the tour company back home had expressly warned against - he already had all the papers he needed. The staff didn't know that. Too bad. Let them sweat. They had told us too many lies to deserve sympathy for their predicament.

Our own was rather more pressing. We had nowhere to stay, and scant chance of catching our train in the morning.

Carol, who until now had been extraordinarily patient, suddenly snapped. Seizing the phone - the receptionist had made another furtive call to Argizuu - she yelled into the receiver, shaking with fury.

"I want a car - *now* - to take us to the Altai Hotel. And I want a representative of Sanjaa there tomorrow at ten, with a full explanation, AND OUR TICKETS!"

In ten seconds she achieved what I hadn't managed in three hours. Within minutes we were back at the Altai. They booked us in without so much as a raised eyebrow. Even the restaurant was still open, serving the most inedible mess yet. We had no complaints. It was good to be back.

*

Miraculously, when the train pulled out the next day, it took us with it. What strings Sanjaa had pulled to save his street-cred with our tour company, we never enquired. We just hoped viciously that the last-minute transaction had cost him a hefty backhander.

The Trans-Sib - or, more correctly here, the Trans-Mongolian Railway, for it doesn't join up with the real thing until Ulan Ude in Siberia - was a shadow of its former glory. The concept was superb: four bunks to each compartment, giving ample space for all, a samovar to every coach for constant hot water, a *provodnik* or attendant to supply bedlinen and generally look after the passengers, and separate loos and washing facilities. Unfortunately the water was off, the samovar cold and dry, the linen non-existent, the loos unutterably squalid and the provodnik blotto throughout.

None of that mattered to us. We had sleeping bags, food, water, and our own six feet of space. Moreover, we were about to set off across Siberia by rail - the greatest train adventure in the world.

Best of all, from my point of view, was the prospect of two days horizontal. I spent most of the first twenty-four hours in the same condition as the provodnik; and so missed the fun. I caught up on it later from Carol's diary.

"The discomfort was made up for by the activities of our carriage mates," she wrote. "We shared with a very sharp lady and her daughter who were trading fashion bags and ghetto blasters illegally in Russia. She was also the train's unofficial source of lager, and as a result our carriage became a sort of speakeasy.

"At 5 am, about two hours before we reached the border, all hell broke loose. Every trader on the train was swapping goods with other traders, as travelling around with seven highly expensive music systems looks just a bit suspicious. The whole process was repeated in reverse the minute we had cleared border customs."

Somewhere inside Russia I struggled to consciousness and began to take in my surroundings. Long-distance trains, I quickly decided, were the perfect solution for the incapacitated traveller with incurable fidgets. All day I lay on my bunk staring out of the window, contentedly scratching my itchy feet without so much as twitching a muscle. Even the landscape played along, changing so slowly and so little that I could switch off for an hour and miss nothing.

Forest, forest and more forest; scenes straight out of Dr. Zhivago, but without the snow. Birch, then pine or larch, then birch again, yellowing slightly now, broken occasionally by meadows in which haycocks prepared to defy the oncoming winter. Every few miles the trees drew back to allow a road to pass through, sometimes tarmac, more often dirt track, leading to a village: a neat settlement of wooden *izbas*, the squat clapboard hut of Siberia. A few cows, a few chickens, dogs barking at the train. Behind every house a garden, brimming with vegetables - potatoes, cabbage, sweetcorn, carrots, a few stunted sunflowers, more potatoes. So much for the short summers - shorter than ever this far north - and so much for prohibition on turning the soil. This was Buryatia, historically part of Mongolia; but the Buryats, it seemed, rolled up their sleeves and dug with the best of them.

A slight slowing of the train, a tiny station, a name flashing past; the Cyrillic indecipherable in those few seconds, but probably too insignificant to raise a dot on our map. At the larger towns the train stopped for a few minutes. Our traders traded frenetically, goods and money often exchanged through the windows to beat the competitor next door on to the platform. Carol and I seized the moments to stretch our legs, wandering briefly with an eye to imminent departure and inspecting the odds and ends for sale on the platform. Mostly junk, car boot sale stuff. A few vegetables. An enterprising lady did a roaring trade in *blinis*, hot pancakes stuffed with jam. On one station the vendors sold factory goods. Production line workers, they were paid in kind for lack of ready money, and this was the only way to turn their wages into hard cash. Saddest of all was a worn peasant lady selling four carrots, the most her garden could come up with. They were scrubbed until they shone like gold, but everyone passed her by. Too late, I hurried for the door to buy them; but the train pulled out, leaving her sitting forlornly on the platform. Her image, the living face of post-Communist poverty, haunted me for four thousand miles.

*

Anna Nikolaevna was a witch.

She had to be. Her nose and chin jutted fiercely, under a huge whiskery mole which split her left eyebrow. She kept a cat, and a broomstick behind her kitchen door. And she lived in a gingerbread house.

Fresh paint dripped pastel blue icing down over the treacle-brown walls of her izba, and white piping drew arabesques over the windows. More paint frosted every available surface, from the wooden outside steps to the kitchen floorboards to the outhouse; even the chicken shed.

226

You took your shoes off and dusted your socks before entering Anna Nikolaevna's house. One footprint on her dazzling floor, and you might be turned into a toad. Deservedly.

A few yards away, and down a bank, was a shingle beach. Beyond, Lake Baikal stretched to infinity, its further shore swallowed by distance. Bolshoi Koti crouched like so many other villages on its edge, deriving its life blood from the immense lake, possessor of one-fifth of the world's fresh water, the Blue Eye of Siberia.

Carol and I had reverted to tourists. Escorted off the train at Irkutsk by Lydia, who was to be our guide and interpreter for the next few days, we had taken a morning to wander through the grand old Siberian regional capital. Its crumbling, ancient wooden houses reminded me of those in Vilnius, at the other end of the former Soviet Empire; while the urgent renovation of the Cathedral, the gleaming gold paint creeping slowly downwards under the scaffolding round its peeling onion domes, shouted the gospel of faith reborn in a land so long kept atheist by decree. In the square outside, red flowers surrounded the eternal flame kept burning to honour the unknown warrior.

Lydia urged us to hurry, for the jetfoil was due to leave. It bore us rapidly up the Angara River, which empties Baikal's water into the distant Yenisei, until the great mouth of Baikal itself opened before us. A swing north, past the resort of Listvyanka and a number of chocolate-drop villages, brought us to Bolshoi Koti. No roads brave the rough landscape of the taiga, so the lake itself is the highway - for boats in summer and, in winter when the ice is six feet thick, for any vehicle you choose: jeep, truck, or - briefly at the end of the nineteenth century - the train itself.

Anna Nikolaevna was waiting to welcome us, hospitality brimming from a heart of gold. The forbidding exterior couldn't have been more misleading. We immediately recast her as white witch at least; then, on better acquaintance, as the kind grandmother. Not that the wolf would have stood a chance against Anna Nikolaevna.

*

Poor, starving William of Rubruck should have come home via Baikal.

Anna Nikolaevna did nothing by halves, least of all cooking. She laid before us plates of food laden as if we were navvies about to fell half the taiga, not idle tourists. That first day she produced a mountainous dish of lepioshki, yeast cakes somewhere between a drop scone and a muffin, well oiled with sour cream and rhubarb jam. After weeks of tightening my belt in Mongolia, I thought I was in heaven. I ate until my stomach groaned, while Anna Nikolaevna beamed, and Carol politely looked the other way.

Then there was her *shchi*... Cabbage soup has been the butt of anti-Soviet jokes since before the Soviet Union itself. But only among people who hadn't tasted Anna Nikolaevna's. All day her stock-pot bubbled and hiccuped like an alchemist's cauldron, huge marrowbones poking their knuckles from under the lid. Sweet, white cabbage and every imaginable other vegetable from her garden went in, and the result might have been served at the Ritz.

Buckets of tea washed down every meal, tea from a small pot of incredibly strong brew often left to get quite cold. Half an inch of this, topped up with water from the ever boiling samovar, came out steaming hot and just the right strength; and saved the hassle of boiling a kettle every half hour.

The garden would have fed an army. Ranks of perfectly ordered onions, cabbages, corn and carrots stood ready to pull. Marigolds and nasturtiums dotted the rows, but not a weed dared to raise its head. Strings of drying herbs dangled from the kitchen ceiling. Meat and dairy foods were produced in the village, while other needs were supplied by the small store, rarely open. Self-sufficiency ranked high in Bolshoi Koti.

As for water, there was no shortage. The water of Lake Baikal, poured in by over three hundred rivers and filtered by sponges sustained by a complex eco-system on the lake floor, has always been held to be the purest in the world. Were the Japanese not paying six dollars a bottle for Baikal water from the bottling plant at Baikalsk on the other side of the lake? Though whether they'd buy it if they knew it was just downstream from the paper mill - that was another matter, said Lydia darkly.

228

For even Baikal's sparkling water isn't secure from pollution these days. Industry, in particular the notorious cellulose factory at Ulan Ude, pours untreated effluent into the Selenge River which, rising in Mongolia and gathering the Tuul among its many tributaries, supplies three-fifths of the lake's water. "The vegetables won't grow properly, the *omul* are tiny and leathery," say people in the vicinity of the Selenge delta. Bad news indeed; for the omul, a kind of salmon unique to Baikal, is both a vital product of the lake and a barometer of its health. It is second from the top of the food chain, so its degeneration signals big problems all the way down to the bottom.

Over on our side, though, there was little sign of trouble. The water here was still crystal clear, the fish plentiful. "There are only small ones for now," said Anna Nikolaevna apologetically, "because the fisherman are all busy haymaking." It was her grandson Dima who set the nets that night. Taking us with him, he rowed well up the lakeside, searching for a good pitch that no-one else had bagged first. Then, handing the oars to Carol, he dropped the net and paid it out slowly, carefully disentangling the cork buoys to float cleanly. As he worked, a full moon rose from behind low cloud to flood the water with light, its beam flickering at the edges as ripples lapped the lake's surface.

The next morning, there were fifty-one fish for breakfast. True to form, Anna Nikolaevna had cooked them all, and looked on with disappointment when we failed to empty the plate.

*

Fifty million years ago, two tectonic plates moved apart to leave a crescent-shaped rift valley one mile deep and four hundred miles long, which sucked in the combined waters of Central Asia and Siberia. Fifty miles at its greatest width, Lake Baikal is still growing at more than an inch a year.

For this is still an area of volcanic activity. Although the Lake is cold - and, through the moderating influence of its great depth, changes temperature slowly, taking until midwinter to freeze and May to thaw -

many hydrothermal vents split its floor, and sulphurous springs feed water of up to 50°C to the surface, creating microclimates in sheltered bays. Earth tremors continue; a major earthquake in 1861 swallowed three Buryat villages and opened up a new gulf.

Baikal's isolation provides a completely self-contained environment. More than a thousand of its species are unique, including the *Ushkaini*, the world's only freshwater seals.

Popular myth says that these seals swam from the Arctic Ocean through underground passages. Even for a creature that can remain underwater for up to half an hour in winter, breathing through holes in the ice, this is a bit extravagant. Zoologists believe that they made their way upriver around the end of the last ice age, and found the Lake to their liking despite the lack of salt water. Much loved by tourists, they are viewed rather more dispassionately by the locals, who hunt them for meat and fur, culling six thousand each winter.

We regretted bitterly that their patch was much further north, beyond the Lake's main island of Olchon. Lydia, though, had seen them, for she had travelled north a year or two before, while translating for a western film about Baikal.

"Everybody needs an extra job these days," she told us as we walked together up the hill behind the village. "The times are so uncertain." A teacher of English at Irkutsk University, she was glad of the tour company work in the summer holidays to eke out her dwindling and irregular salary.

Conversation faltered as the path became rocky. The silence was broken only by the muted piping of a family of long-tailed tits, like feathered flying teaspoons following us with contemptuous ease up the rough slope. At the top we got our breath back sitting among flowers on the edge of a vertical cliff, looking down to Bolshoi Koti and on, endlessly, across the lake. Immediately below us were potato allotments; rows and rows and rows of potatoes. I had wondered at the absence of potatoes in Anna Nikolaevna's eclectically stocked garden. Now I knew where they'd gone.

"So do you think things will get better now that you have democracy? Or worse?"

She shrugged. "Everyone had high hopes of Yeltsin. He was much respected. But now he's slipping in popularity."

Was it the man or the job, we asked? Russia's economy, doing an about turn from Communism to Capitalism, was the ultimate metaphorical supertanker.

"Is there anyone who could do it better? What about Chernomyrddin? We hear good things of him in the West."

The answer, more or less, was "Yuk."

"Zhirinovsky?" This with an apologetic laugh for the absurdity of the question. Zhirinovsky the ranting, extreme nationalist, the man who had assaulted another studio guest under live television cameras.

Double yuk. "And yet," added Lydia, "a lot of people rate Zhirinovsky highly. Those who believe that Russia can only survive under a really strong, hard leader; who'd like a return to the certainties of Stalin, of rule by an iron hand."

"*Stalin?* Do they know what they're saying? Do the people of Russia really know the whole of it, of Stalin's atrocities, of the mass starvation...?"

"Yes, because Krushchev discredited him when he came to power. And yet..." She shrugged, and a look of confusion and despair briefly shadowed her face.

We were out of our depth. Living in our safe little island, after centuries of stability and just rule, where straitened finances meant scrimping a bit to pay the telly licence, where privation meant temporarily running out of fresh milk, we simply couldn't adjust to a world where security took the form of a thriving potato patch and where starvation or civil war or both might be just around the next corner. Insulated in every sense of the word, Carol and I were two of the world's fortunates; living, perhaps, in the top one per cent.

Yet if there was security anywhere in Russia, we decided, it must surely reside in Bolshoi Koti and its sister villages on the edge of Baikal, far from the arena of power, villages whose self-sufficient lifestyle had surely been little changed for centuries; where Russian settler had lived

231

amicably alongside Buryat native, where the old fractious boundaries of Rus and Mongolia had long ago met and merged peaceably.

Back in Anna Nikolaevna's kitchen we found Dima pounding the rest of the fish for *kotleti* - fish cakes - and a wonderful smell of cooking pervaded the cottage. Starvation, we reckoned, wasn't an immediate threat.

*

"Would you like a bath?" Anna Nikolaevna asked us that evening. "My daughter has a bathhouse, and she's heating it up tonight. You can take your washing"

We couldn't believe the offer. There was no running water in Bolshoi Koti, and we washed in the outhouse. We hadn't had a bath for two months. As for the state of our clothes, anything lighter than black was by now a uniform steel grey.

In the dusk we walked through the village, crossed the wooden bridge over the stream and followed a loudly bleating calf up the beaten earth of the main street to Nina's house. She led us across the road to a wooden shack, and we entered to find ourselves in a sauna.

We stripped in the lobby and, carrying armfuls of dirty clothing, climbed the steps to the main room. A wall of heat struck us as the door opened. Inside, three great tins of water stood waiting; one cold, one warm and one steaming on a hot stove. We did our washing stark naked, throwing each bowl of used water over our heads as we finished with it and rinsing away the cleansing sweat that was beginning to pour off us. Then it was our turn for a luxurious wash, spinning out the hot water as long as possible. A final splash down from the cold basin, and it was time to go out into the freezing night, shivering as the breeze ran icy fingers through our wet hair.

At Nina's we drank blackcurrant juice and admired the cat's new kittens from a respectful distance. But the culinary trump card was played, as usual, back at Anna Nikolaevna's.

Kvas, she explained, is the traditional way to finish off a bath night. As we sipped the sweet, fizzy liquid, she told us how to make it.

"Boil three litres of water, then leave it till it's warm. Toast two large slices of rye bread in the oven, then crumble it into the water and boil it again. Add a glass of sugar and a teaspoonful of dried yeast, and leave it to stand for a day or two. Then it's ready to drink."

Kvas flowed freely at births, marriages and deaths, and most other occasions, Lydia told us. As she did so, Anna Nikolaevna's wedding photographs came out. The customs here belonged to pre-revolutionary Russia.

"The bride should wear pink, not white - the groom, too. The morning after the wedding night, the groom wears a white shirt to distribute pink-coloured vodka - if it's not coloured, it means the girl wasn't a virgin. And they should place the poker face down; if the bride is a lazy housewife, a ghost will come and reverse it - and tangle the girl's hair into the bargain."

"At the wedding," chipped in Anna Nikolaevna, "they share a loaf of bread. Whoever takes the bigger bite will wear the trousers!"

There was something not quite right about the photos. They showed her house, but somehow not her house. We puzzled over them, until we realised what was confusing us. It was in the wrong place.

"We had to move it, forty years ago," she said, as if moving house - literally - was the most normal thing in the world. But that's pretty much how it had been, here. Lydia explained.

"It was when they built the dam." The hydro-electric scheme on the edge of Baikal had raised the water level, flooding areas of shoreline. If you wanted to save your house, you picked it up bodily, carried it somewhere high and dry and rebuilt it.

We already knew Anna Nikolaevna to be the former schoolteacher and retired librarian of Bolshoi Koti, as well as gardener and cook *extraordinaire*. Now, it seemed, she was a builder as well.

Was there anything, we wondered, she couldn't do?

*

Before we left the next morning, there were a couple more local traditions to observe.

233

"You must swim in the lake," said Lydia. "People who swim in Lake Baikal add twenty years to their lifespan. And as you leave, you must drop a coin in the water. If you do, it means you will come back."

Back to Lake Baikal? Or Siberia? Or Mongolia? It didn't matter. With that extra twenty years, we would have time for all three.

Though it took me a while to stiffen the sinews. As I sat shivering on the jetty, poking a toe into the freeezing water, I couldn't help thinking of the plankton wriggling below - up to three million per square metre, said the museum encouragingly; or the eighty species of flatworm. Eventually I ran out of excuses and, bit by bit, crawled in for a brief symbolic immersion. Carol did better, venturing quite far out and swimming properly, and returning without so much as having had her toes nibbled.

Warm towels waited for us back at the cottage, followed by thick slabs of Anna Nikolaevna's cake to keep us going on the way back to Irkutsk and the train. This time we hoped for luxury: the *Rossiya*, the classic Trans-Sib express with all the trimmings. So there was no hanging about when it was time for the boat.

We sat in the stern, watching Anna Nikolaevna's figure dwindling into the distance on the quay. When she was no more than a speck, we simultaneously leaned over and dropped our coins into the Lake.

GLOSSARY

Airag   fermented mares' milk
Anda   blood-brother
Aimag   province
Arat   herdsman
Arkhi   spirit distilled from airag, or rough vodka
Batong   water churn
Bag   sub-division of a sumoin
Bus   waist sash
Del   tunic worn by both sexes
Ger   (hard "g") circular felt tent
Gutuls   pointed, upturned leather boots
Khadag   ceremonial blue silk bus
Khakhan   Great Khan
Obo   sacred cairn
Ongghod   family shrine, collection of sacred objects
Stupa   Buddhist shrine
Sum   county town
Sumoin   county
Takhi   Przewalski horses
Tanka   religious painting on cloth
Tarbagan   steppe marmot
Tuman   army unit of ten thousand
Yam   communications/relay system

GENEALOGICAL TREE

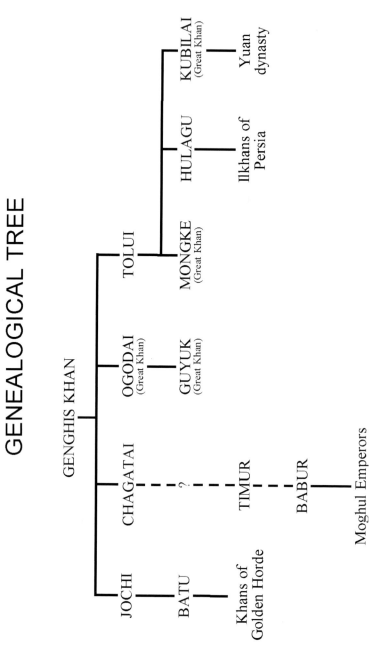

GENGHIS KHAN

JOCHI — CHAGATAI — OGODAI (Great Khan) — TOLUI

BATU — ? — GUYUK (Great Khan) — MONGKE (Great Khan) — HULAGU — KUBILAI (Great Khan)

Khans of Golden Horde

TIMUR

BABUR

Moghul Emperors

Ilkhans of Persia

Yuan dynasty

CHRONOLOGY OF MONGOLIA AND THE MONGOLS

552   Rise of the Altai Turks
745 - 840   Uighur Empire
10th century   Khitans rule Mongolia and China
12th century   Divide and rule policy of Chinese Chin Dynasty
1167   Birth of Temujin, Genghis Khan
1206   Genghis Khan becomes Khan of all the people of the felt tents
1215   Sack of Peking
1218   Conquest of Kara Kitai (descendants of Khitans)
1220   Fall of Bukhara and Samarkand
1221   Death of Ala-ad-Din Mohammed, last Khoresmian Emperor
1227   Death of Genghis Khan
1235   Great Khan Ogodai builds walls of Karakorum
1241   Campaign in Europe of Batu, Khan of Golden Horde
1245-7   John of Plano Carpini travels to court of Great Khan Güyük
1253-5   William of Rubruck travels to court of Great Khan Möngke
1258   Hulagu sacks Baghdad; his dynasty becomes the Ilkhans of Persia
1260   Hulagu's forces defeated by Egyptians
1335   End of Ilkhans of Persia
1336-1405   Life of Timur (Tamerlane)
1370   End of Great Khan Kubilai's Yüan dynasty in China
1502   Russians break free from Tatar Khanate

1586   Founding of Erdenezu Hiid
1730s Mongolia falls under control of Chinese Manchu dynasty
1857   Deposition of Moghul Emperor, last ruling descendant (?)
        of Genghis Khan
1911   Outer Mongolia declares independence from China
1919   Re-entry of Chinese
1920   Mad Baron's invasion
1921   Communist Revolution: People's Republic of Mongolia
        declared
1924   Death of last Khutuktu
1939   Japanese repulsed
1990   Mongolia becomes a democracy

BIBLIOGRAPHY

Bawden, C.R., *The Modern History of Mongolia*, Kegan Paul International, 1989.

Becker, Jasper, *The Lost Country*, Hodder & Stoughton, 1992.

Bökönki, Dr. Sándor, *The Przewalski Horse*, Trans. Lili Halápy, Souvenir Press Ltd, 1974.

Crichton, Robin, *Who is Santa Claus*, Canongate, 1987.

Dawson, Christopher, *Missions to Asia*, University of Toronto Press, 1980.

Dudley Stamp, L., *Asia, A Regional and Economic Geography*, Dutton, 1957.

Fagan, Brian M., *Journey From Eden*, Thames & Hudson, 1990.

Haw, Stephen, *China, A Cultural History*, Batsford, 1990.

Jackson, Peter & Morgan, David, *The Mission of Friar William of Rubruck*, Hakluyt Society, 1990.

Lister, R.P., *Marco Polo's Travels In Xanadu With Kublai Khan*, Gordon Cremonesi Ltd., 1976.

Lister, R.P., *The Secret History of Genghis Khan*, Peter Davies, 1969.

Maclean, Fitzroy, *To The Back of Beyond*, Jonathan Cape Ltd., 1974.

Marshall, Robert, *Storm From the East*, BBC Books, 1993.

Middleton, Nick, *Last Disco in Outer Mongolia*, Simon & Schuster.

Montague, Ivor, *The Blue Sky*, Dobson Books Ltd., 1956.

Morgan, David, *The Mongols*, Basil Blackwell, 1987.

Phillips, E.D., *The Royal Hordes*, Thames & Hudson, 1965.

Polo, Marco, *The Travels*, trans. R.P. Latham, Penguin Books 1958.

Przewalski, Lt.-Col. Nikolai, *Mongolia*, London, 1870.

Severin, Tim, *In Search of Genghis Khan*, Hutchinson, 1991.

Trippett, Frank, *The First Horsemen*, Time-Life International (Nederland), 1974.

Waley, Arthur, *The Secret History of the Mongols and Other Pieces*, Allen & Unwin, 1963.

Waln Smith, Mabel, *Land of Swift-Running Horses*, Harrap, 1956.

Yunden, Ya., Zorig, G., Erdene, Ch., *This is Mongolia*, Ulaanbaatar 1991.

Ziegler, Philip, *The Black Death*, Alan Sutton, 1991.

ARTICLES & PAPERS:

Finch, Christopher, *Mongolia Reintroduces Endangered Przewalski Horse to the Wild*, 1994.

Foundation for the Preservation and Protection of the Przewalski Horse, *Przewalski Horse*, newsletters, 1993 - 1999.

Honhold, Dr. Nick, *Current Situation and Future Options for the Veterinary Services Department of Mongolia*, 1994.

Kaszab, Dr. Z., *New Sighting of Przewalski Horses*, ORYX, Dec. 1966.

Kulchisky, Michael J., *Mongolian Oil Development and Potential*, 1996.

Lawton, John, *The Cradle of the Turks*, Aramco World, Mar./Apr. 1994.

Mongolian Government, *Recommendation & Report for Mongolia's Takhi Strategy and Plan*, 1994.

Montague, Ivor, *Przewalski Horses in the Wild*, ORYX, May, 1968.

Polosmak, Natalya, *Pastures of Heaven*, National Geographic, Oct. 1994.

Tseregmid, D., Dashdorj, A., trans. Ivor Montague, *The Przewalski Horse*, ORYX, Feb. 1974.

APPENDIX

KNOW THINE ENEMY

Reprinted and updated from JAILBREAK, Scimitar Press 1998

"I live in a glass cage," wrote Dr. Clare Fleming about her experience of ME. "Often I seem to be well, so only those close to me see the extent of my disability. Indeed, within my prison of inactivity, there are moments when I feel relatively well. Yet the invisible walls around me are impenetrable. Beyond them lies a barrage of symptoms, and the further I push myself, the greater the deterioration, and the longer the recovery time: hours, days, even weeks... I long to surge ahead, but my glass cage, though expanding, remains firmly in place, and any attempt to break through it is penalised with a setback. I started like Aesop's hare and have had to learn to be a tortoise."

ME, (or Myalgic Encephalomyelitis*, to give it its party name, for the only time in these pages), is seen as an illness of the late twentieth century. Yet it is undoubtedly no newcomer to the human picture, even if it has barely as yet made the pages of the medical textbooks.

The capacity to categorise and minutely define illness is a feature of recent times; in past centuries it was often a mystery what caused an individual to "go into a decline" or "become an invalid". But among some of the more famous invalids, some details of whose ailments were recorded along with their lives, there is here and there documentary evidence giving a strong indication of ME. Just as we can nowadays say with reasonable certainty that Julius Caesar was epileptic and Henry VIII died of syphilis, it is also highly probable that, to give a couple of examples, Charles Darwin and Florence Nightingale were both victims of ME.

The sharp rise in incidence of ME in recent years is, like the rise in childhood asthma, the phenomenon of "sheep-dip 'flu" or organo-

*known in the USA as CFIDS, or Chronic Fatigue & Immune Dysfunction Syndrome, and also - increasingly - as Myalgic Encephalopathy

phosphate poisoning, and the drop in male fertility, possibly linked to environmental causes, such as heavy use of agricultural chemicals. As with Gulf War Syndrome, some ME patients blame their illness on adverse response to vaccination. A number of leading researchers argue convincingly for a viral trigger. These are not mutually exclusive propositions. Far from it; the first two situations could create the ideal conditions for the third to flourish. Until a great deal more research has been done, however, it is impossible to be sure.

For until recently, knowledge of ME was limited by a Catch-22 situation of monumental absurdity. When little was known about it, a baffled medical establishment long continued to deny its very existence as a specific illness. And of course, if it wasn't there, there was nothing to research.

Only when the two groups, the ME Association and Action for ME, had built up sufficient funds to finance research could any investigation into ME begin in this country. Government funding for laboratory research has so far been limited to one very small study, begun in 1998 and still to deliver its findings. It is a pity that its aim, investigating the effect of noradrenaline in the "neuropsychological pathogenesis" of chronic fatigue syndrome, appears to be directed more at the psychiatric end of the wide range of chronic fatigue illnesses than specifically ME.

And so it has taken years to shed the tabloid "Yuppie 'Flu" image, the abiding impression of many people - and not a few doctors - that there is no more to ME than a sort of glorified tiredness.

So what is it really, this elusive plague that has been estimated to affect up to a quarter million people in the UK alone?

ME commonly, though not necessarily, develops after an acute viral infection. It is a neurological illness, involving lesions in the brain similar to those found with poliomyelitis, organo-phosphate poisoning and Creutzfeldt-Jakob Disease, the human form of BSE. Its clinical signs and its epidemiology are markedly similar to those of polio, and the existence in many polio survivors of a Post-Polio Syndrome which is indistinguishable from ME is surely significant. A long-held body of opinion offers the view that ME is caused by an enterovirus - that is, one of the family of viruses containing the polio viruses. Half a century ago, when doctors were still distressingly familiar with the symptoms and behaviour of polio, ME used to be called *atypical* or *non-paralytic polio*, acquiring its present name only in the late fifties. Its hosts exhibit a variety of physiological and metabolic abnormalities: missing enzymes, damaged muscle mitochondria, mycoplasmal (bacterial) infections, reduced blood flow to the brain, to name but a few. Damage to the brain stem disrupts the functioning of the central nervous system; while that in the hypothalamus - a crucial part of the brain stem - may upset the hormonal system, causing adrenal and thyroid insufficiency and lowering metabolic rate. Viral damage has been observed in the heart, thyroid gland and other organs.

Outside the lab, ME shows itself in a bewildering variety of symptoms, which for the luckiest may fade within a year or two, while the more unfortunate - that is, the majority - endure them for life.

First and foremost is debility. Strength and stamina are impaired, and what remains vanishes with indecent haste on activity, taking disproportionately long to replenish. Capacity may vary from the ability, say, to walk a mile down to the inability to feed yourself or walk to the loo. Approximately 20% of those with ME are bedridden for many years. One defining factor of this weakness is the double whammie: exhaustion and apparent recovery after exertion is usually followed by a second, more severe reaction days, or even weeks, later.

Second comes a corresponding blocking of mental faculties: of co-ordination, concentration, memory and so on. Blurred vision may prevent you from reading, or even watching TV; while slurred speech and an inability to walk in straight lines may be misconstrued by those who don't know you're ill.

Thirdly, there is often a great deal of pain. While most experience aches and pains similar to those of 'flu, many sufferers have constant, sometimes severe pain in muscles and joints.

These are the definitive signs. But the biochemical and neurological oddities confuse the issue, with a thousand and one diverse and often bizarre symptoms: frightening heart problems, acute skin sensitivity, hallucinatory dreams, muscle twitching, the embarrassment of hot flushes... the list could go on and on. Food allergies may become a problem, while alcohol intolerance, cruelly, is almost universal. The permutations are endless and, like snowflakes, no two patients are exactly alike.

As to why ME should often develop from what may seem no more than a simple viral infection, marking some people for life, whereas the vast majority catching the same virus should be unaware of anything more than a slight cold - again, as with polio - this is probably a result of predisposing factors depleting immune response; factors such as immune stress (repeated infections, unsuspected allergies or even vaccination), chemical stress (accumulating low-grade OP poisoning, household chemicals, some kinds of printers' fluids), direct physical stress (overwork, overtraining in athletes - even pregnancy and childbirth may be the final straw in the presence of other factors), physical trauma (a bad car crash or serious operation) - or even mental or emotional stress, the lever eagerly and exclusively seized on by the promoters of psycho-babble. Frequently, the ME patient is someone who for a considerable time has been operating on a system running deep in overdraft, and not realising it until the blow strikes.

To live with ME is to live in a looking-glass world, in which normal rules are regularly inverted. It is a world in which to go for a walk in the fresh air, rather than clearing the mind, may blur the vision within a few steps; where regular exercise can steadily undermine, rather than steadily strengthening. The work ethic of a lifetime must be unlearned, because it is not virtuous but actually self-destructive to get up early, or knock off half an hour's work in twenty minutes. It is acquiescence and idleness that now get the Brownie Points. And Brownie Points, failing a better sort of yardstick, are an essential part of the coping strategy, of balancing rest and exercise.

Imagine living on a very low income, permanently in the red, and surviving by credit-card. Then, for financial, read physical resources. You are living in overdraft; and, the deeper the debt, the higher the interest rate - sorry, crash-coefficient - and the longer it takes to pay off what you owe.

Worse, as with plastic money, it is possible - often, indeed, necessary - to overspend on reserves you don't have, until the awful moment comes when the bill drops through the letterbox with a dull thud and you find out just how prodigal you've really been.

This comes back to the double whammie, the partial delaying of body feedback. One of the banana skins is the fact that an effort which feels OK or at least tolerable at the time (be it visiting the supermarket or merely writing a postcard) might hit you very hard a day, week or even a month later. So it is never enough to listen to your body, and stop only when you feel you can't go on. That is far too late; for you must expect the after-effects of the least action to continue to intensify, like those of sunburn, long after the exposure is ended. "You're like a microwave," commented a friend. "You keep cooking well after you're switched off!"

This time-lag is the worst barrier to understanding and managing the illness in the early years. Time and again you're seduced into over-confidence resulting in crash-landing; where the excesses of last month may call you to account at exactly the same time as those of last week, yesterday and five minutes ago, in a sort of simultaneous pile-up like a sonic bang.

So you ride a switchback, in a relentless cycle of boom and bust until the lesson finally clicks. You stop saying, "Last week I was doing so well; what went wrong?" Instead you sit down and work out your average output; then spend your days endlessly totting up, earnestly counting out black marks, like a school monitor, for each activity. Life becomes one long game of Pontoon. The awful threat of going "bust" is implicit in the rules, so you add up your cards with desperate precision, and "twist" or "stick" accordingly.

"Twist" or "stick"? Stick is safe; but if you stick you lose out, you eventually mummify. If you twist you may bust. You never quite know what the next card is. Worse, you can only guess what it would have been. So you learn only the hard way, by your crunching mistakes, and not by what you get right.

So you still succumb to the temptation of that evening out, or the dire urgency of mucking out the bathroom. But at least you to begin to have an idea what that will cost, and may plan accordingly. The randomness is always there, but you can flatten the switchback a little.

Better, you learn to manipulate; to nurse the boom, like an athlete peaking for your own personal Olympics, to encompass something really worthwhile - and then damn the consequences. As an ongoing strategy, that would be suicidal, as each consequent bust could mean serious relapse, and months if not years out of your useful life. But as a once-off, for a really special occasion... such as travelling in Mongolia... it could be worth the risk.

Management and manipulation are crafts which must be thoroughly mastered; for there is no standard medical treatment, except for drugs to alleviate individual symptoms. But painkillers, beta-blockers and the like are mere palliatives, with no effect on the root cause of illness. Many people therefore turn to holistic medicine, finding that, for example, homeopathy or acupuncture may improve overall health status, enabling the body to fire strengthened resources at the enemy within. Others modify their diet, obtaining relief by avoiding food causing intolerance or allergy. Adrenal and thyroid supplementation has helped a number of people significantly, appearing to be one of the most promising lines of treatment so far discovered.

Relaxation techniques, meditation or hypnotherapy are also used to counter the psychological effects of long-term illness. For with such a destructive enemy these are legion: intense frustration, fear of an uncertain future, constant sense of failure and loss of all feeling of self-worth being only a few. Worst of all, perhaps, a disorientating loss of the sense of your very identity, since who and what you are is almost totally defined by what you do - or did, and can do no longer.

And so we come to what has been, for many years, one of the most frightening aspects of ME. For in the days of ignorance, these last signs threw a lifeline to many doctors, baffled by an illness for which there is still no accepted single diagnostic test - bar a brain scan, too expensive to be freely available and in any case requiring analysis by one of a mere handful of specialists, most of whom are in the USA.

"Clinical depression" was entered on many a medical record; psychosomatic disorders, repressed childhood fear, even agoraphobia being pinned on the unfortunate victim. Frustration, fear, failure, loss of self-worth? You're the victim of psycho-social dislocation, you were told, in a glib confusion of cause and effect. Now we've got you pigeon-holed, don't worry: once your mind is straightened out, of course your body will function normally again. Here's your letter of referral; the shrink is the second door on the left.

"To have ME," wrote novelist and former yachtswoman Clare Francis in 1989, "is to experience hell twice over, firstly through the devastation of the disease itself, and secondly through the lack of diagnosis, information and support that most sufferers are still having to endure... family and friends found it difficult to understand a disease which had no name, no visible symptoms, makes you come apart mentally, yet often leaves you looking perfectly well. Rather than test their loyalty beyond reasonable bounds, I pretended my illness wasn't happening. I covered up the gaping holes in my life with lies and evasions: while I slept all day my answering machine said I was out; when I stumbled over words or walked into things I joked about having had a late night; and my social life was reduced to almost nothing by constantly pleading a previous engagement. I began to live the life of a recluse - a lonely, isolated and desperate recluse."

It was the weakest and the inarticulate who really suffered; at best unable to work but often deprived of social security benefits, at worst subjected, with much good intention but little sensitivity, to such "cures" as enforced physiotherapy. And things could be even worse for children. Twelve-year-old Ean Proctor, paralysed and mute from his illness, was forcibly taken away by social workers from his parents, who were accused of being over-protective in contesting a psychiatric diagnosis. Therapists dropped Ean in the deep end of a swimming pool, genuinely believing that they could shock him into regaining the use of his arms and legs. When they fished him out as he was going down for the third time, they were finally convinced.

This happened in the late '80s. When the World Health Organisation listed ME as a neurological illness in 1992, many people drew a sigh of relief. Surely, now, the stigma would be removed; the labels of "Yuppie 'Flu" or "the Me Disease", the implications of social dropping-out, would fade into oblivion. It would be OK to "come out", to admit you had ME. Surely now research would proceed. But it has ever been two steps forward and one - sometimes even two - back.

A study by the Royal Colleges of Psychiatrists, Physicians and General Practitioners published in 1996 was eagerly awaited. Instead, however, of adhering to strict criteria for ME, the "study" - more in fact a review of existing literature on fatigue illnesses than a piece of research, and described by the *Lancet* as "haphazardly set up, biased and inconclusive" - drew references from a wide range of subjects linked by the single, vague symptom of "fatigue", and not already labelled under other illnesses with simple diagnostic tests. The result, by the Report's own figures, appears to have been a heavy weighting of the study towards psychiatric chronic fatigue. As for the quarter of the patients whose illness was purely organic, who "showed no identifiable psychiatric disorder", this didn't inhibit the authors of the Report from recommending psychiatric treatment for them also. The recommended treatment included such therapies as graded exercise - an excellent path for the clinically depressed, perhaps, but disaster for those with ME, where sufficient rest and correct management in the early stages are essential for any chance of full recovery. Moreover, ME, decreed the Report, was to lose its specific identity, to be renamed, subsumed into this much wider spectrum of chronic fatigue illnesses. Thus was born the clumsy hybrid Chronic Fatigue Syndrome, child of a shotgun wedding between the organic and the psychiatric, a name which has only added to the confusion - all the more so in that, in some countries, the terms ME and CFS are truly synonymous.

So information trickles by osmosis rather than via the Establishment. It does so steadily, if slowly. Nowadays many doctors are helpful and informative, although a hard core remain who have nailed their colours too firmly - and too publicly - to the psychiatric mast to haul them down again. And, with ME now the greatest single cause of long-term absence of children from school, when the bad psychiatrists take control (and there are some very, very good ones) it is mostly the children who suffer; for it is with children that their control may be complete. "School phobia" became a label that parents of ME children learned to dread. Ten years on, there are still more Ean Proctors.

A survey carried out jointly by the BBC programme *Panorama* and the group Action for ME found that 59% of relevant families questioned were told that their child's illness was psychological. For refusing psychiatric treatment, 7% were threatened with or actually subjected to court proceedings. Worst of all, 4% of parents were themselves labelled with the psychiatric disorder Munchausen's Syndrome by Proxy - that is, they were accused of being guilty of damaging their own child to gain personal attention.

There have been many recent instances of children taken forcibly from their homes and kept in locked psychiatric wards, sometimes for months, and often with parental visits severely restricted. One father, whose sixteen-year-old son was so ill with ME that he couldn't even swallow, was faced with this threat - even though he had placed the boy under the care of a leading ME paediatrician, who strenuously opposed the psychiatrist's diagnosis. The desperate father sent his son to safety abroad - and was promptly imprisoned for his action. Forced to return, the boy was removed from his home by police and social workers in a dawn raid and placed in a psychiatric ward for several months. By the time the psychiatrist admitted defeat and released him, the boy was even more severely ill and now additionally suffering from post traumatic stress disorder. No, we are not talking of the nineteenth century; this occurred in 1999.

So what of the twenty-first century? Things, as they say, can only get better. But the magic bullet is unlikely to be cast in this country. Britain has some of the leading talent in ME research. Research, though, costs money; and while the ever-beleaguered NHS is wondering how to manage its next 'flu epidemic, it can barely even stretch to the odd ME specialist. At the one or two ME clinics which exist - referral, of course, subject to post-code - the waiting lists run to over two years, a catastrophic situation with an illness whose correct treatment in the first few months can make or break one's entire future. So the labs remain empty, or see small projects ticking over slowly. It is across the Atlantic that most watchers expect the laurels to be gained.

But this is no time for national pride. When the race is won, there will be no losers.

JAILBREAK

A SLOW JOURNEY ROUND EASTERN EUROPE

GILL SUTTLE

A former British modern pentathlon team member, three-day-event rider and the first woman to win a full Oxford Blue for running, Gill Suttle found not just her sport but every significant part of her former life wiped out by the disabling condition ME.

Some years on, she breaks out of the prison of illness by travelling, in a van complete with bed, to Eastern Europe. Sometimes exchanging the driving seat for the saddle, she enjoys some fascinating glimpses behind the scenes of eight former Communist countries struggling to throw off their recent past; and in the process manages to shed at least part of her own.

From the heights of Berlin's biggest big wheel in Europe to the depths of a Czech pothole... mummies in a Slovakian crypt to nudists on an Estonian beach... watching Polish wild beavers to eating Lithuanian elk... riding among Hungarian cowboys to midnight arrest by gun-toting Soviet-style police - this is a wide view of Eastern Europe at its best (and worst), as well as a personal journey.

Gill Suttle comes from near Malvern, in Worcestershire. She now lives at Symonds Yat, Ross-on-Wye, where she runs an ME Support Group.

"A stimulating and lively read from a promising new travel author who vividly conveys the joys and difficulties of her journey across Eastern Europe in the early years of freedom from Communism."

"Excels when she talks about the views and the countryside... her descriptions are evocative but concise and fresh."

"This book must be an inspiration to anyone suffering with ME."

"If you are addicted to horses, travel stories... and chocolate... then this is the book for you!"

JAILBREAK: A Slow Journey Round Eastern Europe is available in bookshops or from Scimitar Press, PO Box 41, Monmouth, Gwent, NP25 3UH. Price direct from the publishers is £4.99 + £1 p&p.

WEBSITE: www.gillsuttle.co.uk

FOR FURTHER INFORMATION ON ME

ME Association
    4, Corringham Rd., Stanford-le-Hope, Essex, SS17 0AH
    Tel: 01375 642466, Fax: 01375 360256
    E mail: enquiries@meassociation.org.uk
    Website: http://www.meassociation.org.uk

Action for ME
    PO Box 1302, Wells, Somerset, BA5 1YE
    Tel: 01749 670799, Fax: 01749 672561
    E mail: afme@afmeuk.demon.co.uk
    Website: http://www.afme.org.uk